THE GOVERNMENT AND POLITICS OF SPORT

Over the past 10 years sport has been increasingly involved with politics. A few well-publicised issues have had great effect. Who now decides and administers the policy and what is the overall effect on sport?

The Government and Politics of Sport identifies the parties involved: central government, local government, the Sports Council, the Central Council of Physical Recreation, and the individual sports governing bodies. It examines their effect on sport's policy and administration through an analysis of three important current sport issues – football hooliganism, drug abuse among athletes, and sports opportunities and facilities for school children. In the course of this examination another important factor is brought to light – the growing importance of internal organizations.

This is the first book to tackle the domestic policy process of sport and to provide a political science analysis of some of the key issues facing sports administrators today.

Barrie Houlihan is Principal Lecturer in Public Administration at Staffordshire Polytechnic. The book is the result of a long standing interest in sports policy and administration and an involvement in teaching sports policy courses for the past 10 years.

THE GOVERNMENT AND POLITICS OF SPORT

Barrie Houlihan

London and New York

First published 1991
by Routledge
11 New Fetter Lane, London EC4P 4EE

Simultaneously published in the USA and Canada
by Routledge
a division of Routledge, Chapman and Hall, Inc.
29 West 35th Street, New York, NY 10001

© 1991 Barrie Houlihan

Typeset in Baskerville by
NWL Editorial Services, Langport, Somerset TA10 9DG

Printed and bound in Great Britain by
Biddles Ltd, Guildford and King's Lynn

British Library Cataloguing in Publication Data
Houlihan, Barrie
The Government and Politics of Sport
1. Great Britain. Sports and games. Policies of government
I. Title   796.0941

ISBN 0-415-05402-8
0-415-05403-6 (pbk)

Library of Congress Cataloging-in-Publication Data
Houlihan, Barrie.
The Government and Politics of Sport/Barrie Houlihan
p. cm.   Includes bibliographical references and index.
ISBN 0-415-05402-8 – 0-415-05403-6 (pbk)
1. Sports – Organization and administration – Great Britain
2. Sports and state – Great Britain.   I. Title

GV713.H68   1991   90–23093
796.06'9'0941 – dc 20   CIP

CONTENTS

FIGURES

TABLES

ACKNOWLEDGEMENTS

Research into public policy would not be possible without the willingness of a large number of people to share their time and thoughts. It is a mark of the enthusiasm of those involved in sport that so many spent time answering my questions, digging out information for me and reading my draft chapters. I therefore would like to record my thanks to the following for their help in enabling me to prepare this book. Janet Eustace of the Sport and Recreation Division of the DOE provided useful information for chapter 2 and also introduced me to her colleagues concerned with football issues and the Council of Europe. Rick Bailey (Birmingham City Council) and Tony Sainsbury (Manchester City Council) offered many valuable insights into the role of local government, and particularly metropolitan authorities, in sport. Denis Artess (Association of District Councils) and Dougal McInnes (Association of County Councils) provided an overview of developments at local authority level and also the role of the local authority associations. The important link between local authorities and the Sports Council was discussed with Joe Larkins (North West office of the Sports Council) and Mike Carey (West Midlands office of the Sports Council), who demonstrated a keen insight and sensitivity to the problems of strategy development.

Chapter 4 on the Sports Council benefited from discussions with a number of Council staff, in particular Derek Casey, Sheila Hughes and Iain Reddish. Mike Collins, until recently head of the Council's research unit and now director of the Institute of Sport and Recreation Planning and Management at Loughborough University, also provided much useful information and analysis. All not only helped me to gather material but also commented on drafts of the chapter. Nigel Hook of the Central Council of Physical Recreation provided information about the Council and its relationship with the Sports Council, and Peter Lawson provided trenchant comments on my draft chapter.

Nick Irvine (Hockey Association), Tony Ward (Amateur Athletic Association), Angela Littlewood (Southern Counties AAA), Bob Allen (Midland Counties AAA), Caroline Searle (British Olympic Association), Jane Pearce (International Amateur Athletic Federation), David Dixon (Commonwealth Games Federation) and David Barber (Football Association) all provided information, opinion and analysis for chapter 5. Professor Eric Dunning (Sir Norman Chester Centre for Football Research, University of Leicester), Roger Ingham (Southampton University) and David Barber (FA) all read and commented on the chapter on football hooliganism. The chapter on drug abuse by athletes was read and commented upon by Michelle Verroken (Sports Council), Mike Gee and Bryan Wotton (both of the IAAF), who all also provided much of the background material for the chapter. Elaine Burgess (Sports Council), Linda Antell and Kate Stephens (both of the National Children's Play and Recreation Unit) were among those who contributed to chapter 9.

If I have omitted anyone who made a major contribution to the preparation of the book may I offer my apologies. May I also offer my thanks to the large number of people who helped in more minor ways through the provision of information and the answering of queries. Needless to say, none of those mentioned bears any responsibility for the way I interpreted and used the information they provided.

B.H.

1

SPORT, POLITICS AND POLICY

> Serious sport has nothing to do with fair play. It is bound up
> with hatred, jealousy, boastfulness, and disregard of all rules
> and sadistic pleasure in witnessing violence; in other words
> it is war minus the shooting.
>
> George Orwell, 'The Sporting Spirit', 1945[1]

> Footballs instead of cannon balls.
>
> Motto of the British Workers' Sports Federation[2]

In the last ten years or so there has been a considerable growth
in interest in the relationship between politics and sport, the role
of government in sport, and the way sport is organised. A
significant part of the explanation of the growth in interest is the
unaccustomed prominence of sport-related issues as major
political, rather than solely sporting, concerns, which has moved
sport from the back pages of national newspapers to the front
page. In Britain, in recent years, there has been a sustained debate
about the appropriate response to the problem of football
hooliganism. Although this problem, unfortunately for sport, has
been the most prominent there have been a number of other
issues which have entered the national arena for discussion, if
only briefly in some cases, including policies to reduce the level
of drug abuse by athletes, the level of government subsidy to
sport, the role of local authorities in managing local sports and
leisure facilities and the position of sport in the national curriculum.

The government has also been involved in a number of
sporting issues which have arisen at international level. In 1979
the Soviet Union invaded Afghanistan and one response by the
United States of America and other Western nations was to

1

suggest a boycott of the forthcoming Olympic Games which were scheduled to be held in Moscow in 1980. The British Prime Minister, Margaret Thatcher, promptly announced the government's support for the American initiative. Strong opposition came from many politicians and from most governing bodies of sport, who argued that while sport and politics could not be separated sport should not be used as a political weapon. Pressure to conform to government policy came in a number of ways, ranging from denying leave to athletes who were also members of the armed forces to withdrawing the special consular facilities normally made available during Olympic Games to any athlete who went to Moscow. More recently, in 1988, the cancellation of the winter tour of India by the English cricket team was the consequence of the Indian government's dissatisfaction with the policy of the Test and County Cricket Board and that of the British government towards apartheid in South Africa and towards those cricketers who insist on playing there. This issue threatened to disrupt the 1990 Commonwealth Games in New Zealand.

The aim of this book is to explore the institutional and political context within which sport is administered in Britain and also to explore the way policy for sport is made. As such the focus is on the identification of those organisations with a significant involvement in the administration of, and policy-making for, sport. Of particular importance are the various governmental organisations involved, including the Sport and Recreation Division of the Department of the Environment, local authorities and the Sports Council. However, it is accepted that policy is not simply the outcome of the pattern of interaction of a set of actors (individuals, institutions and organisations) in the policy process. Historical and ideological factors are undoubtedly important. It would be unwise to undertake a study of policy-making in sport without being aware of the historical development of the governing bodies of British sport and the roots that many have in a public school culture or without examining the significance of sexism, racism and chauvinism for the conduct and organis-ation of sport. While these form an important backdrop to the present study they are not the prime focus and are dealt with explicitly only briefly.

Although the book is primarily concerned with Britain it will

2

quickly become apparent that it is not possible to explore the policy process for issues such as football spectator violence or drug abuse by athletes without taking account of the increasingly important role of a wide range of international organisations, such as the International Olympic Committee, the major international sports federations, and governmental bodies such as the Council of Europe.

SPORT, POLITICS AND POLICY

In order to explore the relationship between sport, politics and policy it is necessary to establish some agreement about the use of these terms. Definition is frequently a soul-destroying exercise, as the more one attempts to capture the essence of the meaning of a human activity or the product of human activity the more one becomes aware of the ambiguities and the compromises necessary to arrive at a plausible definition. However, it is important to establish a common language if political science investigation is to take place.

Allison defines sport as 'the institutionalisation of skill and prowess' (Allison 1986: 5). This definition implies the existence of rules and an authority structure to enforce adherence to rules. Yet as it stands the definition is too vague to distinguish sport from many other forms of social activity. First of all it needs to be made clear that it is 'physical' activity that is essential to sport ('skill' is what we hope to develop but is not a necessary condition) and also that 'competition' is a key ingredient. Coakley provides a more comprehensive definition of sport as 'an institutionalised competitive activity that involves vigorous physical exertion or the use of relatively complex physical skills by individuals whose participation is motivated by a combination of intrinsic and extrinsic factors' (1986: 17). Coakley is at pains to distinguish sport from recreation, play and spectacle. All attempts at definition have grey edges and it would be possible to idle away considerable time debating whether professional wrestling, synchronised swimming and ice dancing qualified as sports. For our purposes Coakley's definition is sufficient to indicate the field of policy that is the concern of this book.

Politics is equally difficult to define. For Millar politics is an activity that 'arises out of disagreement, and it is concerned with

3

the use of government to resolve conflict in the direction of change or in the prevention of change' (1962: 16). The stimulus to political activity is disagreement and conflict. Crick shares Millar's definition of politics as a process for resolving disputes. He refers to politics as 'the activity by which differing interests within a given unit of rule are conciliated . . .' (1964: 21). It might be argued with some justification that the definitions provided by Millar and Crick, while being valuable because of their precision, are rather too narrow. The emphasis is not just on recognised political institutions but also on what one might call 'high' politics involving political parties, governments and major pressure groups.

A different emphasis is one that sees the defining characteristic of politics as the use of power at varying levels in society. Power is derived from the use or control of resources. Resources may be tangible, such as money and the ownership of land, or they may be intangible, such as moral authority (for example, of the Church of England) and political legitimacy (of an elected politician). These resources are sources of power to influence the choices of decision-makers. Decisions which affect our 'life chances' are not just taken by governments but may be taken by a wide range of organisations including schools, the workplace and the family. For the athlete additional powerful organisations would include local clubs, governing bodies of sport and international organising bodies. According to this definition politics is a ubiquitious phenomenon in our lives and cannot be seen as a separate activity. As Leftwich claims, 'politics is at the heart of *all* collective social activity, formal and informal, public and private, in *all* human groups, institutions and societies, not just some of them, and it always has been and always will be . . .' (1984: 63). According to this view politics is closely intertwined with the patterns of decision-making in a society, its ideologies and its distribution of power.

It is proposed to adopt this broader definition of politics for the purposes of this study as it will enable an examination, not just of the political relationship between government and sport, but also of the internal politics of sporting bodies themselves.

Sport and politics are relatively easy to define by comparison with the term 'policy'. The term may be used quite loosely to include what Hogwood refers to as 'policy as aspiration' (1987: 4) as well as more precisely to describe the 'deliberate choice of action or inaction' (Smith 1979: 13). But it is not just governments that can have policies; the governing bodies of sport, physical education bodies and individual clubs, for example, may all have policies which they seek to advance. However, public policy is concerned with the actions and positions adopted by the state.

Dye (1975: 1) defines public policy in very broad terms as 'whatever governments choose to do or not to do'. Jenkins (1978: 15) defines public policy more restrictively, and more valuably, as:

> a set of interrelated decisions taken by a political actor or group of actors concerning the selection of goals and the means of achieving them within a specified situation where these decisions should, in principle, be within the power of these actors to achieve.

As Hill and Bramley point out (1986: 3) this definition suggests a number of attributes of public policy. The stress on 'interrelated decisions' suggests that policy is the product of a pattern of decisions. The reference to 'political actors' draws attention to the relationship between power and policy and that while political actors may not hold formal office (as elected representatives or public officials) they must have control or influence over the use of resources which are a source of power. Third, policy is about setting objectives and making decisions about how they are to be achieved. The final element in Jenkins's definition is that policy should be achievable. This is more controversial, as it has been suggested that policy-makers will, on occasion, deliberately choose a policy for its symbolic properties. A government may announce policies that it suspects, hopes or knows cannot be achieved.

SPORT, POLITICS AND SOCIETY

 It is one of the common clichés associated with sport that 'sport and politics should not mix'. Showing the naivity of such a distinction is fast becoming a sport in its own right. Yet the regularity with which athletes, administrators and politicians express the preference for a clearer distinction between sport and politics is evidence of the widespread feeling that those involved in sport should aspire to some higher ideals than the intrigues and bargains of the political sphere.

For many it is the Olympic Games which best characterise the ideals of sport. In 1956 six national teams withdrew from the Melbourne Olympics, some in protest at the Russian invasion of Hungary and others because of opposition to the Anglo-French invasion of Suez. This action prompted Avery Brundage, former International Olympic Committee president, to comment that 'these countries show that they are unaware of one of our most important principles, namely that sport is completely free of politics' (quoted in Guttman 1984). For Brundage, politics was the 'dark background against which to project the bright world of amateur sports' (Guttman 1984: 96). Expressions of similar views may be found among administrators of British sport. Ron Emes, chairman of the CCPR Executive Committee, made the following plea in his opening address to the Council's 1987 annual conference

> The increasing influence that Government manifestly sought to exert on sport and sport's governing bodies at local, national and international level for reasons which were sometimes unclear, necessitated constant vigilance if sport was to retain the uniquely British tradition of independent management.
>
> (CCPR 1987: 10)

Although it would be easy to find many other examples of demands that politics keep out of sport, there are many involved in sport who recognise that seeking to insulate sport from politics is, at best, a pious hope. Indeed Baron de Courbertin, the founder of the modern Olympics, was well aware of the overlap between politics and sport and argued that the Olympics were an opportunity to foster unity and co-operation between nations. A similar acceptance of the overlap between politics and sport is evident in the report of the CCPR conference mentioned above. For while Emes was warning of the need for vigilance regarding the encroachment of government on sport, the same conference report contained a long list of issues on which the Council intended to lobby government, including privatisation of sports facility management, the content of the national curriculum and rate relief for sports clubs. As McIntosh observes, 'If sport was to influence politics it was hardly conceivable that the interaction should be in one direction only and that politics should have no bearing at all upon sport' (1979: 140).

6

The interweaving of sport and politics is evident at international, national and regional/local levels. At the international level there have been few Olympic Games this century which have not been the source or focus of political controversy. In 1908 the team from Finland, then a part of the Russian empire, refused to march in the opening ceremony under the Russian flag and chose instead to march as a separate group without a flag. In the Olympics immediately after the two world wars the defeated powers were not invited to participate. The 1936 Olympics were blatantly exploited by Hitler and the Nazis to extol the virtues of National Socialism and the supposed superiority of the Aryan race. Although the German team won the largest number of medals the black American athlete Jesse Owens stole the limelight by winning four gold medals and setting new Olympic records each time. In 1976 more than twenty African nations boycotted the Games in protest at the participation of New Zealand, whose government had earlier allowed its rugby team to play against racially selected South African sides. More recently the government put considerable pressure on British athletes not to attend the Moscow Olympics in 1980 following the Russian invasion of Afghanistan in late 1979. The United States refused to send a team to Moscow, with the consequence that Russia sent no athletes to compete in the Los Angeles Games in 1984. (See Espy 1979 and Taylor 1986 for fuller discussions of politics and the Olympic Games.)

Soccer also provides many examples of major international sporting events being used as a forum for government propaganda or as an arena for international politics. At one extreme there is the example of the defeat of Honduras by El Salvador, in a World Cup qualifying match in 1969, being the spark which turned the growing hostility between the two countries into open war. Similarly Whannel provides a number of examples of governments 'cleaning up' their cities prior to major international sporting events by rounding up drunks, the homeless and political dissidents, in order to present the world media with a favourable image (Whannel 1983: 5–6). In 1990 the Asian Games, scheduled to take place in China barely a year after the massacre of students in Tiananmen Square in 1989, will doubtless be used by the Chinese government in a similar fashion as part of the process of rehabilitating the regime in the eyes of the world.

At the other extreme, Denis Howell recounts how, during the World Cup finals staged in Britain in 1966, NATO, through the Foreign Office, first objected to the presence of the North Korean team in a NATO country and then objected to the flying of the North Korean flag and the playing of their national anthem. Howell and Sir Stanley Rous, president of FIFA, resolved the issue regarding anthems by not playing any except at the opening match and at the final, trusting of course that North Korea would not reach the final (Howell 1990: 171–2).

It is not just the World Cup that is a source of examples of the intertwining of sport and politics. 'Friendly' international matches have also been overshadowed by politics. In 1935 the visit by Germany, to play a match at Tottenham Hotspur's White Hart Lane ground, led to protests from trade unions and demands that the match should be cancelled because of the offence that might be given to the large local Jewish population. In 1938 the England team were 'advised by Britain's Ambassador, Sir Neville Henderson, to give the Nazi salute in Berlin's Olympic Stadium four months ahead of the Munich "piece of paper" of appeasement' (Grayson 1988).

Unfortunately most of the examples of the overlap between sport and politics suggest either that politicians have exploited sport for nationalist, racist or other dubious purposes, or that when sport and politics intertwine it is sport that has its ideals undermined and exploited. However, there are some examples of a mutually beneficial relationship where sport has been a positive force for improving international relations. For example, the tentative steps towards a thawing of East–West relations in the early 1970s were accompanied by cultural and sporting exchanges as when the USA sent a table tennis team to China as a first step to more traditional diplomatic relations. A further, more recent, example concerned the holding of a marathon in Berlin on New Year's Day 1990 which followed a route that weaved its way through both East and West Berlin as a way of symbolising the moves towards unification of East and West Germany. Regrettably, similar examples are comparatively rare.

Although many of the most dramatic examples of the links between sport and politics come from the international level there is an equally wide range of illustrations to be found at the national level. The effect of political decisions on sport may be seen in legislation, in the allocation of grants and in the establishment of administrative arrangements for sport. In Britain the law has been used to prohibit particular sports, for example bear-baiting. It has also been used to promote particular sports, for example archery in the time of Edward IV, or sport in general as under the terms of the 1944 Education Act, which made physical education a compulsory part of the school curriculum along with religious instruction.

Although British politicians are maybe more restrained at explicitly exploiting sport for their own, or their party's, advantage there are few who can resist the sporting 'photo-opportunity'. Harold Wilson was probably the first Prime Minister to cultivate an association between his government and sporting success. The holding of government receptions for successful teams, attendance at sporting events and the bestowing of honours on sportsmen and women were all evident during the 1964–70 government. Even Margaret Thatcher was not able to resist being photographed with the England football team or taking part in the draw for the Scottish FA Cup. However, the most significant involvement of the government in sport is in its use as part of a solution to other problems, such as inner-city decline and juvenile delinquency. This aspect of government involvement is explored in more detail in chapters 2 and 3.

At the local government level the relationship between politics and sport is no less intense. Local authorities have used their control of resources to attempt to influence the decisions and policies of individual sportsmen and sportswomen and their clubs. In 1989 Derbyshire County Council withdrew its grant of £14,000 from Derbyshire Cricket Club because of the decision of its captain, Kim Barnett, to join a tour of South Africa. A few years earlier Leicester City Council had banned Leicester Rugby Club from using council playing facilities because a number of club members, selected for the England team, had agreed to tour South Africa. The ban was subsequently overturned by the House of Lords. The involvement of local authorities with sport and politics is not just limited to isolated decisions and conflicts, but also reflects a more general level of interest and responsibility. As will be demonstrated in chapter 4, where the role of local authorities is explored more fully, local government fulfils a major part in defining the character of local provision and sport opportunities. Not only do local authorities make major decisions about the level of provision for their area they also decide where facilities will be located and how access will be controlled, for example through the adoption of a particuar policy of pricing and subsidy. Local authorities frequently fulfil a central role in co-ordinating public, private and voluntary provision for their area by means of planning controls and the distribution of grant aid.

THE POLITICS OF SPORT

Most of the examples referred to above in the discussion of the relationship between politics and sport illustrate how sport serves as an object of political conflict or else as an arena for the furthering of political aims. An emphasis on the use or exploitation of sport by political interests, however, gives only a partial view of the nature of the relationship between politics and sport. To concentrate on the interconnection between politics *and* sport is to risk overlooking the importance of examining the politics *of* sport.

Following Leftwich's broad definition of politics, sport, like any other sphere of human activity, is the product of the distribution of power in society, the dominant ideology and cultural form of the society and its pattern of social organisation. British society has been defined as generally hierarchical, deferential, class-based and democratic (Rose 1980) with a degree of tension arising from localised religious antagonisms (Alderman 1978; Arthur 1983) and rather more widespread racism and sexism (Husbands 1986). If one accepts this description, and there is much scope for disagreement, one would expect these cultural contours to be evident in most institutions and organisations within society, including sports organisations. This therefore raises questions regarding the extent to which sport reflects and confirms, for example, social divisions along racial, sexual, religious and class lines. Now, while the politics of sports organisations is not a central focus of this book it cannot be ignored. Public policy exists on issues such as racial and sexual discrimination, on religious tolerance and on equality of opportunity. It is legitmate therefore to examine the organisation of sport and to assess the degree to

10

which it conforms to the aims of public policy in these areas and also the extent to which sport displays the same cultural characteristics as the rest of society.

One major issue which confronts us in exploring the politics of sport is racism. A superficial survey of sport might lead one to conclude that sport provides one area of human activity free from the stain of racial discrimination. The clear representation of blacks in national athletics and football teams suggests a high degree of equality of opportunity. In terms of general levels of participation the small amount of research evidence available does suggest that, in London, 'at least some groups within the designation black and ethnic minorities are participating in numbers which reflect their proportions in the community' (London Regional Council for Sport and Recreation 1989: 15).[3] The evidence also suggests that ethnic minorities are involved in a range of sports, including athletics, weight training, swimming and football, but that the range is wider among white participants.

Moving away from a focus on the recreational/competitive level to the competitive/professional level, it is again the shortage of research evidence that is most striking. Unfortunately there are few studies of the position of black athletes in British sport to compare with Arthur Ashe's exploration of the black American experience of sport (1988) or Phillip Hoose's more recent analysis of the processes by which ethnic minorities are typecast for particular sporting roles (1989).[4] Hoose's study suggests that the media bear much responsibility for supporting popular prejudices that ethnic minorities are suitable only for some roles in sport and are unsuitable for others. Evidence for this hypothesis is drawn from a wide range of sports and concludes that in many sports in America there exists a 'white centre' (the pitcher–catcher axis in baseball and the quarterback in American football) from which blacks, in particular, are virtually excluded. The explanation for their exclusion lies in media-supported/generated stereotypes of the character of ethnic minorities and the effect on box office takings of too many black sportsmen and women. Hoose accuses the media of portraying 'blacks as undisciplined brutes, Latins as explosive little firecrackers, and whites as heady, gutty leaders who overcome their damned inferior equipment through Puritan effort' (p. xviii). In relation to the box office value of white players Hoose cites the limitation

11

on the number of overseas players in baseball as an example of attempts to preserve the marketability of the sport to white fans. As a result of these attitudes it is not surprising to find that blacks were barred from playing baseball, basketball and football at the highest levels until 1945. Blacks either did not play or else played in their own leagues (Mason 1988).

In Britain there are only a handful of books which address the question of racism in sport directly and there is clearly a need for a more thorough analysis of the issues. Mason reviews briefly the occurrence of racism in British sport. He describes the slow move of ethnic minorities to a position where they could compete for national titles, pointing to the decisions of the British Boxing Board of Control in the 1930s and 1940s not to allow non-whites to challenge for British championships as an example. Mason has also carried out an interesting, though he admits preliminary, survey of the role of black football players in the English first division. His conclusions support those of Hoose regarding the selective positioning of black Americans on the field of play. Mason concludes that in the 1985–86 season there were no black captains in the Football League despite the fact that black players were well established at first division and international level. In passing Mason observes that two of Britain's pre-eminent football clubs, Liverpool and Everton, have a very poor record of selecting black players. Indeed Liverpool has a better record of signing white South Africans than black players. Bruce Grobbelaar, born in South Africa though brought up in what was then Rhodesia, is the most recent in a series of South African signings going back to the 1920s and 1930s (Hill 1989: 75, 105). South Africans apart, Liverpool FC have displayed a consistent willingness to sign local players and the fact that one Liverpudlian in ten is black makes the relative absence of black players more significant. Hill (1989) in his review of the career of John Barnes documents the insidiousness of racism in English league football. Cliff Marshall and Howard Gayle, both black players, made a small number of first team appearances for Everton and Liverpool respectively in the late 1970s and early 1980s, but it was not until the transfer of John Barnes from Watford in 1987 that Merseyside acquired a black footballer who held a regular first team place.

Mason, like Hoose, analysed the positions held by black footballers and concluded that black players predominate in the

Table 1 First division footballers by race and position, 1985–86 (%)

	Attackers	*Midfield*	*Defenders*
All players	27.8	29.4	42.4
White players	23.3	31.2	44.9
Black players	60.5	13.1	26.3

Source: Mason (1988: 16).

attacking positions while the midfield and, to a lesser extent, the defensive positions are largely the preserve of white players (see Table 1). Just as baseball and American football have their 'white centre' so, it seems, does English football.

The clear suggestion is that 'midfield generals' are predominantly white whereas 'mercurial' or 'inspired' goal scorers are black. As Coakley observes, many of the attempts to rationalise the discrimination in field positions have their root in 'traditionally racist beliefs that blacks are best suited for tasks involving speed, agility and quickness, and whites are best suited for tasks involving intelligence, leadership and decision-making' (1986: 152).

It is possible to extend this survey across other sports, including cricket, swimming and athletics. In cricket, for example, Yorkshire County Cricket Club have been accused of racism on a number of occasions largely on the evidence that they do not have any black cricketers in their team despite having large black populations, with strong cricketing traditions, close by. The club's rule that potential players must be born in Yorkshire, which is perceived as an idiosyncrasy by people outside Yorkshire, is seen by some Yorkshire-born blacks as a signal of their exclusion. However, this is an accusation that is strongly denied by officials of the club. Joe Lister, the club secretary, argued that 'in the last few years Yorkshire have made strenuous attempts to involve the ethnic minority cricketers and every boy recommended gets his opportunity.'[5] However, this comment was made at the same time that Brian Close, the club chairman, was publicly apologising for having referred to 'bloody Pakistanis' during a television investigation of allegations of racism in British sport.[6]

Mason has also reviewed the situation in athletics, noting the absence of black middle distance runners. He also considers the circumstances in Rugby Union and League, again pointing out the small number of black players competing at the highest levels. Mason rightly urges caution in ascribing too much significance to his observations. For example, he suggests that the domination of sprint events by black athletes may be explained partly by the strong role models provided by black American sprinters such as Calvin Smith, Ed Moses and Carl Lewis, and partly by the racial stereotyping by white British coaches and trainers who see black runners as lacking the 'staying power' for middle distance running. While this is a plausible hypothesis, it leaves a number of questions unresolved, for example why black British athletes seek to emulate black American sprinters and not the equally illustrious line of black African, and particularly Kenyan, middle distance runners. However, what is most apparent is the woeful inadequacy of research in this area and the consequent caution needed before drawing firm conclusions.

While athletics can claim a high degree of access by ethinc minorities to participation in the sport there is still a significant absence of ethnic minority administrators and coaches. For example, while just under one third of the British Olympic athletics team was black there was not one black coach among the total of nine. However, the Amateur Athletics Association firmly denied any institutionalised racism in athletics and pointed to the increasing number of black athletes who are now in administrative positions in British athletics. In a general survey of the representation of ethnic minorities at official and administrative levels in sport the London Council concluded that:

> the lack of coaches and leaders from black and ethnic minorities was matched, if not exceeded, by the shortage of officials, referees and umpires from these groups. . . . and the limited opportunities available to black and ethnic minorities to play their part in, and to be trained for, leadership, management and administration.
>
> (LRCSR 1989: 24, 38)

If the study of racism in sport is inadequate then the study of sexism in sport is only slightly better. In terms of their involvement in the governing bodies of sport, Whannel and Tomlinson (1984) have noted the absence of women from the administrative hierarchy of the International Olympic

Committee between 1894 and 1981. Bowles and Chappell observe that 'the majority of members on controlling bodies in athletics tend to be men' (1986: 27). This has the consequence, claim Bowles and Chappell, that the more prestigious events, especially those that are televised, include fewer events for women. At Olympic level there were no events for women in the 1908 Olympics, only 32 out of 115 in 1964 and 73 out of 153 in 1984. White and Brackenridge (1985) examined the participation of women in sport both as participants and also as administrators. They found that while the number of female competitors participating in the Olympic Games has steadily increased there was little evidence of a corresponding increase in the proportion of female officials and that the female officials that were present fulfilled 'stereotyped roles such as physiotherapist, interpreter, masseuse and hostess' (1985: 98). In their review of the involvement of women in the governing bodies of British sports they found a similar picture. In badminton, for example, 44 per cent of participants are female but only 12 per cent of senior administrators were female in 1970–71 and only 14 per cent by 1982–83. In conclusion White and Brackenridge comment that:

> There is a greater gender dominance by men in the 1980s than in the 1960s and 1970s. Though women participants appear to be accepting the male model of sport, it seems that relatively few of them remain within the upper strata of the sport structure as administrators and officials.
>
> (1985: 104)

The major governing bodies of British sport have shown a marked lack of enthusiasm for the participation of women in their sports. In the 1920s and 1930s women began to set up their own sporting organisations, often with the aim of affiliating to the national governing body. This was a path followed by women athletes, who formed the Women's Amateur Athletics Association in 1922 only to have their application for affiliation rejected by the AAA. In general women either organise their own organising bodies or have to accept token representation on most national governing bodies, for example the one woman on the FA Council at a time when interest in women's football is rising rapidly.

At a more fundamental level there is much evidence to suggest that within society in general there is a perception that being a woman and being an athlete are incompatible. This is complemented by a perception within sport that to be a woman is to be an inadequate athlete and to be a successful woman athlete is to be an inadequate woman. For men participation in sport confirms and enhances their sexuality but for women participation undermines and questions their sexuality. Consequently women are required to establish their sexuality medically through the indignity of 'sex tests' and also culturally by having 'to demonstrate, often to male sports journalists, that their interest in sport does not detract from their commitment to heterosexual relationships, marriage, and family life' (Critcher 1986).

In 1982 the Sports Council in *Sport in the Community: the Next Ten Years* set a number of broad policy objectives concerning participation. One of the targets was to close the gap between male and female participation in indoor and outdoor sport. Six years later it was forced to conclude that while the gap between men's and women's participation had marginally closed 'women's indoor participation rates still lag some 14 per cent behind' (Sports Council 1988: 27). The Council further concluded that 'participation by women in outdoor sport has fallen whilst that by men has increased . . .' (27). This levelling off in participation rates comes after a decade of steady increase in female participation in sport.

Holt (1989) suggests that much of the history of the growing female involvement in sport does not reflect greater equality between the sexes but rather reflects a process of confirmation of traditional female roles and reinforces the orthodox view of the woman's place.

> Women's sport outside school came to be rooted in a new kind of suburban culture centred around the family garden and the private club, which drew the public and domestic domain more closely together . . . Female sport served as much to enhance woman in her domestic role as to liberate her from it.
>
> (Holt 1989: 118)

The development of more competitive team sports, through the expansion of girls' public schools in the late nineteenth and early twentieth centuries, such as hockey, netball and lacrosse, may also be seen in Darwinian terms that strong sons required strong, fit mothers. Thus fitness and femininity could be reconciled, as both 'were needed to create healthy, moral, middle-class families' (Holt 1989: 119). However, although sport for women was encouraged, it was on a selective basis both in terms of class and in terms of sport. For example, while tennis was socially acceptable as a sport for women owing to its confinement to middle class clubs and suburban gardens, cycling was frowned upon partly because it allowed too much independence.

The slow progress of women's sport at Olympic level has already been noted. What needs to be added is that progress at this level was not uniform across all sports. Prior to 1914 female involvement was largely limited to horse-riding and figure-skating, and before 1948 women's participation in track events was limited to the races under 100 metres (Holt 1989: 130). Even today women may have world championship competitions in football, judo and the pole vault, but they are not allowed to display their skill at the Olympics. As Mason wryly observes, 'One wonders how far the introduction of rhythmic gymnastics and synchronized swimming is a return to the idea of "appropriate" events for women' (1988: 11).

There is a long list of other issues arising from a study of the politics *of* sport of which sexism and racism are only the most prominent. Holt (1989) examines the role of sport in cementing the British Empire and in acting as a basis for anti-colonial nationalism. Jones (1988) explores the interweaving of sport and socialism in Britain between the wars. Knox (1986, 1987) and Sugden and Bairner (1986) both explore the intertwining of sport and politics in Northern Ireland and illustrate the extent to which sport reflects and reinforces the prevailing sectarian divisions. Donnelly (1986) charts the conflict between access to the countryside for the mass of the population with the assertion of property rights by the landowners. James (1963) relates the prevailing political consensus to the way in which sport is played. He conludes that, in the case of cricket, the decline of creative and adventurous batting and its replacement with the long forward-defensive push is a reflection of a security-conscious, welfare state attitude. 'The cricketers of today play the cricket of a specialised stratum, that of functionaries in the Welfare State' (211).

THE STRUCTURE OF THE BOOK

Politics is about 'who gets what when and how' (Lasswell 1958). In studying the politics of sport this means examining, for players and spectators, who plays/watches, what they play/watch, when they play/watch and in what circumstances they play/watch. Questions of class, race, sex, age, etc., are important aspects of issues concerning access to sport and how sport is controlled. They are at least as important as questions of party control of the House of Commons, manifestos and administrative arrangements. The purpose of this book is to explore the administrative context within which these values and attitudes are manifest as a basis on which a fuller investigation of the way in which ideology and administrative structure are integrated in British sport. Consequently the focus for this book is the organisation of the institutional actors in the policy process and the characteristics of the pattern of interrelationships they are involved in.

The book continues, in chapter 2, with a brief survey of the evolution of the government's interest in sport and it examines the way in which governments have perceived sport and illustrates the strong tendency for government to view sport as a means to an end rather than as an end in itself. This leads into an examination of the role of the Minister for Sport and organisation of the Sport and Recreation Division of the Department of the Environment.[7] Chapter 3 focuses on the role of local government and examines the way in which the role has developed from its early association with public health and welfare. The chapter also examines the ways in which responsi- bility for sport and recreation is allocated between levels of local government and within individual authorities. The current range of issues facing authorities are also examined, including strategic planning, competitive tendering and the effects of the local financial management of schools on the policy of dual use. Included in this chapter is a discussion of the particular circumstances surrounding the provisionn of leisure services in Northern Ireland.

Chapter 4 reviews the role of the Sports Council, tracing its evolution from the Advisory Sports Council and also examining its relationship with the Central Council of Physical Recreation. The Sports Council fulfils a central role in the financing and planning of sports policy and is at the centre of a wide network of relationships which stretches to all corners of the sports policy community, both national and international. One especially important link is with the large number of governing bodies of sport, and a consideration of their organisation, financing and activities is the subject of chapter 5. Three governing bodies are selected for a closer examination, namely the Hockey Association, the Football Association and the Amateur Athletic Association. The last two were chosen because they control two of the most significant sports in Britain. Hockey was selected because it was seen as representative of a group of sports, others would include volleyball and badminton, whose governing bodies are having to cope with the problems associated with a rapid growth in popularity. As well as examining the role of these domestic governing bodies the role of the international governing bodies and international organising bodies is also explored. As will be argued, the importance of these international bodies for domestic policy is growing.

Chapter 6 presents a theoretical framework within which the policy process for sport may be analysed. A variety of frameworks are briefly reviewed before the 'policy community' model is outlined and explored in more detail and suggested as the most suitable vehicle for the examination of the sports policy process.

Chapters 7, 8 and 9 provide a detailed examination of three major current issues in sport, namely football hooliganism, drug abuse by athletes and sport in schools. The background to each of the issues is outlined and the membership and operation of the policy network developed to deal with the issue are examined. The final chapter draws together the various themes developed during the course of the book and summarises the main features of the sports policy process.

2

CENTRAL GOVERNMENT AND SPORT

What is the role of a Minister for Sport who has surrendered all his authority to the Sports Council?

Denis Howell (1990: 231)

The role of the state here is that of guardian and foster parent. It cannot invade the institutions of leisure without perverting them to its own uses, and losing sight, in the process, of what those uses are.

Roger Scruton (1980: 100)

Public sector involvement in sport and recreation is divided between a number of levels of government and between a range of functional agencies. Before looking at the development of the government's role in sport it is useful to have an appreciation of the main features of both the administrative map for the policy area and the distribution of decision-making responsibilities. Mapping administrative responsibilities is comparatively easy; Acts of Parliament, statements of account, departmental handbooks, departmental circulars and annual reports all provide information about where the administrative burden falls. It is much more difficult to identify who is involved in the decision-making process. At the centre of the policy process there are those who exercise legitimate authority by virtue of being elected representatives in local councils or the House of Commons or by being a nominee of these bodies, on the Sports Council for example. However, the legitimate authority of these bodies is complemented by political influence which may, for example, be derived from control over economic resources, information or the machinery of implementation, such as that possessed by the national and international governing bodies of sport.

The focus of this chapter is the role of central government in sport and as with many areas of government responsibility the primary function of central government is not to deliver services but to provide the policy framework and to establish the financial guidelines. This is very much the case with regard to sport.

At central government level there are a number of departments that have an interest and involvement in sport policy. The most important is the Department of the Environment, which includes the Minister for Sport, who has a specialist Sport and Recreation Division to provide administrative support. Although the DOE is the lead department on sports issues it does not have any executive responsibilities. Its functions are to determine and administer the Sports Council's grant and to establish the policy framework for the service. The Sports Council, by virtue of its expertise and contacts with governing bodies, has a clear capacity to influence policy. Other government bodies, such as the Countryside Commission and the Nature Conservancy Council, also have influence on sports issues where they overlap with their principal areas of responsibility.

Local authorities are also influential in the policy process, owing in part to the legitimacy derived from being elected bodies and also by virtue of the fact that they control and finance the vast bulk of facilities available to local communities. As a result, despite being increasingly constrained by a steady flow of legislation in the 1980s, local authorities still retain a high degree of discretion concerning the nature and extent of the sports and leisure services they provide.

Turning to the administrative arrangements for sport in the public sector, these rest primarily with the Sports Council and with local authorities. The Sports Council is directly responsible for six national residential sports centres which account for just under one fifth of its grant. The bulk of its income is passed on to governing bodies or to local authorities by way of grant aid and is used to fund new sports facilities or related projects. By far the most important providers of sports facilities and opportunities are the local authorities.

THE DEVELOPMENT OF THE GOVERNMENT'S ROLE IN SPORT

Attempts to explain the evolution of policy are notoriously difficult. There is often the temptation to see pattern and intention in what might properly be described as haphazard and serendipitous. This is certainly the case in reviewing the development of government involvement in sport where it is possible to see the history of sport policy as piecemeal and *ad hoc*, with little coherence and few signs of the presence of strategic objectives determined by the government. This interpretation suggests that government has, at best, a limited role in sport. Indeed the 1975 White Paper, *Sport and Recreation*, stated that 'It is not for the Government to seek to control or direct the diverse activities of people's leisure time' (Department of the Environment 1975: 4). Travis refers to a nineteenth century tradition of 'identifying *separate* or *specific areas* of failure' the solutions to which 'should *not* be seen as a normative planning and management process in a welfare context', but rather as 'a scatter of items of isolated legislation' (1979: 1, 2). Alternatively, it may be argued that much, if not most, sport policy can be explained in terms of class tension and conflict, giving the evolution of policy a coherence resulting from a strategic concern to protect particular class interests and to 'rigorously [regulate] the use made of free time through the state repressive apparatus' (Hargreaves 1985a: 220; see also Hargreaves 1985b). A more accurate interpretation of the development of public policy lies somewhere between these two extremes. Nevertheless as the following review demonstrates there is, particularly in the nineteenth century, a strong relationship between the perception of social change and of social problems by influential social groups, such as landowners, churchmen and some industrialists and a pattern of government policy-making for sport which reflects the recurring themes of social stability, defence of privilege, and paternalism.

Much of the government's past involvement in sport was directed towards particular sports and was designed to prohibit or promote some sports while attempting to restrict opportunities to pursue others. As long ago as 1541 the law was used to prohibit a number of sports and pastimes which were considered frivolous, such as football, but it was also used to require that every healthy man under the age of sixty should possess and practise the use of the longbow. Of all the long established sports it is hunting which best illustrates the variety of uses to which the law may be put in respect of sport. In hunting not only was the law used to control the type of hunting allowed, but it was also used to control access to the countryside. For many hundreds of years the law was used to protect the sporting interests of the powerful. The Game Law of 1671 limited hunting to the rich and imposed severe penalties on poorer people who poached game, even on their own land. Later Game Laws increased the severity of penalties and made the right to hunt more restrictive. The history of the Game Laws is a reflection of the social divisions of the time and the fact that the laws were produced by a Parliament dominated by the landowning aristocracy and gentry and enforced by a magistracy composed of people from the same social classes. Indeed it was not until the early part of the nineteenth century that the most repressive clauses of the Game Laws were modified or repealed. During the nineteenth and twentieth centuries the law has continued to reflect the power of particular sporting and social interests and the weakness of others. For example the 1835 Cruelty to Animals Act outlawed bull- and bear-baiting but did not interfere with hunting and although repeated campaigns have attempted to outlaw fox-hunting they have, so far, proved notably unsuccessful.

The history of hunting is closely linked to the history of access to the countryside. The enclosure of common land dates from the thirteenth century but was at its most intense during the last half of the eighteenth century. Donnelly (1986) charts the campaign to regain the right of public access to land for recreational and sporting purposes. The mass trespass on Kinder Scout (land owned by the Duke of Devonshire) in 1932 marked a turning point in the access campaign, although it was not until 1949 that the National Parks and Access to the Countryside Act was passed. However, the history of access to the countryside in the last century reflects the tension between the political strength and privilege of landowners and the growing concern of industrialists for the poor state of health of their work force. So at the same time (the 1830s and 1840s) that Game Laws and enclosures were depriving the urban working class of opportunities to benefit from fresh air and exercise in the countryside, legislation was being passed that attempted, though not very successfully, to limit the enclosure of common land near large towns and Parliament was voting money for the creation of urban parks.

In addition to parliamentary legislation and local bye-laws that dealt with sport there was an equally important range of policy decisions that, while not specifically concerned with sport, were to have a considerable impact on the development of sports facilities and opportunities. Some, such as the Baths and Wash-Houses Act 1846 and the Public Health Act 1875, were concerned with overcoming the unhealthy consequences of the industrial revolution. The Baths and Wash-Houses Act 1846 was primarily concerned with improving the level of personal hygiene, but a number of local authorities also built swimming baths, and over the early part of this century the recreational and sporting role of baths became dominant. A clear acknowledgement of the importance of the recreational role of baths came with the passing of the Public Health Act 1936, which gave explicit permission to local authorities to build baths exclusively for swimming. The 1875 Public Health Act allowed local authorities to buy land to be used as public parks and while there was no mention of them being used for sporting purposes their gradual establishment provided a basis for the development of urban sport.

In order to understand the significance of the legal changes described above it is necessary to set them within the context of the social dislocation resulting from urbanisation and industrial-isation and the tensions between social classes that these processes generated. The requirements of the capitalist economy for a large, locally available and disciplined workforce and an organised work routine meant that many of the traditional rural sports and sporting occasions were either impossible in the urban context or were considered to be inappropriate or incompatible with the industrial economy. Although Coalter *et al.* overstate the case when they observe that 'the roots of public policy for leisure lay in repression' (1986: 9) there is undoubtedly a strong element of social control over popular sport in much nineteenth century legislation. These economic priorities were complemented and reinforced by the influence of puritan Christianity and its strong opposition to sport on Sunday. Many urban local authorities had bye-laws prohibiting organised sport on Sundays on their land well into the present century. For example, it was only in 1934 that the London County Council, very reluctantly, rescinded its ban on organised Sunday sport in its parks, and then only after the Labour Party had gained control of the council in the elections of that year (Jones 1988: 150–2).

A number of themes run through this brief survey of government policy. The first was a strong element of paternalism towards the 'lower classes'. Nineteenth century philanthropy, which was so important in influencing the shape of education and housing policy, was also significant in affecting the character of policy towards sport. But the motives of social reformers such as the Cadbury family were a mixture of paternalistic concern for the health and well-being of the workforce coupled with an appreciation that a fit workforce was also a more productive one (Holt 1989: 143). The second theme is the concern to defend privilege, as evident in the conflicts over access to the countryside and hunting. Privilege and the determination of the rich to maintain it is also at the heart of the conflicts over professionalism which bedevilled many sports in the late Victorian period. However, these conflicts took place largely outside the formal political arena.

The third theme evident in the survey is the feeling that too much (undisciplined) sport and leisure for the poor was a danger to social stability and that, if at all possible, sport needed to be harnessed as a force for social integration and control. For much of the last half of the nineteenth century there had been growing concern among the middle class about the potential for social instability arising from the swelling ranks of the urban working class (Bailey 1979). This middle class concern was reflected in a mix of religious and political debate over the problem of urban radicalism. As Holt comments:

> Fear of urban radicalism, above all, was what galvanized the rich into thinking about the poor and gave weight to the wider programme of moral reform and education that was proposed by a vigorous minority of evangelicals and idealistic political economists.

> (1989: 137)

The fostering of the development of 'rational recreation' was complemented by an attempt to prohibit the more undisciplined sports of the street and waste ground and was seen by many as an important element in maintaining social stability. Young urban males were the target group and organisations such as the Boys' Brigade and the Young Men's Christian Association relied on the prominence of sport in their activities as a major attraction. Football clubs such as Birmingham, Aston Villa and Fulham have their origins in Christian organisations (Holt 1989: 138). The 'muscular Christian' movement's aim to instil self-discipline in the poor through participation in sport was reflected in the legislation of the time, particularly the 1870 and 1902 Education Acts. However, the emphasis in the legislation was very much on physical training and drill rather than on the development of the team sports that were deemed suitable only for their 'betters' in the public schools.

The first half of the twentieth century was a period during which working class sports, particularly football (Mason 1980), but also rugby league (Delaney 1984) and league cricket (Hill 1987) became more independent of their middle class and aristocratic patrons. It was also a time when governmental concern about the fitness of the nation's youth was clearly evident. The consumption of human capital in the first world war and the approach of a second war with Germany were the main stimuli for the passage of the Physical Training and Recreation Act 1937. This Act was followed a few years later by the Education Act 1944 in which the government required local education authorities to provide facilities for 'recreation and physical training', thus going beyond simply giving local authorities permission or encouragement to provide sport and recreational opportunities. An important consequence of the Act was the growth of sports facilities in schools and also the appointment of trained physical education staff. By the middle of the twentieth century legislation designed to control sport and recreation was balanced by an increasing volume of legislation aimed at promoting sport and recreation. However, most of this promotional legislation was permissive rather than mandatory. It allowed local authorities to provide sporting and recreational opportunities but did not require them to do so. A further characteristic is, as Torkildsen has noted, that 'despite . . . enabling Acts of Parliament, governments consistently viewed recreation as a beneficial means towards some other ends' (1986: 15). These ends might be higher standards of personal hygiene or a fitter nation, but it was not until the early 1960s that government began to consider, with renewed interest, sport (and recreation) as a relatively discrete policy area.

What makes the period from 1960 onwards distinctive is not so much that new issues or themes emerged to replace those of the past, rather it is the acceptance by government that sport was a legitimate governmental responsibility. For Hargreaves the acceptance by government of a more central role in sport policy was due, in part, to a continuing concern with the potential for urban disorder led by young people, but was also due to 'the realisation ... that state aided sport could help to improve Britain's international sporting performance' (1985a: 221) and that this might have diplomatic benefits. The influential Wolfenden Report, while warning that talking 'as if sport could properly be used as a major instrument of international diplomacy ... seems to us to reveal a serious lack of sense of proportion', went on to argue that international sporting contacts had a potential to 'yield rich dividends in international understanding' (1960: 73, 76). A third pressure on government was the growing public demand, supported by effective lobbying by governing bodies, for an expansion of opportunities for sport and recreation. What was also emerging in the 1950s and early 1960s was a growing interest in the pursuit of excellence, partly due to Britain's steady 'decline' in international competition, and partly due to the early sporting successes for the 'systematic planning' of East Germany and the Soviet Union (University of Birmingham 1956; Anthony 1980).

The policy themes of the 1960s of social order, desire for international success and the increasing demand for wider sport and recreational opportunities need to be set within the broader political consensus surrounding the maturation of the welfare state and the ideological pre-eminence of social democracy and also within an economic context of growing affluence. This economic and political context for sport policy was supportive of notions of service planning, public participation and equality of opportunity, all of which were important in affecting the shape of policy development for sport. The establishment of the Advisory Sports Council in 1965, following the recommendation of the Wolfenden Committee, introduced a strong element of planning and co-ordination into the provision of sports facilities and provided a focus for the campaign to expand participation in sport.

The political perception of sport as an element in the fabric of the welfare state was confirmed in the 1975 White Paper, *Sport and Recreation*, which is one of the few attempts by government to provide a comprehensive philosophy of sport and recreation. Much of what was contained in the White Paper reflected the conventional priorities that had been firmly established in the nineteenth and early twentieth centuries. It refers to the role of sport and recreation in contributing to the 'physical and mental well-being' of the population. It repeats the, now familiar, assertion that 'By reducing boredom and urban frustration, participation in active recreation contributes to the reduction of hooliganism and delinquency among young people' (DOE 1975: 3). The White Paper also refers to the benefits for the morale and inspiration of the young that accrue from international sporting success. However, the White Paper was distinctive first in linking these objectives as part of an overall philosophy of the government's role in sport and recreation, and second in asserting that sport and recreation had a legitimate right to a place within the range of welfare services.

The policy guidelines contained in the White Paper stressed the value of sport in the general welfare of the community and gave emphasis to the need to focus on the creation of greater equality of access to sport and recreation. Thus while supporting the principle of mass participation the White Paper highlighted the requirement to target resources on the urban poor, the young, the disabled and the retired. In addition, and in a somewhat contradictory fashion, the government also stressed the importance of 'diverting resources to those who are gifted in sport' (1975: 18).

In the late 1970s and early 1980s the Sports Council was the vehicle for a policy shift which downgraded the 'Sport for All' campaign and gave greater prominence to 'concentrating resources instead on the symptoms, as opposed to causes, of social unrest in the inner cities, and to promoting the elite sector . . .' (Hargreaves 1985a: 223). The stimulus of the 1981 urban riots resulted in a number of urban initiatives (though many would argue that they were palliatives) involving sport, for example the extension of the Urban Programme to cover the provision of sporting and recreational opportunities and the development by the Sports Council of the 'Action Sport' programme (Coalter 1984: 26). In the 1980s sport has generally become more heavily politicised as the dominant consensus has shifted away from welfare state collectivism towards the economic liberalism of the Thatcher governments with their antipathy towards public expenditure, preference for market solutions to problems of service provision and willingness to use sport as a weapon in international relations.

As Britain moves into the 1990s government policy for sport retains a number of traditional features, but it has also developed a number of priorities derived from contemporary Conservative philosophy. The current preoccupation with football hooliganism is a manifestation of the traditional concern with the problem of 'too much' leisure for the young. The direction of recreation provision towards the inner cities is also a long-standing feature of government policy despite the lack of 'firm evidence that vandalism, delinquency and anti-social behaviour can be changed by increased recreation spending' (Henry 1985). The privatisation of leisure services' management is a logical application of the Conservatives' commitment to limit state activity and to introduce market competition. The commitment to wider participation is still evident within the Sports Council although there are signs that the fostering of excellence may become a more central priority again.

At the end of the 1980s the Minister for Sport initiated a number of policy reviews, including an examination of sporting opportunities for the disabled, coaching and sport and recreation in the inner city; the last two were carried out in conjunction with the Sports Council. Although the reviews do not constitute, in themselves, the development of a comprehensive strategy, they are gradually expanding the scope of interest of the Sport and Recreation Division and represent the adoption of a more promotional role by central government

GOVERNMENT ADMINISTRATION AND SPORT

One of the key developments of the last thirty years, apart from the creation of the Sports Council, has been the establishment of the Sport and Recreation Division (SARD) and the appointment of a Minister with special responsibility for sport within the Department of the Environment.[1] These changes have provided a focus for policy co-ordination and formulation, and this section discusses, not only the operation of SARD and the way in which the role of the Minister has evolved, but also the problems faced in administering and developing policy for sport and recreation and the extent to which they have been overcome by these new administrative arrangements

The nature of the problem of co-ordination is easily illustrated. In the early part of 1989 a number of parliamentary questions relating to sports issues were asked by Members of Parliament. Each question was duly answered by the relevant Minister. On 23 February Tom Pendry asked a question concerning financial management in the Sports Council. This was answered by the Minister for Sport, Colin Moynihan, who has overall responsibility for the Sports Council. In reply to a question on 22 March from Mr Menzies Campbell concerning the proportion of health expenditure devoted to sports medicine, Michael Forsyth, on behalf of the Secretary of State for Scotland, stated that the information was not available. A month later, on 20 April, David Blunkett asked a question regarding the eligibility of sports clubs for exemption from the national non-domestic rate. Although a matter of intense interest to many non-profit-making sports clubs the answer was given by the Junior Minister at the DOE responsible for local government finance. On the same day Tony Banks asked a question concerning the implementation of the recommendations of the Popplewell Inquiry into the question of safety at football grounds. The reply was given by the Home Office Minister, as this issue was defined as primarily one of crowd safety and control rather than as a sports issue. Finally, a few days later (26 April) a question was asked by Anthony Favell about the government's plans to encourage tne participation of school-children in sport on Saturdays. Angela Rumbold answered for the Department of Education and Science. The involvement of so many government departments poses formidable problems of co-ordination for the Minister for Sport and his civil servants.

In 1973 the Cobham Report of the House of Lords Select Committee on Sport and Leisure clearly identified the confusion of responsibility within government for sport as a major hindrance to the development of coherent policy. The committee noted that 'The multiplicity of organisations involved with recreation nationally is reflected in the fragmentary nature of Government responsibility. The organisations report to different Ministers, and nowhere can one say that Governmental interest in recreation is centred' (para. 114).

The extent of the fragmentation can be indicated by the existence of six government departments with a significant responsibility for sport and recreation. The most important department is Environment, which is the department to which the Minister with responsibility for sport and recreation is attached. However, it is important to note that although the DOE has a major responsibility for sport, sport is a very minor part of the range of responsibilities within the department. Out of the ten main divisions within the department the Sport and Recreation Division and the Directorate of Rural Affairs are the two with the greatest involvement in sport.

The Sport and Recreation Division has an Assistant Secretary at its head and has approximately twenty staff out of a total DOE staff of 6,488.[1] Although SARD is small it is divided into three sub-sections with the pattern of responsibilities shown in Figure 1.

During 1988 and 1989 the complement of the division rose because of the preparation for and passage of the Football Spectators Bill and SARD C, which had responsibility for football hooliganism policy, established a sub-unit of specialist staff to concentrate specifically on the Bill and to deal with the large amount of correspondence it generated.

The Directorate of Rural Affairs is also split into three sub-sections, confusingly referred to as divisions. The Country-side Division has responsibility for long-distance footpaths, the amenity aspects of woodlands, conservation policy, and liaison with the Countryside Commission. The two remaining divisions are responsible for wildlife and matters relating to the establishment of a statutory Broads Authority respectively. Other DOE divisions dealing with inner cities, local government, planning, environmental protection and water also have an involvement in sport and related issues.

While the DOE is undoubtedly the lead department in matters concerning sport there are a number of other departments that make an important contribution to the policy area. The Department of Education and Science with its responsibility for

Figure 1 The organisation of the Sport and Recreation
Division and the allocation of responsibility

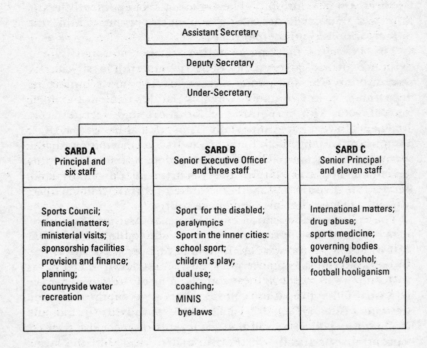

schools and the curriculum has considerable influence over the
range of sports facilities available in schools and how they are
used. In recent years the decision to encourage local education
authorities to sell surplus playing fields has raised a clear example
of an issue, of considerable importance to SARD, being discussed
in another department. In this case SARD was involved in the DES
discussions and in the words of one civil servant 'would expect to
be invited to "sit in" on the departmental discussions'.

The Football Spectators Bill, which dominated the work of
SARD during 1989, was the product of much interdepartmental
discussion between the DOE and the Home Office. Other
sporting issues on which the Home Office would expect to be
consulted include public safety at sports events, and gaming and

lotteries. The Department of Trade and Industry has also been closely involved with promoting the development of sports facilities as sources of employment creation. The present Minister for Sport's policy initiative to expand sports opportunities for the disabled is being supported by £500,000 from the Department of Social Security, which has general responsibility for the disabled. Other departments with a clear functional interest in sport are the Ministry of Agriculture, Fisheries and Food, respon- sible for the use of agricultural and forest land for recreational and sporting purposes; the Ministry of Defence by its control of a large number of armed services sports facilities, some of which are also open to the public; and the Health and Safety Executive, which provides advice and guidance to local authorities on safety at swimming baths and children's playgrounds, etc. There are, in addition, the Welsh Office, the Scottish Office and the Northern Ireland Office, which have a territorial responsibility for sport.

Co-ordination between departments is achieved mainly by informal contacts at senior civil service level. Although previous Ministers for Sport have attempted to regularise co-ordination by holding quarterly meetings of representatives of departments with an interest in sport, these fell into disuse partly owing to the lack of issues which concerned more than two departments and partly as a result of apathy. Civil servants develop, maintain and foster contacts with colleagues in other sections and departments as and when the need arises and only involve Ministers when matters of policy need to be settled. In these situations meetings at ministerial level will be arranged. The same *ad hoc* approach to co-ordination applies to the relationship between SARD and the local authorities. While the mediating role of the Sports Council must be acknowledged, SARD seems to have little contact with the main providers of sports opportunities for the mass of the public. This may seem a little surprising given the lobbying expertise and organisation of local government through the various local authority associations, such as the Association of Municipal Authorities and the Association of District Councils. However, the present government made it plain in the early 1980s that it wished to downgrade the level and intensity of consultation with local government and it is therefore in keeping with this attitude that SARD should not be encouraged to develop extensive consultative links with local government. The effect is that contact is sporadic and arises only when it is unavoidable, as for example over the introduction of compulsory competitive tendering in leisure centres or when the local authority associations were invited to comment on the Minister's recent policy documents such as those on sport in inner cities and sport for the disabled.

As should be clear the number of departments with an interest in sport creates formidable problems for policy development and co-ordination. To make matters worse the fragmentation of responsibility and interest is not confined to central government but is echoed at all levels in the administrative framework. Outside government departments, and with varying degrees of independence from them, are a large number of government-created agencies, sometimes referred to as quangos (quasi-autonomous national governmental organisations). The most significant of these for sport is undoubtedly the Sports Council and the network of Regional Councils for Sport and Recreation, but others with a prominent role in the policy area include the Countryside Commission, the Forestry Commission, the Training Agency and the Nature Conservancy Council. These organisations have relatively clearly defined functions but, as will be suggested in chapter 4, the degree of specialism of these bodies magnifies the problems of administrative and policy co-ordination.

Quangos have a limited range of executive functions, as the primary responsibility for providing and staffing public sector sports facilities falls on local authorities. Within Britain's two-tier system of local government the heaviest responsibility for sport falls on the lower tier, district councils, although the upper tier, county (or, in Scotland, regional) councils, also has some important responsibilities in the area. As has already been shown, local authorities have a framework of, largely permissive, legislation to work within. In addition central government is able to influence policy development and service delivery at local level through a pattern of administrative and financial controls, and the provision of advice. Central government departments and the major quangos all possess a network of regional offices through which they are able to maintain close relations with individual authorities.

THE MINISTER FOR SPORT AND THE ROLE OF THE DOE

It was not until the 1960s that sport and leisure began to be recognised as a relatively coherent and unified cluster of services that required, if not common planning, then at least common consideration. Given that most of the responsibilities of government are organised on a functional basis, for example education within the Department of Education and Science and health within a Ministry of Health, it would have been quite consistent to have created a Ministry of Sport. Unfortunately, as we have seen, unlike education or health, sport has not been able to establish a clear administrative framework within which to develop the service, and responsibility has remained scattered among a wide range of departments, agencies and levels of government. In addition the existing post of Minister with responsibility for sport is that of a Junior Minister in charge of a small section within a very large and busy department.

Although Lord Hailsham can claim to be the first member of a government to have been given specific responsibility for sport the first member of the government to be designated 'Minister for Sport' was Denis Howell in 1974, who held the post until the election of 1979. Since 1979 the job has been held by Hector Munro (1979–81), Neil Macfarlane (1981–85), Richard Tracey (1985–87) and Colin Moynihan (1987–90) with the present holder being Robert Atkins. It is most important to note that for all 'Ministers for Sport' responsibility for sport has been only a part of their duties in the DOE. Denis Howell was, in addition to his responsibilities for sport, responsible for the admittedly related services of the countryside, environment policy, the Property Services Agency and water resources. Colin Moynihan had a similarly broad range of duties in the DOE such that only about a quarter of his time was devoted to issues associated with sport. Indeed, during the 1988–89 session Moynihan was responsible not only for overseeing the passage of the Football Spectators Bill through Parliament but also for the equally controversial Water Bill.

It should also be noted that although the Minister for Sport is the main focus of the policy area in the DOE at least one other Junior Minister has an interest in some aspects of sports policy. As Grayson (1988) points out, the development of sport in urban areas and the redevelopment of inner cities are frequently closely related and both within the remit of the DOE, yet, since at least 1987, the responsibilities have been divided between two different Junior Ministers, one the Minister for Sport and the other the Minister for inner cities and urban development. A similar overlap exists with the Minister responsible for the countryside, with the additional complication that the Directorate of Rural Affairs is located at Bristol while SARD is in London.

A number of explanations may be suggested for the persistence of the existing administrative arrangements. First, sport was emerging as an area of government concern at a time when the administrative capacity of central government was already stretched and when the management fashion was for the creation of large broad-based or 'giant' departments. The process of merging minor, though related, departments or functions to form 'giant' departments was well under way by the end of the 1960s. In 1968 the Foreign Office absorbed first the Commonwealth Office and two years later the Ministry of Overseas Development. Also in 1968 the Department of Health and Social Security was formed by the merger of the Ministry of Health and the Ministry of Social Security. This was followed two years later by the creation of the DOE as part of a further round of departmental reorganisation in 1970, under the Conservative government of Edward Heath. The fashion for a small number of large departments lasted well into the 1980s. Unfortunately when the fashion did change it was to be replaced by an interest in 'hiving off' functions to specialist agencies (quangos) rather than an interest in the establishment of specialist departments at the centre.

Second, not only did sport have a generally low salience to political parties, but also when they were pressed to comment on the role of government in sport there was a broad consensus that a strong central ministry was not the preferred model. In the debate about the role of government in sport stimulated by the inquiry of the Wolfenden Committee (1960) into Sport and the Community both the major political parties rejected the idea of a central Ministry of Sport. The Conservatives while calling for the establishment of a 'Sports Council of Great Britain' 'absolutely rejected the creation of a Ministry of Sport' (Anthony 1980: 53). The Labour Party also favoured a Sports Council of Great Britain and also rejected the notion of a Minister of Sport or of Culture (Anthony 1980: 53). It should be noted in passing that despite seemingly strong support for a 'hands off' approach to sport by government there is a surprising amount of legislation which affects sport (Wolfenden 1960: appendix). As Hargreaves suggests, a carefully cultivated myth of the British political culture is that there exists a deep antipathy towards the 'state formally "interfering" in the way people spend their free time' (1985a: 220).

A third explanation lies in the nature of sport and recreation services. As the Cobham Report (1973) made clear, when explaining the fragmented nature of government responsibility:

> Since recreation is often a by-product of some primary function – forestry and education are examples – there can be no hope of collecting into one Department all those bodies whose decisions impinge on recreation. The primary function of each body will decide where it is located and to which Minister it is responsible.
>
> (para. 114)

At present there is little enthusiasm within the government for a stronger focus for its responsibilities for sport. At the 1987 general election both the Labour Party and the Conservative Party produced explicit policy statements on sport and recreation though neither made reference to a stronger role for government. The Conservatives, in a very brief reference to sport, stated that they would 'continue to work with the Sports Council and, through our funding of the Sports Council's National Centres, we will encourage the pursuit of excellence in our sports' (Conservative Party 1987). The Labour Party in a fuller discussion of its policy for sport put a similar emphasis on the central role of the Sports Council in developing government strategy, commenting that 'The role of the Sports Council will be reviewed and strengthened with proper Ministerial involvement' (Howell 1987).

The limitations on the role of the Minister for Sport and the Sport and Recreation Division should not be overstated, for the Minister may exert considerable influence on the policy area if he chooses, as Colin Moynihan has clearly demonstrated. In general the degree of involvement sought by the Minister depends on a number of factors, including the salience of sporting issues to the government, the quality and ambition of the Minister and the style of the department. Denis Howell, for example, attempted to develop a strong interventionist role for the Minister. Despite his commitment to the essentially voluntaristic nature of sports administration he was keen to establish the Sports Council as the Minister's vehicle for policy initiatives. He acted as chairman of the Advisory Sports Council until Labour lost office in 1970. On the return to office of the Labour Party in 1974, two years after the creation of the Sports Council, he even considered attempting to alter its royal charter in order to give him more influence over its activities and particularly so that he could resume the chairmanship. When told that it would be impossible to alter the charter and that he might not even be able to attend meetings of the council he declared, 'What is the role of a Minister for Sport who has surrendered all his authority to the Sports Council?' (Howell 1990: 231). His attempts to determine the spending priorities of the Council led swiftly to the resignation of Roger Bannister, the chairman. Following Bannister's resignation Howell appointed a new chairman 'with whom I could do business and who understood the position I had taken up' (Howell 1990: 233) and who also agreed that he had a right to attend meetings. Howell established a relationship between the Minister and the Council which, in general, has persisted. The main difference between Howell and Moynihan was that, whereas the former wanted to use the Council as his forum for executive action, the latter tended to limit his intervention in Council business to strategic matters and relied more heavily on his civil service staff in SARD.

Sports issues, particularly drug abuse and football hooligan-ism, have been all too prominent in the 1980s and have propelled sport on to the national political agenda. Colin Moynihan seemed determined to prove that he would be an exception to the rule that being Minister for Sport is a graveyard of political ambition. Moynihan consequently seemed determined to reorient the political style of SARD away from its *laissez-faire* attitude of the 1970s to a more interventionist and promotional role. The attempt to develop a more interventionist style in SARD is reflected, not only in the content of the Football Spectators Bill and the series of policy reviews initiated by the Minister, but also by the adoption of a more active role in fostering international, and particularly European, co-operation on sports issues.

The Minister for Sport and SARD have always had the responsibility to maintain links with international bodies on sports matters, though this has frequently taken place under the wing of the Foreign Office. In recent years these international contacts have become of much greater significance to the success of domestic policies. Combating football hooliganism and drug abuse are two examples of the growing number of issues in sport which have a clear international dimension. Perhaps the most important international body at the present time is the Council of Europe, which has played an important role in promoting and co-ordinating anti-doping measures in member countries.

At first sight the Council of Europe is an unlikely body for such a role. Established in 1949 by a grouping of non-communist European nations, the Council is best known for the development of the European Convention on Human Rights and the creation of a European Court to adjudicate in cases. In structure the Council consists of a Consultative Assembly, composed of delegates chosen by the national parliaments of member states, and a Committee of Ministers. It is the latter body which is of greater significance. The committee meets twice a year and has the power to decide conventions (policy statements) which are then recommended to member states, who, if they accept them, are bound by their terms. The main focuses of the Council have been on cultural, sporting, educational and environmental issues. Among the sports issues discussed in recent years have been the economic effects of sports investment and sport for prisoners. Furthermore, it has produced two important conventions on doping in sport and has proved to be an important forum for co-ordinating policy towards football hooliganism, with Neil Macfarlane, then Minister for Sport, calling an informal meeting of the Committee of Ministers after the Heysel stadium disaster. Colin Moynihan has also used the Council as a forum for developing support for sporting competitions (paralympics) for the disabled.

Partly because the Council of Europe has proved a successful forum for the discussion of sporting issues and partly because it has such a wide membership, the European Community rarely discusses sport and its problems, although there was a recent unsuccessful proposal to organise a European Community athletics competition. Some money has come from the European

Community to finance sports initiatives, through its European Social Fund, but the overall amount is slight. Apart from the provision of small amounts of finance there is little involvement by the European Community in sports issues and policy.

The other major international body with an interest in sport and recreation is the United Nations Educational, Scientific and Cultural Organisation (UNESCO), an autonomous body related to the United Nations. Its main function is to develop and promote projects aimed at raising the standard of education in the world. As such it is closely concerned with the development of physical education and held a conference on this topic in Moscow in the mid 1980s. However, the United States is no longer a member of UNESCO and Britain withdrew its membership in 1987, and the potential of this body to act as a foundation for the development of world-wide initiatives on sports issues such as drug abuse is now severely limited.

The Minister or his representatives from SARD do have contact on an irregular basis with a number of international sports organisations such as: the International Olympic Committee, over Colin Moynihan's proposal to build a 'para-lympics' competition into the Olympic calendar; the International Amateur Athletics Federation, concerning the development of a concerted response to drug abuse by athletes; the Commonwealth Games Federation, over the question of potential boycotts of competitions; and UEFA, over proposals to combat football hooliganism.

Although much of the contact with international political and sports bodies is sporadic and irregular it is an important element in the policy-making process, given that many of the most pressing problems facing sport in Britain have a clear international dimension. Consequently, during the last ten years or so, contacts between the British government and international organisations have become more frequent and more regular.

THE ORGANISATION OF SPORT IN OTHER COUNTRIES

France

The administrative pattern of sport in Britain, and especially the fragmentation of responsibility, is evident in many, though not all other countries. Where there is a clear difference between Britain and many other countries is in attitudes about the appropriate role of government in the policy process for sport. France, for example, provides a contrast with Britain. Sport is considered to be part of a broad range of services with come under the ambit of the Ministry of Culture, not only one of the most prestigious of the central departments, but also one that has attracted a number of prominent incumbents such as Jack Lang. The Ministry of Culture is a strongly interventionist department, in keeping with the tradition of centralism in France, and, as Hantrais remarks, 'has not hesitated to intervene directly and to initiate what are often high prestige projects' (1987: 328). The degree of devolution of responsibility to quangos such as the Sports Council or to local government evident in Britain is not to be found in France.

In 1936 a Ministry of Sports and Leisure was established and, as in Britain, the prime concern was with the health of the population. However, sport in general had a low priority during this period, and it was not until the late 1950s that, through the newly created Ministry of Cultural Affairs, sport began to be considered seriously as a specific policy area. Even then the development of sports policy in France was, and to a great extent still is, closely linked with the development of tourism. Given the advantages of the French climate and geography, much state funding of sport has been directed towards outdoor sports such as skiing, swimming and sailing. Part of the 1960 'National Plan' provided for a major expansion of the skiing industry, while strong pressure from governing bodies and local city councils led to a significant and rapid expansion in the number of swimming pools. Both these developments were supported by substantial central government finance and a general eagerness to produce potential Olympic champions. (Bauer 1988)

The highly centralised pattern of administrative responsibility for sport in France during most of the post-war period has resulted in some clear differences in policy emphasis. The most notable is the concentration of capital funding in Paris, particularly for the arts but also for sport, 'on the grounds that Paris is the shop window of France and that such investment does create jobs on a large scale' (Hantrais 1987: 329). However, there are some clear similarities, especially regarding the tension

41

between policy designed to encourage greater participation in sport and a concentration of resources on the production of elite athletes. The election of a Socialist government in 1981 heralded a period where the emphasis of policy was clearly first to broaden the base of participation and direct resources towards disadvantaged groups, and second 'to combat social problems among youth' (Hantrais 1984: 141; 1989). As part of the implementation of this policy the administrative capacity of the centre was greatly strengthened by the appointment of a Minister of Free Time (to help people use their leisure constructively), and two Junior Ministers, for Youth and Sport, and for Tourism respectively (Hantrais 1984: 136). This reform at the centre was also complemented by a restructuring of local government aimed at a greater decentralisation of power. In the three-tier structure of local government the two upper tiers, the regions and the departments, are broadly responsible for countryside recreation and planning. It is the lowest tier, the commune, that has explicit responsibility for sports centres, youth centres and open spaces. However, there are some 36,000 communes with an average population of under 1,500 and only thirty six with a population of over 100,000 (Norton 1987: 26). The difficulty of funding capital investment in sport at the commune level is obvious and consequently while the communes have the responsibility few have the necessary resources. In general, communes rely on their power to use educational establishments for purposes of sport.

Leisure and sport administration in France is characterised by strong central direction (and funding) and limited scope for local government initiative. There are many similarities between France and Britain regarding policy objectives. Among the most prominent similarities are a concern to use sport policy as an element in a broader strategy to redistribute opportunities in society, as an aspect of inner city/social control policies, and to improve the quality of elite athletes.

Canada

Canada has a three-tier structure of government: federal, provincial and city/regional. Although Canada has a more centralised and directive approach to sports administration than Britain, each level of government has an important role to play.

42

At federal level the department charged with specific responsibility for sport is the Department of National Health and Welfare. Located within the department is the Fitness and Amateur Sport Branch (FASB), which is headed by a Minister of State, who is supported by an Assistant Deputy Minister. FASB is subdivided into a number of specialist units, the net result of which is to maintain a division between the requirements of elite athletes and the fitness and health campaigns for the mass of the population. In 1961 the federal government created the National Fitness and Amateur Sport Advisory Council, a purely advisory body with no executive powers or programme funds. The main purpose of the council is to advise the Minister and link federal and provincial policy development. The major governing bodies of sport are heavily dependent on federal finance but attempt to retain their independence and seek to influence policy through an umbrella organisation, the Sports Federation of Canada.

Despite the stronger and more coherent role of central government in Canada there is still a high degree of administrative fragmentation. (Redmond 1985). At federal level a number of other Departments have major interests in sport policy; for example, the National Parks Service, the Department of Indian Affairs and Northern Development, and the Department of Defence. The jealously guarded autonomy of the provinces has resulted in a wide degree of variation in the extent of federal–provincial co-operation and the amount of complementary financial and administrative support at second-tier level. Although most provinces now have a Ministry with primary responsibility for sport it rarely has exclusive control of the policy area and must normally share it with departments such as Parks or Health Education. Much of the recent expansion of sports opportunities is due to the efforts and investment of Canada's cities, particularly those that have hosted major international sporting events. In consequence municipal governments are influential actors in the development of sport policy and provision in Canada.

Financial support from the federal government to provinces, governing bodies and individual athletes grew rapidly from about $0.25 million in 1962 to over $50 million in the mid 1980s. Olympic preparations are also heavily subsidised by the state, amounting to over $37 million per year in the run-up to the 1988 Olympics.

There are some clear similarities between administrative arrangements in Britain and Canada. For example, both countries have a central department with a Junior Minister and civil service support; both suffer from the problems of administrative fragmentation arising from the number of functional departments with an interest in the policy area and the diffusion of responsibility between levels of government; both have established agencies or quangos to provide advice and both face a well organised pressure group representing governing bodies. However, there are also considerable differences; first, the administrative capacity of the central government in Canada is far greater than in Britain; second, responsibility for policy formulation and execution lies with the federal government and FASB; and third, the salience of sport to governments in Canada has been far higher than in Britain.

There are a number of similarities between the development of sport policy in Britain and Canada. For example, the National Physical Fitness Act 1943 was prompted, as was Britain's Physical Fitness and Training Act 1937, by the poor state of health of military recruits and was aimed at improving the general level of health in the country. The subsequent Fitness and Amateur Sport Act 1961, which aimed to widen access to sport, can also be seen as part of the general welfare state philosophy dominant in this early post-war period. However, a distinct theme in Canadian sport policy, by comparison with Britain, is the conscious use of sport for 'nation-building' and as a vehicle for enhancing national prestige through the development of international sporting excellence (Harvey and Proulx 1988: 97). In 1961 the Canadian Parliament passed sweeping legislation which greatly increased the grant aid available to governing bodies of sport, established a National Advisory Council on Fitness and Amateur Sport (broadly similar to Britain's Sports Council) and sought to generate interest at provincial level. During the 1960s there were important debates about the best way to achieve sporting success, the proper relationship between mass participation and elite sport, and the relative priority between sporting success and an improvement in the health of the nation. The culmination of this debate was reflected in the policy document *A Policy of Sport For Canada*.

This major policy statement resulted in a massive increase in federal government intervention in sport ostensibly directed at improving nation-wide fitness, preserving stability in an increasingly urbanised society and fostering national integration. The Minister's intention was to place the pursuit of excellence within the context of a broader range of policy goals or, in the Minister's words, to put 'the pursuit of international excellence in its proper perspective, as a consequence and not a goal of mass participation' (Munro 1970: 28). However, as Harvey and Proulx (1988: 100) state, the Minister's promise to shift the emphasis from elite sport to mass participation was 'just an empty promise'. The needs of elite sport and the pursuit of international success dominated government policy to the point of obsession throughout the 1970s and, following the success of Canadian athletes in the 1976 Olympic Games and the Commonwealth Games two years later, these objectives persisted into the 1980s (Macintosh 1988). The pursuit of international competitive success came to a jarring halt with the Ben Johnson drug scandal at the 1988 Olympics.

German Democratic Republic

The collapse of the German Democratic Republic (GDR) in the winter of 1989–90 has provided an opportunity to gain more information about how sport was organised in one of the most successful sporting nations of the last twenty years. It is still too soon to identify the pattern of state involvement and support that will emerge in the eastern part of unified Germany. While there are signs that the level of state support will diminish it will be interesting to see the extent to which the highly successful framework of sports administration will be dismantled.

At the heart of East German sports organisation was the *Deutscher Turn und Sports Bund* (German Gymnastics and Sports Union), established in 1957. The DTSB was an 'independent', though publicly funded, organisation which was a union of all sports federations in the country and, until the recent elections, had strong administrative and membership links with the government and the ruling Socialist Unity Party. At central government level there was a Sports Minister with a limited range of responsibilities, including sports science, the College of

Physical Culture in Leipzig which educates coaches, and (shared with the Education Ministry) some elements of school sport. As Gilbert observes, 'the State Secretary for Sport, though controlling an immense budget quite apart from DTSB funding, tends to take orders from the DTSB rather than issue them' (1980: 47). That the Ministry was very much the junior partner in the relationship with the DTSB was reflected by the fact that the Minister in 1957, Manfred Ewald, stepped 'down' to become the DTSB's first president. The other major sports organisation in the GDR was the National Olympic Committee, which must, according to the Olympic Charter, be independent of government. However, owing to the ostensible independence of the DTSB, Ewald was also able to hold the position of president of the GDR's National Olympic Committee and thus bring all major sporting organisations firmly under the control of one umbrella body.

The DTSB was run by a Presidium comprising the president and seven vice-presidents, each responsible for a particular functional area such as international relations, elite competition, etc. The Presidium reports to an Executive Committee which was elected by a Gymnastic and Sports Congress which met every four years. The Presidium was at the head of a four-tier national structure which had organisations at club, district, county and national levels. The 8,000 or so individual clubs were financed in a number of ways. Buildings were usually provided by the state, through the municipality, while running costs were met through members' subscriptions and by grants from unions or other social organisations. There was a close relationship between clubs and their local schools. Factory sports clubs frequently provided additional coaching services for schools, and pupils were expected to join their local sports club.

Obtaining information on public expenditure on sport and recreation for the GDR is difficult but an increase in staff involved in sport of 160 per cent and the opening of nearly 7,000 new sports facilities between 1971 and 1985 give an indication of the scale of investment (Strietzel and Heigel 1987: 210).

The importance of sport in the history of the GDR was reflected, not simply in the administrative and financial support provided, but also by the emphasis given to sport in the constitution. Article 25 stated that 'the participation of citizens in cultural life, physical culture and sport is guaranteed'. In addition,

Gilbert has noted that over half the members of the GDR parliament were also members of the DTSB (1980: 49). In explaining the consistent success of the GDR in international competition Sutcliffe refers to 'objective planning . . .the strategic use of scarce resources and the total integration of sport into the social and political structure of the country' (1988: 1). The role of sport in the GDR must be seen in the context of the post-war division of Germany and the subsequent establishment of a separate East German state. In the early years of the republic sport was seen as a key element in fulfilling the twin imperatives of 'denazification' and building a sense of national identity for the nascent East German state. For Eric Honecker, in 1948 the chairman of the Free German Youth movement and later leader of the GDR, 'The sports movement must make its contribution to the democratic revival of our nation' (quoted in Hardman 1980: 124). In the late 1940s and early 1950s the emphasis was clearly on the development of opportunities for mass sport, such as swimming, athletics and gymnastics, as part of the ideological re-education of the German people. The abortive uprising in 1953 led to a greater emphasis on para-military sports, such as orienteering and shooting, which were prominent in the school sports curriculum for much of the 1950s (Hardman 1987).

From the late 1950s the emphasis in sport policy slowly shifted away from using mass participation in sport as a means of eradicating the past to a concern to use elite sport as a vehicle for the creation of a new national identity for the socialist future. Sport was used in three ways: first, as a means of gaining diplomatic recognition for the nascent GDR within the world political system; second, to establish the GDR as a force within the communist bloc; and, third, as a way of showing the superiority of the socialist system (Sutcliffe 1988: 1–2). The International Olympic Committee proved to be a valuable arena for the GDR to press its case for international recognition of its independent statehood. Banned by the IOC from participating in the 1952 Games, the GDR was allowed to participate in the two subsequent Games only as part of a combined German team and under an IOC-designed flag. However, the GDR was able to use the independence of the IOC to its diplomatic advantage in the early 1960s after the building of the Berlin wall and the subsequent attempt by Western nations to isolate the GDR.

Participation in Olympic competition fulfilled the dual purpose of keeping the issue of the integrity of the GDR in the diplomatic limelight and also demonstrating the 'superiority of the "new man" in a socialist democracy over the capitalist bourgeoisie' (Hardman 1980: 135).

By the late 1980s the GDR had created a sports administration that gave strong support to the elite and had projected the image of sporting achievement as a reflection of the superiority of socialism. However, when refugees began to leave the GDR in autumn 1989 there were many sportsmen and women among them. During the early months of 1990 the exodus of sporting talent was such that a number of clubs simply ceased to exist and governing bodies were keen to develop all-German competitions and leagues as a way of attempting to retain their players. At the same time bitter criticism was emerging of the lack of sporting opportunities for the mass of the people. The movement 'New Forum' criticised the 'medal mania' of the past. By December 1989 even the DTSB had announced its commitment to mass sport. However, it was not long before the twin pillars of the GDR's sports administration, the DTSB and the national Olympic committee, were confronted by the need to reform. By early January 1990 the president of the GDR's NOC, Manfred Ewald, had resigned and his successor was talking of negotiations with the West German NOC and the need for more democracy. By the same time the Executive Committee of the DTSB had also resigned, leaving the organisation in disarray.

The political collapse of the GDR was so sudden and the willingness of the Germans to vote for the staunchly anti-communist Christian Democrat Party of Helmut Kohl so apparent that it must call into question the success of the GDR policy of using sport to contribute to the development of a new socialist national identity. As in Canada, where separatist pressure is again building up in Quebec, it suggests that the citizenry of a country have a different view of the significance of sporting success from that of their leaders.

CONCLUSION

The role of central government in sport varies according to country, party ideology and time, and as such makes generalisations unwise. This qualification notwithstanding, what does seem to be common is the willingness of governments to use sport for other purposes, whether that purpose is nation-building, as in Canada and the German Democratic Republic, or control of the young, as in Britain and France. Only in France, with the socialist conception of 'free time', is there an impression that leisure and sport had an intrinsic value. Even in France the promotion of free time was short-lived, as the government became more concerned with what people did with their leisure than with how much of it they had, and consequently the innovative Ministry of Free Time was wound up after only two years.

Britain

The administrative arrangements for sport in Britain are characterised by a high degree of fragmentation, both between central government departments and between levels of government, and a heavy reliance on local government to provide facilities and opportunities for sport and recreation. Central government's concern with policy is sporadic, but on the occasions when it chooses to intervene it is able to act in a determined fashion and greatly influence the choices of the policy community, even if it is not quite able to impose policy solutions. The nature of central government intervention is affected by a tradition which seems to have combined, on the one hand, a desire to leave sport and recreation as a sphere of private life and, on the other, a clear inability to do so. More cynically one might suggest that government was content to allow free choice in sport provided that the public, particularly the young male urban public, made suitable choices.

British governments and Ministers, Howell notwithstanding, have generally preferred to leave responsibility for sport with the Sports Council rather than developing a stronger civil service capacity within the DOE. Among civil servants there is limited enthusiasm for working in SARD, as it is perceived as being outside the main career tracks of the DOE. As reflected in recent MINIS[2] returns SARD has not been keen to widen its responsibilities in order to achieve a more comprehensive oversight of policy. Indeed in 1988 it was reported that SARD had not been able to transfer responsibility for the Gleneagles agreement to the Foreign and Commonwealth Office, and that the Department of Health and Social Security was not prepared to accept responsibility for monitoring the voluntary agreement between the tobacco industry and the government.

Ministers therefore have tended to develop a relationship with the Council which allows them the opportunity to make strategic interventions on policy yet leaves in the hands of the Council the primary responsibility for policy-making and the development of administrative and technical expertise. Ministers have achieved this aim in different ways. Howell preferred to be part of the Council itself, and chairman if possible. Moynihan established his influence by altering the membership of the Council and by taking a series of policy review initiatives, thereby setting an agenda for the Council. However, most Ministers have worked within a ideological framework which puts the voluntary governing bodies of sport at the heart of sport development and which sees the local authorities as the key public sector provider. The role of local authorities is examined in chapter 3 and that of the Sports Council and its relationship with the government are explored more fully in chapter 4.

3

THE ROLE OF LOCAL GOVERNMENT IN SPORT

In the past twenty years [local authorities] have made the most significant contribution to extending the 'sporting franchise'. . . . the [Sports Council] is concerned that any diminution in the role of local authorities as providers of sporting facilities and opportunities will substantially undermine the achievements of the past *and* the Council's strategy for the future.

Sports Council (1988: 58)

THE EMERGENCE OF THE LOCAL AUTHORITY ROLE IN LEISURE

In 1988–89 the Sports Council had a total of just over £45 million to cover its own running costs and to distribute in grant aid to governing bodies, local authorities and voluntary sports organisations. By contrast, also in 1988–89, local authorities in England and Wales spent approximately £738 million.[1] As a provider of sports facilities and staff local government fulfils a central role. As was noted in the Yates Report:

Many other interests, voluntary, private, commercial and public have played their part in the development and management of facilities for sport and outdoor recreation, but the main burden of capital investment in purpose-built sports facilities for sport and recreation has been borne by local government.

(Yates 1984: 5)

Between 1971 and 1989 the number of swimming pools

51

provided by local authorities has increased from approximately 500 to more than 1,200. There has been an even more dramatic growth in the provision of sports halls, with their number increasing from about 20 to over 1,200 over the same period. As these figures show, the growth in the significance of local authority involvement has been recent, rapid and accomplished without the benefit of a statutory foundation of mandatory services on which to base bids for central government funding.

The history of the emergence of the leisure function at local authority level is one of unco-ordinated, frequently inadvertent growth. The nineteenth century roots of leisure provision lay largely in a concern with public health which resulted in the piecemeal accumulation of legislation to encourage the provision of municipal washhouses, public baths and open spaces. Outside the large industrial cities the development of leisure facilities at spa towns and at coastal towns was stimulated by the growing prosperity of the Victorian middle class and the opening up of the countryside by railway construction. In the early part of the twentieth century the popularity of outdoor recreation and physical fitness led in part to the passing of the Physical Training and Recreation Act in 1937 which gave local authorities the powers to provide and develop facilities for sport and recreation. The 1937 Act was typical of the legislative activity regarding sport and recreation in that it was primarily permissive in content and consequently left individual authorities to determine the extent of provision.

The uneven development of leisure at local level continued until the late 1960s, when for the first time local authorities came to see their leisure provision as a distinct cluster of services. During the late 1960s and 1970s a number of factors emerged which, collectively, contributed to the acknowledgement of sport and recreation as a discrete local government responsibility and also stimulated local authorities to reflect on the most appropriate administrative structure for service delivery and planning. Veal and Travis (1979) identify seven important factors in all. The first was the establishment of the Sports Council in 1972 (and the Countryside Commission in 1968 and the Tourist Boards in 1969), which in turn did much to stimulate the development of the second factor, namely new types of facilities such as sports and leisure centres, and country parks. Both these developments were reflections of a broader underlying change in people's leisure patterns, largely stimulated by a steady rise in disposable income. Recent data presented by the Sports Council show that there has been a steady rise in both the proportion of the population participating in indoor and outdoor recreation and also in the frequency of participation. The proportion participating in at least one outdoor activity rose from 28 per cent in 1977 to 32 per cent in 1986; for participation in indoor activities the figures were 21 per cent in 1977 and 28 per cent in 1986. The annual frequency of participation shows a similar increase, from 28.8 per cent (1977) to 37.8 per cent (1986) for outdoor recreation and from 20.2 per cent (1977) to 26.1 per cent (1986) for indoor (Sports Council 1988).

Of great importance for local government was the discussion of structural reform which took place during the 1960s. The debate on reform concentrated not solely on the perceived need to establish larger and, so the current thinking went, more efficient and effective units of local government. An important additional element of the debate concerned the appropriate pattern of internal organisation for the new, larger authorities. The emerging consensus was that there was a need for a small number of large departments (Chandler 1988: 102). Both the Maud Report (1967) and the more influential Bains Report (1972) strongly advocated the move towards what the latter referred to as 'directorates' or comprehensive service departments. The Bains Committee suggested that a comprehensive department would be suitable for leisure services.

The actual reorganisation of local government took place in 1974 and established the two-tier structure of local government which broadly still persists today, although metropolitan counties and the Greater London Council were abolished in the late 1980s. The consequences for sport and recreation of the restructuring of local government were in part beneficial and in part unfortunate. On the positive side the restructuring created authorities which now had a range of sports and leisure facilities, whereas in the past there might have often only been one important facility for each authority. For many of the new district councils leisure services gradually achieved a higher political profile owing to it being one of their most significant responsibilities in terms of expenditure, manpower and capital assets. A rather more negative consequence of reform was that responsibility for the service was split between the two tiers of local government. Thus in the non-metropolitan areas the districts were broadly responsible for indoor sport and recreation and urban parks, whereas responsibility for informal outdoor recreation in rural areas lay primarily with county councils. This arrangement created serious problems for co-ordination and strategic planning of the service.

The fashion in the 1970s for structural solutions to social and administrative problems was complemented by a high level of confidence in planning. For example, underlying many of the suggestions made by the Bains Report was strong support for corporate planning within the new authorities. Planning was also a feature of service design in a number of policy areas, and one of the first tasks of the newly established Regional Councils for Sport and Recreation was to devise a Regional Recreational Strategy.

In the mid 1970s two reports from Westminster gave additional impetus to local service development. The first was the report on sport and leisure from the House of Lords in 1973 and the second was the government White Paper *Sport and Recreation* in 1975. The net effect of these reports was to help to reinforce the emerging identity of the leisure service as a coherent and discrete policy area at local level.

THE STRUCTURE AND ORGANISATION OF LEISURE SERVICES DEPARTMENTS

The coincidence of these factors reinforced the underlying groundswell of demand for a wider range of leisure opportunities coming from a younger and more affluent population. However, while the 1970s were undoubtedly a period of sustained expansion there was a lack of consolidation of the service such that a number of authors were still able to refer, in the late 1970s, to the fragmentation at local level. For example, the Association of District Councils (1978) could point to a lack of 'corporate identity' for the service. Similarly, Travis (1979), in contrasting leisure services and other policy areas such as housing and education, noted that the former straddle and overlap many facets and sectors of government responsibility.

During the 1980s a considerable maturing of the policy area

Table 2 The distribution of leisure responsibilities, 1990
(1979 figures in brackets) (%)

Type of department	Non met. districts		Met. districts		London boroughs	
One leisure services	39	(30)	54	(22)	52	(27)
One non-leisure services	44	(47)	0	(0)	6	(0)
Two leisure services	7	(10)	29	(53)	18	(24)
One leisure, one non-leisure	2	(7)	6	(6)	6	(30)
Two non-leisure	1	(1)	0	(0)	12	(0)
Three or more leisure	6	(4)	11	(17)	6	(15)
Three or more, one non-leisure	1	(2)	0	(3)	0	(3)

Sources: adapted from Veal and Travis (1979); figures in brackets from Veal and Travis, remaining figures from *Municipal Yearbook* 1990.

has taken place, as reflected in the allocation of responsibility for leisure services, the pattern of expenditure, and the pattern of service planning. In terms of the allocation of responsibility for leisure services at local level the Chartered Institute of Public Finance and Accountancy (CIPFA) was still able to comment, as recently as 1980, that 'Leisure as a unified programme area is still a relatively new concept in local government terms . . .' (1980: 4). This observation is confirmed in Table 2, where the data for 1979 show that, among district councils, only between one fifth and one quarter had a single comprehensive leisure department, and in the more numerous non-metropolitan districts just under half allocated responsibility for leisure to a non-leisure department such as technical or operational services. However, the table also shows that by 1990 the picture had changed considerably. In all three types of districts surveyed there has been a clear move towards the creation of comprehensive leisure services departments, with over half the metropolitan and London districts now having leisure as the responsibility of one specialist department. The slow pace of change in the non-metropolitan districts is in part owing to the small size of some authorities. The table also shows that, while the popularity of maintaining two leisure services departments has slowly declined it is still the second most common administrative arrangement in the larger towns and cities. Where two departments exist it is usual for one to be responsible for cultural activities and the other to be responsible for sport and physical recreation.

One important explanation for the range of solutions to the problem of allocating responsibility for leisure is that the term is so loose and the boundaries of the policy area so ill-defined. It is possible to identify five overlapping clusters of services which may be included in a comprehensive leisure services department: sport and physical recreation, education, tourism, social, and cultural. Sport and recreation would cover those aspects of the service most clearly reflected in the provision of opportunities for competitive sport or recreation such as sports centres, playing fields and ski slopes; the cluster of education-related services would include swimming pools and also libraries; tourism-related services would include museums and conservation areas as well as many aspects of countryside recreation, including country parks, picnic and camping sites; community centres and youth clubs would be examples of the cluster of leisure services within the social category; the cultural aspects of leisure would include theatres and art galleries.

From the above description of the span of many leisure services departments it is important to note that sport is but one element, albeit an important element, in the range of leisure activities of an authority. Two further points are important in understanding the nature of leisure provision at local level; the first is that, for most of the country, responsibility is divided between two levels of local government, and the second is that most leisure services are discretionary rather than mandatory. Table 3 indicates how leisure services are distributed between the two levels of local government in England and Wales and Table 4 indicates the distribution of expenditure between districts and counties, also in England and Wales. As indicated in Table 4 most expenditure is by the district councils and the emphasis of their spending is on indoor and outdoor sport and recreation. The figures also show how stable the pattern of expenditure has been, even when the abolition of metropolitan counties is taken into consideration. In addition Tables 3 and 4 both show that few elements of the service are the exclusive responsibility of one tier of local government, thus generating potential problems for planning and co-ordination.

There are two explanations for the fragmentation of

Table 3 The distribution of responsibilities between tiers of local government in England and Wales

Service	Non-met. districts	Met. districts	Counties
Outdoor sport and recreation	/	/	
Indoor sport and recreation	/	/	
Informal outdoor recreation	/	/	
Countryside recreation			/
Cultural activities	/	/	/
Youth and Community		/	/
Libraries		/	/
Tourism	/	/	/
Conservation	/	/	/
Entertainments	/	/	/
Social services facilities		/	/

Note: If the school sport facilities are taken into account then county councils have a strong involvement in both indoor and outdoor sport.

Table 4 Distribution of net expenditure on leisure and recreation, 1989–90 (1983–84 figures in brackets) (%)

	County councils		Districts councils	
Indoor sport and recreation	0.40	(0.33)	31.58	(26.46)
Outdoor sport and recreation	0.21	(2.87)	32.70	(33.23)
Cultural facilities	2.74	(3.10)	11.20	(10.60)
Grants and contributions	1.17	(2.52)	2.22	(2.23)
Other (including country parks)	4.62	(2.30)	13.16	(16.36)

Source: CIPFA, Leisure and Recreation Statistics 1983–84 and 1989–90.

responsibility for leisure services. The first is the variety of services inherited by local authorities following the reorganisation of local government in 1974. Prior to 1974 few local authorities had extensive leisure responsibilities; rather there was a wide range of small-scale projects, facilities and programmes. Thus, at reorganisation, leisure services might have been conceptually distinct, but in practice there were few experienced practitioners or politcians at local level to lobby for a more unified and coherent allocation of responsibility. The picture in Scotland is little different, with the regional councils having a broadly similar range of responsibilities to the counties south of the border and with the major responsibilities lying with the district councils. The distribution of responsibilities in Northern Ireland is quite different and will be discussed later.

A more important element in the explanation of the fragmentation of responsibility for sport and leisure is the absence of a strong statutory base requiring the mandatory provision of leisure services. As Travis *et al.* state, 'where services are mandatory they tend also to be the responsibility of a specific tier of local government' (1981: 54). Apart from the provision of allotments, libraries and a youth service, and the management of National Parks, there are a few other duties placed on local authorities in the broad field of leisure provision. On the other hand a local authority may, according to Section 19 of the 1976 Local Government (Miscellaneous Provisions) Act, 'provide . . . such recreational facilities as it thinks fit'. It is upon this legislation and similar earlier legislation that the present provision of swimming pools, sports and leisure centres and outdoor recreational facilities is based.

Given the discretionary nature of much local provision it is not surprising to find a wide variation in the level of expenditure on leisure. The most recent figures from CIPFA show that in 1989–90 the *per capita* expenditure on leisure, even when comparing the aggregate spending by counties and their constituent districts, is still subject to wide variation. For example, the average expenditure on indoor recreation was £7.08 but the range was from Norfolk (£2.68), East Sussex (£2.85) and Dorset (£2.80) to Northumberland (£12.39), Durham (£14.08) and Humberside (£14.90). As regards outdoor recreation the average was £7.56 and the range from Norfolk (£1.40), Wiltshire (£1.62) and Cornwall (£3.82) to Staffordshire (£9.78), Leicestershire (£10.04) and Northumberland (£10.42).

Although there is still considerable variation in the pattern of spending by individual authorities it is significant that, taking the service as a whole, the proportion of total local government expenditure allocated to leisure has remained broaadly steady (Table 5). This is despite the pressure that local spending has been under during much of the 1980s and the non-statutory nature of most of the service.

Explaining the stability of spending on recreational and

Table 5 Expenditure on recreational and cultural activities as a
percentage of total local authority expenditure, 1979–88

1979	1980	1981	1982	1983	1984	1985	1986	1987	1988
4.8	4.8	4.7	4.7	5.0	4.9	4.7	4.8	4.7	4.7

Source: *National Income and Expenditure*, 1989.

cultural activities by local authorities is difficult and caution is
needed. In general leisure services are rarely valued as important
in their own right and arguments for investment in leisure are
normally couched in terms of the benefits it may have for other
policy objectives such as better health or reducing vandalism. The
investment in leisure provision as part of a solution to other
problems may be a view expressed by central government but it
is less explicit in the debate over resources at local level (Coalter
et al. 1986: 140; Knox 1989: 73–5). However, interviews with
officers in local authorities suggest that a perception of leisure
investment as an instrument for the achievement of non-leisure
policy objectives may be becoming more common. While they
agreed that part of the stability of local expenditure can be
explained by the strength of popular demand for a widening of
provision, part of the explanation lay in the increasingly common
perception of leisure services, by both central and local government, as an element in economic development. During the 1980s,
as the government's regional policy has been wound down, local
authorities have become more concerned to market their area to
investors, and recreational and cultural facilities are seen as
important in attracting investment. Also for many areas tourism
has been identified as a potential growth industry and this has
resulted in local expenditure on the leisure infrastructure as well
as on the promotion of special leisure events such as arts festivals.

It is possible to argue that the maintenance of the leisure
budget as a proportion of total local expenditure is to be
welcomed. But if its maintenance is the result of fulfilling the
objectives of other departments or committees it is a sign of the
continuing weakness of leisure services relative to other policy
communities. In order for the officers and councillors involved
in administering leisure services to establish control over its
development and to have that control recognised a number of

criteria must be fulfilled. Many are similar to the list mentioned by Travis and Veal earlier and include a mandatory basis for the service, a single leisure services department, and strong central government support. However, one important element in the recognition and establishment of an area of local government activity as a discrete service is the development of a profession.

A number of authors have commented on the central role of professionals in local authorities. Cunningham and Fahey (1976) refer to their dominance of senior positions in local government as 'unique', while Poole (1978) suggests that it is a primary characteristic of the local government service. Local government may be characterised by the dominance of professions in all major departments and with the culture of the department reflecting that dominance. Indeed it has been argued that the attempts to develop corporate management and establish programme-based departments have frequently failed owing to the strict demarcation of areas of competence by the professions (Houlihan 1988: 71). It is within this highly professionalised model of local government that the leisure services have had to compete for resources.

Professional organisations have existed in the leisure field for some time, the Institute of Baths and Recreation Management dating from 1921 and the Institute of Parks and Recreation Management from 1926. Unfortunately these professions found it difficult to establish themselves as a major source of policy influence within local government. This was owing largely to the location of leisure as a subsidiary function within departments led by stronger professions, such as engineering or planning. One consequence was that the qualifications offered by these professional bodies have frequently been viewed, with some justification, as technician or craft-level training. The comment in the Yates Report sums up their role when it suggests that the leisure manager:

> may have been consulted about the design and use of the facility; he was able to give the last word on the quality of the grass in his recreation grounds, or of the water in his swimming pool, but his professional skills and experience were not seen to qualify him for much beyond that.
>
> (Yates 1984)

During the 1980s two factors contributed to an enhanced opportunity for the development of a strong leisure profession. The first was the expression of interest by government, reflected in the establishment of two committees of inquiry into the training of recreation managers. The Yates Committee, appointed in 1976, to cover England and Wales, and the Gunn Working Party, appointed in 1979, for Scotland, both grew out of the White Paper *Sport and Recreation*, which recognised the 'need for improvement of management and career prospects in the recreation field' (DOE 1975). Central government support for an aspiring profession is an essential ingredient in the slow process of professionalisation. Unfortunately, the committees were appointed by the Labour government but reported to a far less sympathetic Conservative government. Nevertheless, both reports came out strongly in favour of a single professional body for recreation management (Yates 1984: 98; Gunn 1986: 85).

Paralleling the work of the committees was a series of discussions among the major existing professional bodies about the possibility of merger. The clear aim being to replace the fragmented voice of leisure managers with a unified, and hopefully more influential, voice. The outcome was the formation, in 1983, of the Institute of Leisure and Amenity Management, which incorporated four of the largest existing bodies. The major body to refuse to merge was the Institute of Baths and Recreation Management, which feared that the new body would weaken the cause of professionalisation owing to a dilution of expertise resulting from its attempt to cover too wide a definition of the service.

The position of leisure managers in the early 1990s is that they have done much to establish the conditions for progress along the road to professional recognition and the influence over policy that comes with it but they are still a relatively weak profession within local government.

THE POLICY PROCESS IN LOCAL GOVERNMENT

Following the reorganisation of local government in 1974 most authorities adopted a management structure similar to that recommended by the Bains Committee (1972). On the officers' side the report suggested that authorities should appoint a chief executive officer to replace the town clerk, who should have responsibility for the general management of the authority and act much as a managing director in the private sector. Supporting the chief executive there should be a series of broad-based departments responsible for a number of services, each with a chief officer or director who, collectively, would comprise a chief officers' management team to advise the chief executive. On the councillors' side, there is commonly a parallel committee for each department, although in some authorities one committee may be responsible for two or more departments. Those councillors who chair committees form the membership of a policy (and resources) committee which complements the discussions of the chief officers' management team. Finally, the majority party leader normally chairs the policy and resources committee and forms a close link with the chief executive.

Identifying the common features of the local policy process is extremely difficult. Obvious caution is needed in generalising about processes in over 400 authorities with different sets of service responsibilities, different party political make-ups, and different population sizes and socio-economic characteristics. However, some attempt at generalisation is necessary in order that the context for the formation of specific items of leisure policy may be appreciated.

First of all, local authorities work within a legislative frame-work which is broadly the same. Some variation is present between Scotland and Northern Ireland on the one hand and England and Wales on the other. Over the last ten to fifteen years that legis-lative framework has become an increasingly tight constraint on the autonomy of local authorities. In the fields of housing, education and social services, central government has used legislation, or the ministerial powers derived from legis- lation, to impose common policies on local government and thereby limit ability to respond to problems in ways determined locally. Thus local authorities have been obliged to sell council houses to tenants, if the latter expres-sed the wish to buy; schools are preparing to adopt a national curriculum; and social workers have had to follow rules of procedure laid down by the Minister in child care cases. Although leisure services have not been seriously affected by this type of direct central government intervention, largely owing to the essentially discretionary nature of the service, they have been affected by the general contraction of local authority financial resources.

All local authorities have been affected by public expenditure cuts during the 1980s. While the severity of financial constraint has varied, it has forced all authorities to examine their capital and revenue spending programmes carefully. A number of further factors may be identified as having a general impact on the context of local decision-making. Among the most important are the influence of the Audit Commission and the imposition of compulsory competitive tendering. A key influence of the Audit Commission has been on the management practice within authorities, which has become progressively more concerned with efficiency and effectiveness. The introduction of compulsory competitive tendering has reinforced this concern for value for money and the economic and efficient use of resources.

Within this context local authorities display a number of similarities in the way in which policy is formed although, as with all generalisations, they are more clearly evident in some authorities than others. Of particular significance are the influence of professional officers, the growing importance of partisan divisions within local party politics, and the tension between competing priorities of services.

The centrality of professions in local government has already been noted, but in order to appreciate fully the role of professionals it is important to set professionalism within the context of 'departmentalism'. Departmentalism refers to the long-standing problems arising out of the tendency within local authorities to establish single (or, as is increasingly common, dual) service departments, associated within a specific profession and reporting to a single service committee. For example, social workers will work within a social services department which will report to a social services committee. Within the field of leisure services the pattern is less clear and uniform, but the most common pattern is of the leisure services committee having responsibility for the recreation or leisure services department, which is staffed by professional career leisure services officers. At best this pattern creates a strong triangular alliance, with the common aim of protecting and furthering the development of the service. At worst, however, it produces an introspective, insular and self-seeking culture which sees other service departments, and indeed the authority as a whole, as rivals for resources.

A key relationship in the policy process involves the committee chairperson and the service director. These two plus their senior colleagues will exert substantial influence, if not complete control, over the agenda of the committee and will generally rehearse issues and possible solutions prior to exposure at full committee. According to Elcock:

> [the] agenda meeting creates a valuable interface where officers can keep the chairman and vice-chairman informed about recent developments, consult them about issues which are likely to cause political controversy and discuss with them recommendations they wish to make to committee about whose political acceptability they are doubtful.
>
> (Elcock 1986: 104)

To an extent senior officers and councillors are the filters in the process of identifying issues for deliberation, but they are also competitors for control over access to the decision process.

A major aspect of this relationship is where the boundary between officer influence should be. For many authorities the relationship is uncontentious and boundaries are recognised and respected. However, for an increasing number during the 1980s the relationship has been subject to frequent renegotiation. One undoubted source of tension has been the rise of what has been referred to as 'manifesto politics'. Laffin refers to the decline in consensus politics at local level and the 'emergence of a new breed of elected member' who is 'less deferential and more sceptical of professional advice' (Laffin and Young 1985).

In summary the policy process at local level is becoming increasingly politicised and is focused on the relationship between senior officers and politicians. This relationship is set within a broader context which is influenced partly by central government legislation and resource control and partly by the characteristics specific to each authority.

LOCAL GOVERNMENT AND SPORT IN NORTHERN IRELAND

A significant exception to the above generalisations about the nature of local policy processes is Northern Ireland, where not only are the structure and responsibilities of local government distinctive, but so too is the relationship between central and local government and the significance of leisure as a political issue.

In one of the most recent studies of the consequence of party politics for local government policy towards sport and recreation the general conclusion was that a broad consensus existed that 'everyone was "in favour of leisure", leisure *per se* was not a party political issue, [and] although it may have achieved a relatively large financial allocation, its status on the political agenda was relatively low' (Coalter *et al.* 1986: 127). Coalter and his colleagues also observed that:

> it would seem that the apolitical nature of much of the debate concerning leisure policy derives not solely from political apathy but also from the perceived nature of the realm of leisure. It was regarded by many as an area of personal opinion, freedom and choice, and as such a 'depoliticised' arena, properly outside the realm of adversarial politics.
>
> (Coalter *et al.* 1986: 127)

On the surface at least the same cannot be said for Northern Ireland and as such the fact deserves a brief explanation.

The Local Government (NI) Act 1972 which reorganised local government in Northern Ireland was the outcome of a compromise between the desire for management efficiency and service effectiveness on the one hand and the reality of sectarian politics on the other. During the 1960s, as sectarian conflict intensified, local government in the province had been gradually stripped of a number of important functions. The most notable was housing, the allocation of which by local authorities, frequently along sectarian lines, had been a serious cause of friction. The reorganisation of local government followed the Macrory Report (1970) and resulted in the creation of twenty-six district councils responsible for local services, including leisure, with other services, such as education, being directly administered by Westminster through the Northern Ireland Office. The new district councils were responsible for the delivery of a narrow range of comparatively minor services such as refuse collection and disposal, burial grounds and crematoria, tourist amenities and recreation. Within this range recreation was relatively important and, it must be added, in contrast to England and Wales, a mandatory service.

The weakness of the system of local government, where many services, such as education and housing, are administered without any process of local electoral accountability, is an important element of the context for the administration of leisure services in the province. The limited powers of the districts have led to increased frustration among local councillors who feel marginalised within the broader political system. Added to this is the deeply entrenched sectarian loyalties that make inter-party political co-operation extremely difficult. The net effect has been that for much of the 1980s the normal processes of local government decision-making have been periodically disrupted by, for example, boycotts and the refusal to set a rate.

Provision of recreational facilities in Northern Ireland was far poorer in the early 1970s than in the rest of the United Kingdom. As Knox points out, 'It was not until 1973 with the reorganisation of local government and the formation of the Sports Council for Northern Ireland that the impetus for leisure provision came' (1989: 79). Knox also makes clear the degree to which the new local authorities relied on the guidance of the Sports Council in matters of the scale, location and type of facilities to be built. The methods used to determine need and location were a combination of spatial analysis combined with the notion of a hierarchy of provision throughout the province. This rational approach to location and type was complemented by strong Northern Ireland Office support for investment in leisure, which was perceived as a key means of reducing the level of inter-community tension.

On the face of it local government leisure services were in an enviable position. Leisure provision was mandatory, there was strong political and financial support from government, and there was technical and planning expertise provided by the Sports Council. Unfortunately what soon became clear was that the provision of leisure facilities had become subsumed under the weight of sectarian politics, just as council house allocation had before it. The location of new facilities, the Sunday opening of facilities and the flying of flags were all used by the various religious/political factions as means of seeking sectarian advantage. The location of leisure centres was determined less by rational planning than by the need to balance investment in Catholic and Protestant areas of cities such as Belfast and Derry. Hence a new leisure centre in a Protestant area would almost certainly be followed by one in a Catholic area (Knox 1986, 1987). The attempt to prevent Sunday opening of facilities was pursued by the Unionist, Protestant councillors partly for sabbatarian reasons but mainly because Sunday opening was supported by Catholics.

Although provision for sport and recreation in Northern Ireland has improved dramatically in the last twenty years, this has been despite the difficulty faced by local authorities in identifying and pursuing recreational planning objectives. The formation of a local leisure policy community has not proved possible, given the strength of other policy communities to impose the policy priorities of sectarianism on the policy concerns of leisure (Sugden and Bairner 1986).

A NETWORK OF RELATIONSHIPS

Within England and Wales local authority leisure departments operate within a network of relationships with other organis-ations. Among the most important are the Sports Council and its regional councils, local voluntary bodies (for example, local sports clubs) and the local education authority. Other organisations with which the local authority would have less significant contact would include the Department of the Environment, national governing bodies of sport and their local associations, and the Central Council for Physical Recreation. It is suggested that policy is the outcome of the pattern of interaction between organisations involved in the policy area. This model of the policy process is explored in chapter 6. The purpose of this section is to identify the main characteristics of the relationships, including the frequency/regularity of contact; the mode of contact; the issues which activate a relationship; and the basis of the relationship.

Key relationships for local authority leisure departments are with their Regional Council for Sport and Recreation and their regional office of the Sports Council. The Regional Councils are independent of the regional offices of the Sports Council although the latter provide administrative support for the Regional Councils. Most significantly the regional director acts as secretary to the Regional Council. Members of the Regional Councils are nominated by the Minister and the chairman of the

Sports Council and appointed by the Minister. The Regional Councils have a planning, advisory and liaison role within their area, but they control no resources, as it is the regional offices that control finance and human resources. The most important role for the Regional Councils in recent years has been the preparation of regional sport and recreation strategies.

Generally the contact between a local authority and its regional office is influenced by a wide range of factors, including the relative importance of leisure services within the authority, the existing level of provision, and the degree to which the particular region seeks to adopt a proactive role in policy development. In the West Midlands region, for example, contact with local authorities takes place at a variety of levels and with differing degrees of formality. At the most formal are the meetings of the Regional Council itself, which is dominated by local authority representatives and has a number of sub-committees which undertake the discussion of policy. This formal contact is supplemented by a cycle of meetings between staff of the regional office and the chairman of the Regional Council, and senior officers and councillors from each local authority. These meetings, which occur about every two years, provide the regional bodies with the opportunity to acquire and confirm information about the level of provision, and also to discuss policy development and how the plans of the authority might be supported. A third level of contact is at the county level, where, two or three times a year, all the districts within a county will meet staff from the region. A wide range of issues may be raised at these meetings, including Sports Council campaigns and local innovative projects. However, not all these county-wide meetings are perceived as valuable by the region. The more successful meetings are those where the local authorities send senior staff and also staff from a range of interested departments, for example education and planning, and not just from leisure services. The less successful meetings tend to be those where officers sent are too junior to be in a position to reflect or interpret adequately local authority policy. At the final level of contact within each region there is an officer who has a geographical responsibility for a group of authorities who will be responsible for developing and maintaining the day-to-day contact between the organisations.

From the point of view of the regional office of the Sports Council, the relationship with its local authorities, and that between the Regional Council and local authorities, are crucial to the achievement of its objectives. Its resources are limited and the success of its regional strategy therefore depends on the co-operation of a number of organisations, of which the local authorities are the most important. The Regional Council sees its role as being to bring organisations together and to encourage and support their sports development activity within a planned framework. However, it is the Sports Council, through its regional offices, that provides the more tangible support to local authorities, including technical advice and pump-priming finance, though the extent of support will depend on the degree to which the policy of the authority is consistent with the regional plan.

A few examples will illustrate the general approach of the Regional Councils and the range of projects supported. In the North West the Regional Council, through a series of functional panels, was a major source of support for local authority initiatives. For example, Manchester City Council was strongly committed to the Sports Council's national initiative 'Action Sport', aimed in part at stimulating involvement among social groups with a current low level of participation. The Regional Council supported the regional office, who engaged consultants to monitor the implementation of the policy by Manchester, thereby providing the Recreational Services Department with significant data to use in its attempts to obtain local authority funds to continue the policy once the start-up finance had been exhausted.

The provision of start-up or pump-priming finance for projects is one of the main ways in which the Sports Council seeks to support and influence local authority policy. Manchester's finance for the early stages of its 'Football in the Community' scheme at Manchester City FC came from the regional office. As the scheme became established and was recognised as successful, finance was obtained from the Manpower Services Commission, which in turn led to direct funding by the DOE. In Birmingham revenue and capital finance has been made available for a number of projects. Revenue finance has been provided for the appointment of a number of staff, including development officers for football, hockey and one to work in the Muslim community. The council has also provided Birmingham with contributions, up to £75,000, towards the capital cost of laying synthetic pitches.

In summary the Regional Councils and the regional offices of the Sports Council fulfil a number of important functions in the local policy community. Most significant of all, they provide strong support for strategic planning of sport and recreation. The support comes partly through the role of the Regional Council in developing regional strategies and also in the form of the technical advice and expertise provided by the regional offices. In some authorities there is some suggestion that the planning priorities of the Regional Councils have altered such that the socio-economic elements of strategic plans have been downgraded and have been replaced by a concern to maximise the efficient use of resources. To suggest that a concern with the social effectiveness of policy has been superseded by the priority of efficient resource utilisation would be to oversimplify a complex pattern of change. However, despite strong denials from the Sports Council to the contrary, a number of authorities share this perception of a shift in regional policy.

The second function, the supply of 'pump-priming' finance, was, and still is, important in enabling the provision of mainstream facilities and also for the success of the more innovative projects. In general the regional offices and the Regional Councils provide local authorities with expertise and legitimacy when arguing for support for leisure within the local council, and also with modest finance as a means of stimulating more substantial local authority finance.

A second important relationship is with governing bodies, or more usually their local associations. Many of the larger towns and cities have local 'sports councils' on which are represented the local authorities and the governing bodies. The prime function of these organisations is to provide a forum for the exchange of information, to act as a sounding board for local authority initiatives, and to facilitate a degree of co-ordinated planning. In addition to contact through local sports councils the local authority's officers will maintain more informal contact with the local or county associations of the major governing bodies of sport. Where a local sports council exists the pattern, frequency and intensity of contact are highly variable. A number of local sports councils have become defunct owing to the lack of regular meetings or, more commonly, a perception by one or more groups of participants that the body is a 'mere' talking shop. However, there is evidence that local clubs and associations are giving greater commitment to developing their relationship with the local authority either through local sports councils or through direct contact. There are a number of reasons for this, the first being a reaction to the persistent accusations of elitism levelled at governing bodies by government and the Sports Council. The Sports Council is requiring governing bodies to prepare a corporate plan as a basis for grant aid and there are clear signs that one ingredient of a successful plan is an explicit commitment to the grass-roots development of the sport. One symptom of the growing concern with sports development is the increase in the number of development officers being appointed by governing bodies. Because it is only a minority of sports that can afford to fund development officers out of their own resources they frequently seek the support of other agencies such as the Sports Council and local authorities. Frequently, therefore, the Regional Council will look for evidence of co-operation between the governing body and local authorities on grass-roots development work as a condition of continued or increased grant aid.

A second reason for a closer relationship with local authorities arises from the realisation by governing bodies that they are operating in an increasingly competitive market for young talent. The increasing range of sports to choose from, the decline in school sports and the decline in the number of teenagers and young adults have combined to put pressure on governing bodies to market their sport. The involvement of governing bodies takes a variety of forms. In some areas bodies provide coaching for school teams or may even help to organise competitions. In the Manchester area, for example, the local authorities have helped to finance and administer the Greater Manchester Youth Games, but have relied heavily on the local governing bodies to provide coaching and to undertake some of the organisation, a role the latter have been very willing to fulfil. In the West Midlands the Midland Counties AAA has for some time been encouraging its clubs to build closer contact with schools through help with the running of school sports teams and with coaching. A number of athletics clubs have also designated a schools liaison officer. These initiatives are by no means limited to athletics, as other sports, including basketball, hockey, swimming and both rugby union and league, have also strengthened their commitment to sports development work through closer links with schools.

The third key relationship involving the local authority is with the local education authority, which in the metropolitan areas is within the same authority. Under the 1944 Education Act local education authorities are required to provide physical education as part of the school curriculum. They are also required to provide recreational activities for 'any persons over compulsory school age who are willing to profit by the facilities provided for that purpose'. As a result schools and colleges control a vast store of indoor and outdoor facilities. One of Denis Howell's first priorities, following his appointment as Minister for Sport in 1964, was to examine how school facilities could be opened up for community use. A reflection of the lack of progress is given in the comment by James Munn, the recent Director of Recreation and Community Services for Birmingham, on the relationship between education and leisure when he noted the 'marked absence, since the 1960s, of inter-departmental and inter-agency strategies within a public sector which has been perhaps too preoccupied with the systems of fragmented and traditional bureaucracies' (1985: 40). Indeed in the twenty-five years since Howell's expression of priority, progress on the dual use of educational sports facilities has been, at best, uneven. Part of the problem, which is discussed more fully later, lies in the problematic relationship between the departments responsible for education and for leisure.

In the larger metropolitan areas both services are the responsibility of the same authority. Although this should have made co-operation easier such was rarely the case. The perennial problems of inter-departmental and inter-professional rivalry, and a culture where resource acquisition and control were symbols of status, were major impediments to joint policy development. In many authorities policy development in sport and leisure aimed at young people generated squabbles over 'ownership' of the new service. For example, in Manchester the plan by the Leisure Services Committee to establish a sailing centre was challenged by the Education Committee on the grounds that it should be seen as an educational resource. For many authorities service development frequently results in debates over the location of service boundaries, with departments and committees often seeming to be more concerned with territorial issues than with improving and developing services. In Munn's words 'the various specialisms within education and leisure services had little or no corporate awareness, seeing conflict as an alternative to specialism' (1985: 42).

ISSUES FACING LOCAL GOVERNMENT LEISURE SERVICES

Compulsory competitive tendering

In September 1987 the DOE published a Green Paper which aimed to initiate discussion of the form of compulsory competitive tendering (CCT) most suitable to leisure services. This consultation process took place while the enabling legislation was being debated in Parliament. The subsequent Local Government Act of 1988 introduced the framework of compulsory competitive tendering for a range of local government services. In 1989 the terms of the Act were extended, by Parliamentary Order, to include the management of local authority leisure services. The terms of the Order were such that the tendering for leisure services would begin in 1992 and that by January 1993 all facilities covered by the Order would have to be subject to CCT. The Order covered most major facilities and provided a broad definition of management.

CCT differs from other forms of privatisation in that local authorities will still own the facilities and will still be able to control the prices, set quality standards and influence the programming. They will also retain the ability to decide policy matters such as who is to receive subsidy. According to the Audit Commission, CCT is expected to reduce unit costs by up to 20 per cent (Audit Commission 1989: 17).

Although the number of authorities that have gone out to tender is still relatively small it is undeniable that the process of preparing for CCT has been, for many authorities, a traumatic experience. Most local authorities have decided to prepare an in-house bid for the tender, which means in effect that the existing management team will compete with private companies for the contract to run their present facility. For many manual employees the result has been a worsening of pay and conditions of service as in-house management teams attempt to cut costs to a level found in the private sector. Although it is too soon to make an assessment of the consequences for the role of local government in the provision of facilities and for sports opportunities in a locality, one or two tentative observations may be made.

Regarding the impact of CCT on the future role of local government in leisure provision one consideration will obviously be the proportion of authorities seeking to win contracts and the proportion actually winning contracts. If leisure follows the pattern of tendering in other services such as cleaning and catering then the vast majority of authorities will prepare an in-house bid and the majority will be successful. However, there is some, albeit slight, debate about the desirability of seeking to win the tender. There are obvious benefits accruing to those authorities that do win the tender competition, including the day-to-day control and the ability to initiate innovation more easily during the life of a contract. On the other hand 'there is some feeling amongst local authorities who have used contractors that being freed from the day-to-day problems of staffing has enabled them to concentrate to a greater extent on service provision and planning considerations' (West Midlands Chief Officers' Group 1987). If this view were to be widely accepted it would be consistent with the Minister for Sport's preference for local authorities to move away from direct provision and to concern themselves more with an enabling role which involves planning, co-ordinating, and facilitating the provision of leisure services by other organisations, whether commercial or voluntary.

In a number of local authorities, and at Regional Council for Sport and Recreation level, there is a strong view that the consequences of CCT may well prove beneficial for sport in the medium to long term. In particular CCT is forcing an increasing number of local authorities to think strategically; for example, to identify and make explicit their objectives when planning new capital projects and to ensure that target groups are identified on the basis of some market research. CCT may also prove to be an important catalyst in encouraging local authorities to review their use of manpower and especially to alter the balance between service delivery staff and management in favour of the former. Finally, a view strongly expressed by the Regional Councils was that CCT has encouraged local authorities to think more creatively about how they can achieve their policy objectives. Examples of this include schemes where authorities arrange for bowls clubs to be responsible for the management and maintenance of municipal bowling greens, or where swimming clubs agree to provide coaching at leisure centres in return for cheaper hire rates for club activities.

There is also some very limited evidence available from those authorities that have already put their services out to tender. In Westminster City Council, where the major leisure services have been contracted out for over five years, there are signs that use is greater and provision wider. The manager of the Queen Mother Sports Centre quotes the increase in the numbers swimming as being 26 per cent between 1987–88 and 1988–89, with similarly large increases for aerobics and use of the fitness room (*The Times*, 10 March 1989; see also Bottomley 1989).

Notwithstanding the expressions of optimism from local authorities and from Westminster City Council, the CCPR has mounted a strong campaign against CCT, arguing, in the words of Peter Lawson, the CCPR general secretary, that 'This is a very serious attack on a tradition that sport in Britain is based on public facilities' (*The Independent*, 2 December 1987). Foremost among the governing bodies concerned at the potential consequences of CCT is the Amateur Swimming Association (ASA). The ASA argues that its sport is almost totally reliant on public facilities and it fears that CCT will result not only in higher prices but also in less access to the pool as managers seek the highest return. Similar concern is expressed by the Football Association and by the Amateur Athletic Association.

In conclusion CCT may well be good for the local authority revenue budget and may well result in an expansion of participation in leisure activities. Unfortunately the cost of those undeniable benefits may well be a decline in the opportunities for team sport and a decline in the contribution made by local government to the planned development of sports skills and the improvement of sports performance. In many authorities the main concern is over the impact of CCT on the provision made for minority groups or voluntary clubs. Despite the Audit

Commission's assurances that local authorities will be able to determine management priorities, much of the impact on the programming and special provision will take place during the pre-tender stage as the existing management attempts to minimise costs and maximise the cost recovery rate before competing with private companies (Gaughan 1989).

At present local authorities are fairly optimistic about being able to keep contracts in-house, and consequently progress towards a clearer conceptualisation of their role in terms of strategic planning, enabling and acting as a catalyst is uneven and generally cautious. However, it is likely that it will take the private sector between five and ten years to 'gear up' to bidding effectively for a substantial proportion of local leisure contracts and it may be only when the private sector is a more effective competitor that authorities will be forced to make choices about their preferred role in leisure provision.

Dual use

'Dual use' refers to the policy of opening up sports and recreational facilities to as wide a public as possible. The policy covers a broad range of facilities, including those controlled by local education authorities and those controlled by private companies, government departments and universities. In some authorities, such as Walsall and Birmingham, dual use is part of a broader policy of community development where access to sports and recreational facilities is complemented by a process of service decentralisation. For many other authorities dual use was a much more limited policy designed simply to increase the range of facilities locally available. The prime target of this policy has been the extensive sports facilities attached to schools and colleges which generally are open only during term time and school hours and where use is restricted to pupils. Ideally, under dual use, once pupils went home, members of the local community would come in to use the facilities, thus utilising the expensive capital resources possibly twelve hours a day, seven days a week and fifty-two weeks of the year.

A policy with such laudable aims deserves to succeed. That its achievements have been modest is surprising, given the influential organisations that have expressed support, including the Sports Council, the DOE, the Department of Education and Science and the CCPR. Despite this high level of support the policy has failed to become a widespread feature of local authority provision. In the 1990s there are a number of success stories set amidst a general picture of policy failure. Birmingham and Walsall provide good examples of relatively successful dual use policies in action. In Walsall, for example, a network of community schools are the basis for a hierarchy of provision ranging from simple facilities available at local primary schools, through more sophisticated and specialist facilities at secondary schools, to specially built centres of excellence (*Sport and Leisure* 1985; Nixon 1985).

At the heart of the implementation of the policy of dual use are three issues, namely what to share, how to manage the sharing and how to finance the policy. Resolving these issues has proved extremely difficult. Part of the explanation lies in the location of responsibility for education and leisure with different tiers of local government in the non-metropolitan areas. Even within the metropolitan districts agreement has often proved elusive. An additional problem concerns the relative importance of the policy to the two services/departments. For leisure services departments dual use is frequently a key element in a community recreation strategy. However, for an education department dual use is likely to have a much lower priority. In addition it must be acknowledged that within the school and its curriculum, physical education often holds a position of low status. Not withstanding the relative priority of the policy there is the further potential difficulty of the attitude of the head teacher, the governing body of the school and the local education committee. From the point of view of the schools and the education department there often seems to be little to be gained from the use of their sports facilities for non-educational purposes during times when the school is closed. Indeed many felt that the benefits were all one-way and to the advantage of the leisure services department. In the 1970s many attempts to introduce dual use foundered on the opposition of the head teacher and/or that of the education department and committee.

In the future the opportunities for dual use to expand will undoubtedly be affected by the delegation of financial responsibility to most schools. 'Local management of schools', which came into effect in 1990, gives school governing bodies extensive control over their budgets and facilities. For those authorities that have organised dual use as an extension of the management responsibilities of the head teacher there should be less of a problem. However, many authorities have organised dual use under a separate management structure for non-school use. In this case the problems are more substantial, as the Education Reform Act 1988, on which the local management of schools initiative is based, makes the continuation of these arrangements extremely difficult.

A number of leisure officers have suggested that this will encourage governing bodies to see their sports and leisure facilities and equipment as assets which should be valued commercially. This in turn may have the consequence that school sports facilities may be conserved, owing to the high replacement and maintenance costs, or only made available to leisure departments or community groups at market rates of hire. The net effect may be to make dual use more difficult to negotiate. On the other hand it may result in a renewed interest in, and an expansion of, dual use schemes as schools come to see their sports facilities as a potential source of additional revenue and, more importantly, as ways of projecting a positive image of the school in the community.

In Birmingham, for example, the council has already reached agreement between the Recreation and Community Services Department and the Education Department on the basis for the continuation of the city's extensive, and highly successful, dual use programme. Agreement has been reached on the management structure, which includes a full-time manager for each dual use centre, and the level to which the Recreation and Community Services Department will reimburse individual schools for the additional revenue and materials costs they incur (£50,000 in 1990–91). One indication of the success of Birmingham's experience is that in 1990 it had four schools waiting to be accepted as centres for dual use development. Unfortunately, Birmingham, Walsall and the small number of others like them, are not typical of local authorities in general and it is debatable whether dual use will thrive under the pressures of the 1988 Act where its roots are less deep. It is too soon to draw firm conclusions about the general impact of these recent developments on dual use. But there is sufficient anxiety within the sport and recreation policy community for the Sports Council and the major local authority associations to have launched a major survey of existing dual use provision and the effect of 'local management of schools'.

Finally, whether the delegation of greater responsibility for the management of schools to governing bodies acts as a stimulus to or restraint on the development of dual use, one unavoidable consequence will be to fragment control over the stock of sport and recreational resources even further, making the development of an authority-wide strategy for leisure more difficult to achieve.

Strategy development

For local authorities the 1980s were a difficult period during which to devise and sustain corporate plans or strategic plans for particular services. At the corporate level Greenwood and Stewart (1974; see also Greenwood *et al.* 1976) among others have shown the problems encountered in establishing corporate planning and its gradual decline throughout the 1980s. Attempts to plan strategically for particular services such as housing, social services and transport have experienced varying, but generally limited, degrees of success and consequently the commitment to planning and strategy development has declined.

Although in recent years the leisure policy area has been acquiring some of the requirements for strategy formation, such as a greater number of single comprehensive departments and committees, and strong support from the Regional Councils for Sport and Recreation, progress in strategic planning has been slight. Attempts to plan have been undermined by a variety of factors, some general to all local services, others more specific to the leisure field. The general factors include the uncertainty surrounding central government grants, the consequences of economic decline and the pace of legislative change during the decade.

Factors with a more specific effect on strategy development in leisure included the variety of sources of finance. Leisure, while enjoying a generally stable financial base, has often relied on a variety of funding sources, such as the DOE's Urban Programme and the Sports Council, for experimental projects. The availability of alternative sources of funds is always welcome in times of a shrinking revenue base but it has a number of potentially undesirable effects. In particular it may lead to the distortion, or even abandonment, of a service strategy, however vague that strategy may be. The second specific factor concerns the relative political and financial weakness of leisure services in the larger metropolitan districts. In these authorities leisure has a small budget relative to other services such as education, social services and housing. In addition, unlike the non-metropolitan districts, it is less likely to be a service which attracts the politically influential councillors, who will normally seek a place on the Policy and Resources Committee and the major service committees before considering leisure. Its relative lack of salience to local politicians makes strategies difficult to develop and difficult to sustain.

Finally, while there has been an increase in the number of single service and broad-based leisure departments significant elements of the service are none the less normally excluded. Among the excluded services would be schools sports facilities and the community facilities developed by social services departments. In commenting on the problems of developing a corporate approach to leisure planning Munn observed that:

> The emerging scene is therefore one of a public sector which has been unable to harness its existing and programmed resources effectively and is bound by a host of separate bureaucracies and agencies, who see the development of any inter-department strategy as an area of identity erosion, *not* an opportunity to improve the quality of the living environment in a host of 'village communities' – rural and urban.
>
> (Munn 1985: 42)

Birmingham's success in overcoming these problems has, in large part, been due to a forceful director and the strong political support of councillors to overcome resistance from other departments to the changes necessary to enable strategy development, including the transfer of adult education and the youth service from the Education Department to Recreation and Community Services.

A recent report by the Audit Commission criticised local authorities severely for their general lack of strategy regarding leisure services. The report noted the lack or vagueness of strategic objectives, the confusion of social and financial objectives, and the poor quality of management information on which to base strategy development (Audit Commission 1989). The report drew particular attention to the frequent lack of any explicit justification for the range of facilities provided or for the pricing and subsidy structure. Finally, the report noted that 'overall, many authorities do not ... know what they are achieving with the money they spend' (Audit Commission 1989: 12).

The net effect of the general lack of strategic direction at local level is that the character and development of the service are influenced either by financial opportunism or even by political or professional whim or enthusiasm. In a number of authorities, in England and Wales, political bargaining over the location of facilities was considered routine. As Benington and White observe:

> At worst the pattern [of distribution of provision] sometimes seems to reflect the individual predilections of officers and members rather than the particularities of local need. Even at best, innovative programmes are not easily co-ordinated with the long term objectives of the service and tend to become monuments to the changing fashions of the policies of grant giving bodies.
>
> (1986: 7)

In conclusion, there are a number of authorities who have developed leisure strategies, of which sport has been a recognisable element, and have been able to sustain their strategies through the challenges of, for example, financial constraint and CCT. Unfortunately the overall picture of the health of local authority leisure services is not reassuring. White (1986) in a major sample survey of the attitudes of chief leisure officers to the changing role of leisure services, found a group of officers trying to come to grips with the pace and direction of change. While most officers seemed to be aware of the major challenges facing them a number doubted whether local authorities had the skills to tackle them or the strategic framework within which to formulate policy responses to the challenges.

4

THE SPORTS COUNCIL AND THE ROLE OF GOVERNMENT AGENCIES

The Royal Charter meant that the Sports Council was, in effect, untouchable: never again would a politician become the supremo of an umbrella organisation of British sport.

Neil Macfarlane (1986: 79)

It is not only the Sports Council but also the BBC and the Arts Council which are finding out that the protection of their Royal Charter is meaningless when the appointment of their entire membership, and most of their funding, is entirely at the disposal of the Government of the day and controlled by a Government which is determined to exercise its patronage to achieve its policy objectives.

Denis Howell (1990: 217)

QUANGOS

One of the most significant developments in the machinery of government in the post-war period has been the growth in the creation of quasi-autonomous national government agencies, popularly referred to as quangos. If one were to move through a continuum starting with traditional central government departments, such as the DOE, at one end and arriving at private companies at the other, one would pass through a bewildering array of organisations which possess some features of government departments and exhibit varying degrees of independence from government. 'Quangos' therefore is an extremely loose term, used to refer to a large, and growing, number of organisations that are not under direct parliamentary control but are clearly linked to government by, for example, financial arrangements, lines of accountability or statutory obligations (Anderson 1977; Bowen 1978). The Sports Council is an example of a quango, relying as it does on an annual government grant and being headed by a council appointed by the Minister for Sport, but retaining a significant degree of independence derived from its royal charter. There are a number of other organisations operating in the broad area of sport and recreation that would also qualify for the description quangos, the most significant of which are the Countryside Commission (rural recreation), the Forestry Commission (leisure uses of Commission land), Tourist Boards (promoting visitor programmes and attractions) and the Nature Conservancy Council (habitat conservation, and including an interest in major leisure activities such as bird watching).

Defining quangos is not easy, as there are few, if any, characteristics that they hold in common. Among the most frequently identified characteristics are that they tend to be funded directly by the Treasury, they tend to be under the direction of a board which is usually appointed by the relevant Minister and their staff are not classed as civil servants (Hood 1979). However, there are many exceptions and much disagreement concerning the boundaries between quangos and more orthodox units of government. The difficulty in agreeing a list of common organisational characteristics of quangos led to attempts to identify the distinguishing features of quangos in terms of their role in the administrative and policy process. While the range of functions performed by quangos is nearly as diverse as their organisational arrangements it is possible to identify a number of recurring functions (Hood 1978b; Doig 1979). Among the most common functions are promotional or developmental activities (i.e. New Town Development Corporations, Tourist Boards, Sports Council) and controlling/licensing (the Gaming Board). Quangos may also be used where a particular specialist expertise is not available within the civil service, for example the skills of new town development or indeed some of the services provided by the Sports Council such as technical advice on sports centre design. In addition quangos may be established when the government desires to avoid direct political involvement in an issue. For example sport, like the arts, was not seen as a proper sphere for party political or direct governmental action and consequently government involvement has been mediated through quasi-governmental bodies. An alternative, and more cynical, motive for the avoidance of direct responsibility is where the government creates a 'buffer zone' between it and sectional pressure, as might be the case with equal opportunities, where the oversight and monitoring of policy to combat racial and sexual inequality are both the responsibility of quangos. Just to confuse matters, not only have quangos been used to depoliticise an issue or to create a 'buffer zone' between the government and a sensitive political issue, they have also been used in quite a contradictory fashion to facilitate direct government control over an issue or area of policy. This has been the case particularly regarding services that are normally provided by the local government sector. In the case of housing and education the government has created or expanded quangos in order to by-pass local authorities. For example, the Housing Corporation and the Training Agency may be seen as more amenable vehicles for the execution of government policy than the housing and education committees in Labour-held local authorities.

As should be evident by now, quangos fulfil a wide range of functions within the machinery of government and, importantly, the initial motive for quango creation may be subsumed by different motives as new issues arise and existing problems evolve. Because of the position of quasi-governmental organis-ations in that grey area between government and non-government they pose particular problems when attempting to identify their role in the administration of services and in the policy process. Among the general problems arising from the use of quangos is the difficulty that sometimes exists in co-ordinating their activities with the strategic objectives of government. Quangos may 'go off the rails' and pursue objectives or adopt methods out of step with those of government (Hood 1978a). More commonly quangos increase the number of 'clearance points' in a policy community. As the number of interest-specific quangos increases so too does the degree of bargaining required to get a broad policy accepted and implemented. Thus the more an administrative structure is fragmented the more compromise is required and the slower the process becomes (Pressman and Wildavsky 1973; Hood 1979). A further problem concerns accountability, including how Ministers use their power of patronage in making appointments to the boards of quangos, and how quangos are held accountable for their use of public money often received as grant in aid. A constant theme during the post-war period has been the inability of Parliament to hold the government to account for its actions.

The problem of parliamentary oversight of quangos is much greater and is, as will be shown later, a particularly significant element in Parliament's relationship with the Sports Council. At the heart of much of the concern with the accountability of quangos is the fear that they may 'go native', in other words that they may 'forget' that they are ultimately government agencies and become more like a pressure group on behalf of the interests that they deal with. Thus, for example, how can the public and Parliament feel confident that the Sports Council is reflecting government priorities to its clients rather than acting as a conduit for the promotion of client interests in the heart of government (Hood 1980; Davies 1979; Barker 1981)?

A further issue specific to sport is whether the large number of quangos and their significant role in the policy area increases further the problems of administrative fragmentation. It may be argued strongly that having a series of narrow specialist quangos responsible for related aspects of sport and physical recreation makes the problem of the strategic development of sport considerably more difficult. For not only do these agencies develop their priorities without regard to those of related bodies, they also present a complex maze for those involved in policy implementation to negotiate.

A final issue that needs to be addressed is whether the initial rationale for the creation of a series of specialist quangos still holds good today. The 'hands off' approach of the 1950s and 1960s has been replaced by a far less precious attitude towards sport. The Conservative government has intervened forcefully to lead policy development on drug abuse by athletes and football hooliganism and has restructured the Sports Council with little regard to the sensitivities of that body. Similarly, it may be argued that the specialist expertise initially focused in the Sports Council is now much more widely available in local authorities and in the commercial sector. These issues will be discussed further at the end of this chapter.

THE SPORTS COUNCIL

Of the quangos operating in the sport policy area the most important is the Sports Council. Although it was established relatively recently the origins of the Council may be traced back to the 1930s and are closely intertwined with the fortunes of the Central Council of Recreative and Physical Training. The 1930s were a watershed in the development of sport and recreation in Britain. As with other social services the development of sport as a recognised focus of public policy is best seen as a series of steps rather than as a process of gradual acceptance. The analogy of steps is more appropriate because periods of rapid progress were often followed by longer periods when very little organisational or policy development took place. The latter half of the nineteenth century and the early twentieth century were marked by flurries of activity in which, for example, governments would define more clearly their attitude towards sport or where interest groups were formed or became better organised. The result of these changes was further consolidation and definition of the contours of the policy area.

A particularly important burst of activity took place in the 1930s. By that time sport/physical activity was firmly established in the school curriculum and the growing number of physical education teachers were able to challenge the dominance of 'drill' in the PT curriculum. The emergence of an increasingly well organised group of teachers with a professional interest in sport complemented the newly established National Playing Fields Association (1925) and its concern to improve the quality of outdoor sport facilities. The creation of other related organisations, such as the Women's League of Health and Beauty (1929) and the Youth Hostels Association (1930), also contributed to and reflected the flourishing interest in fitness and sport. The emergence of these organisations took place against the growing preoccupation of the government and influential groups, such as the British Medical Association, with the state of health of the nation's youth and the increasing threat of war with Germany.

It was against this background that the Central Council of Recreative and Physical Training was established in 1935. The initial aim of the CCRPT was to stimulate provision for the community as a whole although particular attention was given to the needs of post-school physical education with the aim of helping to improve the level of fitness among the nation's youth. Although established by a group of enthusiastic individuals the CCRPT, by the end of its first year, was rapidly becoming an umbrella organisation for a wide range of bodies already active in the field of sport and recreation. In consequence, individual membership soon gave way to a system of affiliation by national organisations, especially governing bodies of sport and youth associations (Evans 1974). During the 'National Fitness Campaign' which followed the passage of the Physical Training and Recreation Act in 1937 the CCRPT greatly expanded its activities to include the training of physical education teachers and coaches. By the end of the war the now renamed Central Council of Physical Recreation had established a regional structure and was accepted by central government and local authorities as the main source of advice and expertise in the area of physical recreation. The CCPR relied heavily on grant aid from the Ministry of Education to fund its coaching development work with the national governing bodies. The Council was also involved, at this time, in organising British teams for some of the early post-war international competitions and in the development of national centres for sport, the first of which was opened at Bisham Abbey in 1946.

During the 1950s the CCPR became more closely associated with the government's emerging youth sport policy. Indeed it is probably fairer to say that the government supported the CCPR policy both politically and financially because the government lacked any clear policy on either sport or youth of its own (House of Commons 1957). The growing concern about the absence of a government youth policy and the weakness of the administrative capacity in this area prompted the CCPR to establish a committee of inquiry under the chairmanship of Sir John Wolfenden in 1957 (Evans 1974: 91–4).

The Wolfenden Report, published in 1960, was a watershed in the development of sport policy. The committee was given very broad terms of reference:

> To examine the factors affecting the development of games, sport and outdoor activities in the UK and to make recommendations to the CCPR as to any practical measures which should be taken by statutory or voluntary bodies in order that these activities may play their full part in promoting the general welfare of the community.
>
> (Wolfenden 1960: 1)

The main recommendation of the committee was that a Sports Development Council (SDC) be established, to be supported by a grant from government which it would distribute among sport's governing bodies and organisations such as the British Olympic Association and the CCPR. The aim of this suggestion was to support the development of voluntary activity with state financial assistance, but not to replace voluntary activity. The report also suggested that the new body should be responsible to the Treasury or the Lord President of the Council rather than being responsible to the Ministry of Education. This recommendation was due partly to the questionable success of the National Fitness Council, which had been accountable to the Education Ministry, but also to the Ministry's narrow focus, which the committee feared might not give due weight to adult sport and recreation and the international aspects of sport. In addition the committee was emphatic in its rejection of the '"official" control . . . of private leisure activity' (1960: 97). The proposal that the SDC should remain independent of any department would help to ensure the preservation of the 'non-political' nature of sport and prevent sport being submerged within the work of a large department (Coalter *et al.* 1986: 47). As a result the committee opted for a quango based on the model of the Arts Council and the University Grants Committee. (See Coalter *et al.* 1986 and Evans 1974 for a fuller discussion of the analysis and conclusions of the committee.)

In addition to the central recommendation that the SDC be established the report contained over fifty other recommendations covering, *inter alia*, coaching, amateurism, Sunday sport and facilities. The ideological context of the report was that associated with the welfare state and the necessity for positive state action in the face of the dislocation arising from industrial and social changes in the post-war period. Sport and recreation were seen as contributing to social control of the young, the improvement of the nation's health and also as playing an important role in instilling positive social values. Thus the report argued that 'if more young people had opportunities for playing games fewer of them would develop criminal habits' and that participation in competitive games would develop qualities 'valuable both to the individual and to society such as courage, endurance, self-discipline, determination [and] self-reliance' (1960: 4, 5). The report was clearly consistent with the prevailing conventional wisdom regarding the role of the state. As Coalter *et al.* crisply observe:

> there was a central ambivalence in the proposed solutions – a recognition of the necessity for increased state involvement and yet the fear of undermining voluntary effort. Within the classic Beveridge tradition state activity was only defensible as a framework for voluntarism. The concern of Wolfenden was to achieve reforms which would not introduce major structural change, but would assist existing organisations to perform more efficiently.
>
> (1986: 46)

The early 1960s were a period of steadily increasing government support for sport. It is not surprising that the political reception of the report was generally positive. Not only was government financial support for sport becoming more significant but the government had acknowledged the importance of sport by the appointment, in 1962, of Lord Hailsham as Minister with special responsibility for sport. However, there was a marked reluctance to implement the committee's key recommendation concerning the SDC, reflecting 'a mixture of a traditional Conservative commitment to minimal state intervention, a concern not to "politicise" or "professionalise" sports administration and a desire to preserve the valuable role of the volunteer . . .' (Coalter *et al.* 1986: 48). It was not until after the election of a Labour government in 1964 that a political climate more sympathetic to the idea of a SDC emerged. The new government was committed to administrative reform and also held a strong belief in the power of central planning. Consequently in 1965 the Advisory Sports Council (ASC) was established to provide the government with advice on expenditure priorities and the development of amateur sport and also to attempt to improve co-ordination among statutory and voluntary providers.

The ASC lasted seven years until it was replaced by the Sports Council in 1972. During that time the ASC made considerable progress in stimulating debate on sport and recreation issues in government and in establishing closer co-ordination between providers. However, the period also brought into sharp relief the tensions and ambiguities of role which caused the Sports Council so much concern in the late 1980s. On the positive side a lasting contribution of the ASC was the establishment of a network of advisory Regional Sports Councils consisting primarily, but not exclusively, of representatives of local authorities with the aim of advising on the regional co-ordination and provision of facilities for sport and physical recreation. The valuable initial work of the Regional Sports Councils focused on the survey and analysis of existing provision and the preparation of regional priorities for action. A further benefit of the ASC was the central role adopted by the Minister, Denis Howell. The Minister chaired the meetings of the ASC, on which from 1967 the CCPR was represented, and thereby provided a very direct link between the advisory function of the ASC and the CCPR and the executive capacity of the Ministry, creating for the first time a clear focus for policy development for sport and recreation.

Unfortunately the positive consequences of the establishment of the ASC need to be qualified. The most important qualification concerns the continuing ambiguity of the relationship between government, the ASC and the CCPR. By the early 1960s the CCPR was closely enmeshed in the web of government through its receipt of considerable grant aid from the Ministry of Education and its involvement in the implementation of the government's sports/youth policy under the 1937 Physical Training and Recreation Act. In consequence the CCPR was firmly in that grey area between government and non-government discussed at the start of this chapter. For Coalter *et al.* this represented a corporatist strategy on the part of government, which aimed to 'incorporate', and thereby exercise influence over, voluntary interests within the ambit of a government-sponsored organisation (1986: 48–51). However, such a view is difficult to sustain, as the appearance of corporatist features in the organisation of areas of government interest does not demonstrate the existence of a corporatist strategy. It is more likely that the relationship between the CCPR and the government was the outcome of the growing influence of the maturing sports lobby on the one hand and, on the other, the absence of clear policy objectives (short-term preoccupations not withstanding) on the part of government. Thus the relationship is better explained as the outcome of pluralist politics rather than of a corporatist strategy.

Prior to the establishment of the Sports Council its forerunner, the Advisory Sports Council, had a close relationship with the CCPR. The CCPR, from its existing regional network, provided the administrative support for the newly formed Regional Sports Councils. Walter Winterbottom, secretary of the CCPR, was seconded to the ASC to act as its first director, a position he was later to hold jointly with his post as General Secretary of the CCPR. Although there were initially no 'reserved' seats on the ASC for CCPR representatives, from 1967 the CCPR was allocated two places. In addition, upon Winterbottom's completion of his secondment to the ASC the CCPR undertook to 'provide the Sports Council with such services as might be agreed'. As Evans comments, 'During this period (1965–71) it became increasingly difficult to detach the work of the CCPR from that of the [Advisory] Sports Council and the Regional Sports Councils . . .' (1974: 209). The creation of the Sports Council in 1972 added considerably to the ambiguity of the relationship between the British Olympic Association, the CCPR and the government.

The decision to create an executive Sports Council by royal charter was warmly welcomed by the sports community but it posed serious problems for the relationship with the CCPR. Initially, at least, the CCPR accepted that the creation of an executive Sports Council as proposed by the recently elected Conservative government would necessitate 'some form of merger or absorption with the Sports Council' (Evans 1974: 218) and a merger between the two organisations was formally proposed by Eldon Griffiths, the Minister for Sport. The eventual outcome of the protracted negotiations between the two bodies was that the CCPR agreed to the transfer of its staff to the Council, but that the CCPR should remain in existence to act as a representative body for the governing bodies of sport and to act in a consultative capacity in relation to the Sports Council. The assets of the CCPR (national centres and regional offices in particular) were to be transferred to a charitable trust, with the Sports Council as trustee. This arrangement reflected the CCPR's misgivings at losing control over major sports resources.

Organisation and financing of the Sports Council

In 1988 the Minister for Sport announced that the size of the Sports Council would be cut from a membership of thirty-two to fourteen. According to the Minister the rationale for the change was that 'The Council, going into the 1990s, needs an input from present-day sportsmen and women, [and] from the private sector, to act as a catalyst for generating more income for the elite and at the grass-roots level' (quoted in the *Guardian*, 29 October 1988). Underlying reasons included the desire to break the pattern of political in-fighting between rival interests on the Council and also to streamline decision-making.

Prior to the 1988 changes the membership of the Council included seven nominees of the CCPR, all ten chairmen of the Regional Councils for Sport plus representatives of local authority interests. The Council therefore contained three fairly distinct and, at times, incompatible interests, namely the governing body/elite interests represented by the CCPR nominees, the local authority/mass participation interests represented by the local government appointees and a local/regional interest represented by the ten Regional Council chairmen. The consequence of this pattern of membership was that the Council, on occasion, divided along interest group lines, making the development of corporate policy more difficult. However, one positive consequence of a large Council was that it was capable of taking a closer interest in the process of policy formation, owing, for example, to its ability to establish sub-committees.

The present structure of the Sports Council is shown in Figure 2. The new Council meets once a month with a strong emphasis on strategic decision-making and the approval of grant allocation. The Council relies heavily on its sub-committees to carry out the preliminary reviews of policy options, in relation to the national centres, and to vet grant applications. The Council and its sub-committees are supported by a series of consultative groups whose membership is a mix of Council members and nominees from interested organisations. The groups are of two types and fulfil two important functions; the first type is likely to be permanent and links the Council with the wider sports community and the second type usually has a limited life and is established to deal with specific problems. An example of the former is the CCPR consultative group which fulfils the consultative role required by the Sports Council's charter, and the Performance and Excellence consultative group, which is examining the needs of top athletes, and more likely to be

Figure 2 The structure of the Sports Council, 1989

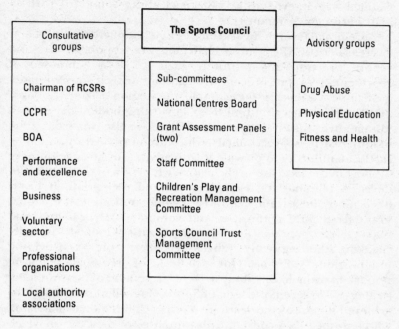

disbanded once its deliberations are complete, is an example of the latter. In addition to the consultative groups and sub-committees of the Council, a small number of advisory groups remain, such as for drug abuse, and, in general, fulfil a similar role to the consultative groups. As the new Council organisation has been in operation for only a short time it is too soon to reach a final judgement on its impact. However, the initial view of Council officers and governing bodies is optimistic and there is a feeling that the speed of decision-making has improved and that policy is more consistent.

For the new Council the consultative groups act as its 'eyes and ears' and are a major source of policy initiative. Another important channel by which policy issues reach the agenda of the Council is through the meetings of the Committee of Chairmen of the Regional Councils for Sport and Recreation, which take place three or four times a year, part of the meeting being with the Minister and part with members and officers of the Council.

Other sources of policy initiation include individual clubs, Council staff, international bodies such as the Council of Europe, and central government.

At regional level there are ten Regional Councils for Sport and Recreation (RCSR), whose chairmen are appointed by, and report direct to, the Minister. Each RCSR is composed of representatives and officers of local authorities, sports-related government agencies (for example, the Regional Tourist Boards and National Parks Committees), governing bodies and a small number of ministerial appointees. There are also representatives of local/district sports councils, which are normally organised by the local authority to provide it with advice on the development of sport in the local area. The primary function of the RCSR is to devise a regional strategy for sport and recreation. It has a particularly important role in reviewing applications for capital grant from local authorities and voluntary organisations and making recommendations to the Sports Council. Broadly speaking the regional councils see their role as providing pump-priming finance for schemes of regional or local importance which contribute to the achievement of their regional strategy. The recent pruning of Sports Council membership was achieved in part by the decision to remove all regional chairmen, who now meet as a consultative committee of the Council which is chaired by the chairman of the Sports Council.

The revision of its size and membership followed a major reorganisation of the Council's management structure. The management restructuring was prompted by repeated criticism of the Council's approach to corporate planning and particularly its capacity to achieve effective financial control. The House of Commons Environment Committee's investigation of the Sports Council criticised the Council for failing to exercise effective control over the finances of its national centres and over the grant it distributed to governing bodies (House of Commons 1986: xxv, xxvii). In the same year a highly critical report from the National Audit Office was presented to Parliament which drew attention to a number of weaknesses which included the poor monitoring and control of finances at headquarters and at the national centres, the unreliability of asset records and the inadequacy of invoicing systems, as well as confusion over the financial arrangements between the Council and the CCPR (NAO 1986).

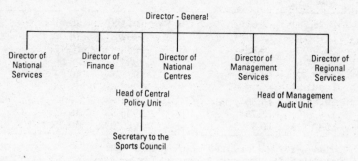

Figure 3 The Sports Council: senior management structure

The report was supported by an investigation by the House of Commons Public Accounts Committee during 1986–87 (House of Commons 1987). The latest report by the NAO is still critical of the Council's capacity to exercise effective financial control and concludes that despite 'various improvements being set in train . . . it remains to be seen whether, and how quickly, the remedial measures now in hand or under consideration will be fully effective' (NAO 1989).

The new management structure of the Council is shown in Figure 3 and is designed to strengthen the strategic capacity of the Council by creating a small senior management group and to enhance financial control by adding the Head of Management Audit to the management team, at third-tier level.

A key concern of the Council is to strengthen financial control not only over its own running costs but also over the grant distributed either centrally or through the Council's regional bodies. In 1988–89 the Council received a total income of £45.67 million of which £38.41 million came as grant aid from the DOE and represents a slight decline in the proportion of Council activities funded publicly (84 per cent in 1988–89; 85 per cent in 1983–84; 91 per cent in 1972–73). The remaining income came from fees for the use of the national centres, running training courses and conferences, from the National Coaching Foundation and from sponsorship.

Staff costs accounted for £9.4 million in 1988–89,[1] with the bulk of Council expenditure being on sports development work (£14.7 million), the provision of local and regional facilities

Table 6 Grant in aid to the Sports Council 1972–73 to 1989–90 (£ million)

Year	Grant	Year	Grant
1972/73	3.60*	1981/82	20.91
1973/74	5.00**	1982/83	28.00
1974/75	6.58	1983/84	27.12
1975/76	8.33	1984/85	28.60
1976/77	10.20	1985/86	30.11
1977/78	11.52	1986/87	37.35
1978/79	15.03	1987/88	37.15
1979/80	15.73	1988/89	38.41
1980/81	19.31	1989/90	39.95***

*　　Excluding £37,869 from the Ministry of Education.
**　 Excluding £53,643 from the Ministry of Education.
*** Planned expenditure.
Source: Sports Council Annual Reports and 1988 Corporate Plan.

(£8.6 million) and the running of the national sports centres (£6.4 million). The remaining income is spent on a range of activities including research, training courses, children's play, and publicity. About two-thirds of all grant money is distributed centrally by the Council, the rest being allocated through recommendations from the Regional Councils for Sport and Recreation. Grant is distributed nationally to the national governing bodies of sports, to national organisations with a specialist or multi-sport interest (such as the British Deaf Sports Council), or else for specific projects (such as the Action Sport scheme in inner city areas).[2]

Policy development

Policy development, from the creation of the Advisory Sports Council in 1965 to the present, has been dominated by a debate over the social function of sport, the relationship between the state and the voluntary sector and the relative priority of elite sport. These themes, which weave their way through the history of the Sports Council, are set within the context of recurrent economic crises and the consolidation of the philosophy of economic liberalism associated with Margaret Thatcher.

The Advisory Sports Council was established in 1965 at a time of great confidence in the capacity of government to plan the development of the welfare state. The role of the Regional Sports Councils was to contribute to the organisational co-ordination required for the systematic analysis of recreational 'needs' and the integration of planned service provision. Much of the early activity of the ASC was directed at stimulating an overhaul of the organisational apparatus for sport and recreation at local authority level and among the governing bodies of sport. In addition to overhauling and strengthening the administrative framework for sport the ASC also aimed to develop a pool of expertise, particularly on technical matters. The sharpening of the identity of sport as a discrete policy concern of government was assisted by the transfer of responsibility for sport from the Department of Education and Science to the Ministry of Housing and Local Government. This transfer freed the ASC and the nascent sport policy community from the constraining influence of an 'educational' definition of sport and allowed a broader interpretation based on the responsibilities of local authorities for the general welfare of the local community. In many ways this early period in the history of the Sports Council is dominated by the concern to define the policy area and to establish the foundations of a policy community for sport and recreation. National policy towards sport was only very vaguely articulated and was focused on a number of broad principles. These included the belief that sport had a role to play in combating the rise in juvenile delinquency (Wolfenden 1960; Kilmuir 1961), that the role of the state was to support voluntary activity rather than replace it (McIntosh and Charlton 1985: 7), and a commitment to the policy of 'Sport for All' as expressed by the Council of Europe in 1966. That sport was a 'good thing' was taken as a motherhood statement.

The period from the early 1970s to the present marks a steady increase in the interest taken by government in the public policy of sport and its administration. It is not possible to point to a particular event and mark it as the catalyst for the changing attitude of government. The explanation lies in a series of related developments which combined to stimulate a more active role for the government in the policy area. One important element was the strength of public demand for leisure facilities, while a second was the growing sophistication of the sports lobby. A third explanation lies in the emergence of urban deprivation as a more clearly defined area of government concern and the subsequent inclusion of sport and recreation in the range of policy 'solutions'. Against this background three tensions are especially evident during the period; first, between investment in elite sport as opposed to promoting mass participation; second, between increasingly interventionist governments and the relative autonomy of the Council implied in its charter; and third, between the Council and the rump of the CCPR.

Elite or mass sport?

The establishment of an executive Sports Council in 1972 and its absorption of the assets and many of the functions of the CCPR introduced a much more significant actor into the policy arena. With the new Council being so heavily dependent on the expertise and staff of the CCPR it is not surprising that the Sports Council retained, in its early years at least, the policy concerns and modes of implementation of the CCPR. Of particular importance was the Council's reliance on the governing bodies of sport as channels for the distribution of grant. Consequently although there was mounting support for the promotion of mass participation in sport the Council moved only slowly away from its preoccupation with the elite athlete.

The aim to 'encourage wider participation in sport and physical recreation' was included as one of the Council's four stated aims in the first annual report. The others covered the promotion of a general understanding of the importance of sport and physical recreation in society, increasing the provision of new sports facilities and the use of existing sports facilities to serve the needs of the community, and raising standards of performance in sport and physical recreation. In the same year, 1972, the Sports Council launched its own 'Sport for All' programme some six years after the government's endorsement of the Council of Europe's 'Sport for All' campaign, and a year before the Cobham Report (House of Lords 1973) argued for a stronger policy towards mass sport. In the early and mid 1970s the Council devoted its own limited resources to the provision of pump-priming finance aimed at stimulating local authority investment or voluntary activity. There was little discernible tension between the interests of the elite and of the mass, as there was a consensus, reinforced by the Cobham Report on 'Sport and Leisure' (1973), that an increase in facilities was the first priority. However, it was apparent from the outset that 'Sport for All' meant different things to different people. For the first director of the Council it meant 'all sport [including] competitive, international sport' (Walter Winterbottom, quoted in Coalter *et al.* 1986).

It is doubtful if 'Sport for All' ever became more than a slogan. From the mid 1970s onwards government was expecting (and at times directing) the Sports Council to target its resources at specific groups in society. Thus 'sport for all' slowly became 'sport for the disadvantaged' and 'sport for inner city youth'. In the White Paper *Sport and Recreation* (DOE 1975) the government gave explicit direction to the Sports Council and to the Regional Councils for Sport and Recreation that 'it would be right for the highest priority in grant-aid to be accorded to suitable recreational projects in such areas [where living conditions are particularly poor]'. Sport was therefore seen as part of the Labour government's inner city strategy, with effort directed towards 'recreational priority areas', thereby complementing the expanding Urban Programme. From the mid 1970s the government began to earmark small amounts of the Council's grant for specific projects related to its inner city strategy, which helped to reinforce the policy shift away from 'Sport for All' and towards selectivity.

While the Sports Council acknowledged the shift in policy, and incorporated it into its policy statement in 1982, the Council remained committed to providing substantial support for elite sport and exhibited remarkable tact towards the governing bodies of sport with regard to the role that they might play in developing participation. Thus the Council's bid for resources outlined in its policy statement allocated 35 per cent of its bid for 'encouraging excellence' (Sports Council 1982: 42). In the same document the Council, in discussing the possible contribution of the governing bodies to the promotion of participation, refers rather deferentially to discussing 'with governing bodies the role they wish to play' (1982: 34). The continued support for elite sport is explained, or more accurately rationalised, in the evidence given by the Council to the Environment Committee of the House of Commons in 1985. Stating that the Council spent 25 per cent of its budget on promoting excellence (a figure that prompted some scepticism from the committee), John Wheatley, the director-general of the Council, argued that 'Our support of excellence is very largely, though not entirely, due to the stimulatory inspirational effects on mass participation' (House of Commons 1986: 89).

During the 1980s the Council gave considerable thought to locating mass participation within a broader, strategic approach to sports development. To this end the Council has identified four relatively discrete building blocks in sports development. The first is the *foundation* level, where the emphasis is on awakening interest in sport, especially among school age children, and may be seen as developing 'physical literacy'; the second block relates to *participation* and is concerned with promoting participation, whether the reasons are social, health-related or the result of the intrinsic value of sport; the third block is concerned with improving *performance* from the participant's present level of ability, whatever that might be; the final block concerns *excellence*, where success is the primary motive. This conceptualisation of sports development is consistent with the long held view in the Council that an emphasis on mass participation cannot be separated from a concern with the elite level.

The key role of the Sports Council in sports development is to create awareness among the public, ensure that activities and the necessary facilities exist, and to consolidate interest. The implementation of this strategy has been aided in the late 1980s by the easing of tension between provision for the elite athlete and the mass participant. This is partly because many governing bodies and also the British Olympic Association, which is primarily concerned with elite sport, are now better able to support athletes from their own funds. It is also partly due to a slight slackening in the government's concern with urban problems, which has enabled the Council greater room for manoeuvre over the allocation of finance. The Council's latest policy document maintains the twin objectives of the development of elite and mass participation. However, most of the additional resources it was bidding for would go on providing opportunities for mass participation, with the emphasis concerning elite sport being on the improvement of co-ordination and the development of regional plans rather than the allocation of substantial new funds.

The Sports Council and government: degrees of independence

The concept of 'independence from government' is particularly difficult to define. In general, quangos retain the degree of independence that it suits government to allow them. It is difficult to recall an issue or policy area where the government has allowed the status of the quango (such as those possessing a royal charter) to obstruct the implementation of its policy. Housing, broadcasting, vocational training and health are all policy areas where the existence of strong quangos has not deterred the government from the strenuous pursuit of its policy priorities. Even local government, with its much stronger claims to legitimate autonomy from the centre than quangos, has been forced to concede ground on matters of policy when faced with a determined government. It should therefore not be surprising that the Sports Council has become progressively an agent of central government policy. This is not to suggest that it has lost its scope for discretionary action; rather, it is suggested that the scope is now severely constrained by central policy priorities. Thus the cause for comment is not that autonomy has largely been lost, but that it survived for so long.

The relationship of the forerunner of the Sports Council, the Advisory Sports Council, to government was extremely close. The Minister for Sport, Denis Howell, was to act as chairman, thus creating a situation where he was chairman of a body set up to advise the government on matters relating to sport while also being the Minister who would receive, and presumably accept or reject, that advice. The establishment, in 1972, of a Sports Council with executive functions and under a royal charter increased the degree of autonomy. However, the royal charter, frequently seen as a bulwark against government intrusion, was sufficiently vague to enable the relationship to be reinterpreted to suit the prevailing management attitudes and policy priorities of government. Not only did the Minister retain the right to approve the appointment of the Council's director and its members, but also he was allowed, under the terms of the charter, to appoint assessors to the Council. Assessors are civil servants acting on behalf of the Minister not simply as observers but as the 'voice' of the Minister. In addition the charter contains the broad stipulation that the Council 'shall have regard to any general statements on the policy . . . that may from time to time be issued by Our Secretary of State'.

In the early years of the Council the degree of independence it enjoyed was due to the absence of any clear government objectives rather than to any deference on the part of the government. As Coalter *et al.* observe, 'The independence of the Council was secured because it operated within a policy vacuum' (1986: 67). However, from the mid 1970s onwards central government began to intrude more forcefully into the work of the Council for a number of reasons. The first was that sports issues were beginning to impinge on the mainstream concerns of government. For example, football hooliganism linked the sports policy area to the much more important law and order policy area. The second reason for increasing government interest was that a number of government policy objectives could be met using sport as a convenient medium. For example, sport was seen as part of the solution to inner city problems and it may also be argued that a sporting boycott of South Africa, based on the Gleneagles agreement, was preferable to an economic boycott which would seriously harm Britain's trading interests. Third, in the 1980s, the Sports Council suffered from the Conservative government's initial suspicion that quangos are less careful with public money and run the risk of being 'captured' by their clients. Finally, sports facilities and management, like many other public services, were considered suitable candidates for experiments in privatisation. It is possible to add a fourth reason, which is that the economic recession of the mid 1970s was bound to put all areas of public expenditure under greater scrutiny. Finally, the election, in 1979, of a radical reforming Conservative government was bound to lead to a more interventionist style from the centre.

The greater involvement of central government in the work of the Sports Council may be illustrated in a number of ways. Of particular importance was the practice, begun in the late 1970s, of including within the Council's general grant sums allocated for specified purposes. For example, in 1978–79 the government gave a specific grant of just over £800,000 to assist directly with schemes in deprived urban areas. In broader terms the government has made it clear that it expects the Council to fall into line behind the government's priorities, especially those related to inner cities. More recently, in late 1988, Denis Howell, the Labour shadow Sports Minister, accused Colin Moynihan of manipulating the Council into supporting his proposals for sports sponsorship by presenting the proposals to a Council containing a number of new and relatively inexperienced appointees.

The exercise of the Minister's powers of patronage provides a further example of the increase in government involvement in the Council. In 1985 the chairman of the Sports Council, Dick Jeeps, was replaced amid suggestions that the government felt he was out of step with both the new business orientation of the Council and the firmer line on severing sporting links with South Africa. More recently the Minister halved the size of the Council, leaving only seven experienced members and bringing in seven new members. The motive was to produce a more dynamic, business-oriented Council. Not only was Moynihan intent on introducing a new culture to the Council, he also created a potentially very powerful niche for himself within the new Council structure. One of the Council's key consultative groups comprises the ten chairmen of the Regional Councils for Sport and Recreation, chaired by the Sports Council's chairman, whose meetings are attended by the Minister, thus, according to John Rodda, providing the Minister with a channel through which he may by-pass the Council (*Guardian*, 2 July 1988: 13).

The Relationship with the CCPR

The Wolfenden Committee, whose report provided the primary stimulus for the government's decision to appoint an Advisory Sports Council, was a creation of the CCPR. The establishment of an ASC and the subsequent creation of an executive Sports Council were significant victories for the sports lobby and the CCPR in particular. However, the establishment of an executive Sports Council and the transfer of responsibility for the national sports centres from the CCPR left the CCPR with a vague and somewhat marginal role in the sports policy community. It is the attempt by the CCPR to redefine its role that has bedevilled the relationship between the two bodies at the heart of British sport.

The present CCPR membership covers a wide spectrum of sport and recreation organisations.[3] Most, if not all, major governing bodies are members, but in addition the CCPR provides a representative organisation for armed forces sports organisations, a broad range of umbrella bodies (such as the

Figure 4 The structure of the Central Council of
Physical Recreation

British Universities' Sports Federation and the British Sports
Association for the Disabled), professional bodies (Institute of
Leisure and Amenity Management), youth, teaching and medical
organisations. It is therefore with a high degree of legitimacy that
it can claim to be the 'voice of British sport'. However, one should
add that the CCPR may well be representative of *organised* sport,
as it represents organisations with a total membership of over 6
million members, but total adult sports participation is over 17
million. The majority of participants are therefore outside the
ambit of the CCPR, though some will none the less share similar
interests on many issues. The CCPR's aims are to 'formulate and
promote measures to improve and develop sport and physical
recreation', to facilitate co-ordination between specialist sports
bodies and to 'act as a consultative body to the Sports Council and
other representative or public bodies concerned with sport and
physical recreation' (CCPR undated: 2). The income of the CCPR
comes primarily from the Sports Council. In 1987–88, out of a
total income of £637,465, £589,660 (92.5 per cent) was received
in grant from the Council, £10,659 in member subscriptions, £24,646 from services and publications and £12,500 in
sponsorship.

This income supports a small headquarters staff of about
twenty whose responsibilities parallel the divisional structure of
the Central Council, which is shown in Figure 4. The Executive
Committee is chosen by the membership as a whole and it is the
Executive Committee's responsibility to allocate members to
one of the six interest-based divisions. However, while an

organisation may be allocated to one division it may well have 'observer' status on another if it feels that it has interests which span more than one division. With a total membership of over 260 plus a number of individual members, many of the divisions are very large and they therefore tend to operate through a system of working parties, with the divisions receiving and discussing their reports before forwarding them to the Executive Committee.

Although the CCPR does not have a regional organisation there exist a series of independent Regional Standing Conferences of Sport and Recreation (RSCSR) which comprise representatives from Regional and County Sports Associations. The function of the RSCSRs is to provide the collective view of sport in the region and as such they fulfil a similar role to the CCPR at national level. The RSCSRs also act as a constituency from which representatives to the Regional Council for Sport and Recreation may be chosen. While a number of RSCSRs meet on a regular basis, with secretarial support provided by the Sports Council's regional office, others meet only infrequently, usually for the purpose of electing representatives. At national level the CCPR has a Regional Committee comprising two representatives from each of the RSCSRs which functions as the link between the national organisation and the regions and aims to provide a channel for communication and a means of injecting a regional view into the CCPR's national policy discussions.

The decision by the government to establish an executive Sports Council and the subsequent failure to arrive at a satisfactory agreement for merger between the new Council and the CCPR created, as mentioned earlier in this chapter, a running sore in the body of the policy community. The decision by the CCPR to continue in existence as 'a standing forum for sports bodies' (Evans 1974: 226) was followed by a memorandum of agreement between the two bodies which contained a clause that obliged the Sports Council to provide the CCPR with 'such resources and facilities as the CCPR might reasonably require in carrying out and implementing its new objects'.

In the mid 1970s the Central Council was given increased representation on the Sports Council, to seven members, in an attempt to placate the growing criticism from the CCPR that it was being marginalised in the policy process. But writing in 1980 Don Anthony observed that the CCPR had still not found an acceptable role in relation to the Sports Council. From the late 1970s onwards the CCPR seemed determined to compete with the Sports Council rather than advise it on policy. Anthony criticises it, though maybe too harshly, for lobbying independently of the Council (Anthony 1980: 11-12). More importantly it also attempted to recreate an executive role for itself largely financed by public money. During the early 1980s the CCPR commissioned a number of major pieces of research, for example into sports sponsorship and satellite broadcasting. In addition it organised a training scheme leading to its Community Sports Leader's Award. Matters came to a head when the report of the Environment Committee of the House of Commons made a series of fundamental criticisms of the role of the CCPR and its relationship with the Sports Council. In particular, the report observed that 'whatever its aspirations . . . the CCPR is, at present, essentially an organisation for making representations on behalf of governing bodies' (House of Commons 1986: xiv). Given this definition of its role, the Committee went on to suggest that 'It is for governing bodies to say whether they want an umbrella organisation of this kind but we do not see why it should be financed from the public purse' (1986: xiv). The Committee noted that the CCPR had doubled its bid for resources from the Sports Council for 1986 to over £600,000 and that its agreement with the Sports Council gave the latter, at best, little scope for regulating the CCPR's use of public money. In conclusion the Committee stated, 'We see no significant role for the CCPR other than to represent the collective views of governing bodies. We do not see why the CCPR should be financed from the public purse' (1986: xvi).

The most recent report of the Public Accounts Committee reinforces these comments and observed that 'given the substantial sums the [Sports] Council is committed to paying to the CCPR, it could not clearly identify commensurate benefits' (House of Commons 1989: vii–viii). Despite these comments and similar expressions of concern voiced by the National Audit Office (1989: 4, 5) the Central Council received £612,000 for 1986–87 and £590,000 for 1987–88. From 1983–84 to 1987–88 the CCPR grant has risen by 137 per cent (£249,000–£590,000) whereas the income of the Sports Council has risen by 37 per cent (£27.1 million–£37.2 million) over the same period.

In many respects the Central Council is in an impossible position. It is at present, and for the foreseeable future will continue to be, heavily dependent on government grant.[4] However, its primary role is to represent the interests of the voluntary sports organisations in general and the governing bodies in particular. It is difficult to see how this relationship is acceptable to anyone. In particular the tension arising from the government subsidy of pressure groups must continue to surface over the coming years.

The future role of the Sports Council

At the beginning of this chapter it was suggested that quangos might fulfil a number of functions for government. At its establishment the Sports Council was seen as fulfilling a promotional role and as providing a focus for the development of expertise absent within the civil service. In addition the Council provided a buffer between government and party politics, on the one hand, and the voluntary organisations involved in sport on the other. However, a lot has changed in the years since the creation of the Sports Council and it is legitimate to ask whether the same rationale is still valid or whether a new set of functions have emerged to provide a justification for the continuance of the organisation.

Regarding the promotional work of the Council, this is still a central feature of its activities, as reflected in its recent corporate plans and its latest strategy document. Of the Council's bid for additional resources of £11 million it proposes to spend £9 million on capital projects, of which £7 million is to be spent on projects associated with promoting mass participation (Sports Council 1988: 78–9). Promotional activity is clearly the primary element in the rationale for the Sports Council. Could any other organisation do the job as well or better? The CCPR considers that it could fulfil most of the functions of the Sports Council more effectively. The CCPR, referring to 'the quango stigma of the present Sports Council' (House of Commons 1986: 115), argued that the Council is too obviously the government's tool and too remote from the day-to-day activities of the governing bodies of sport. In evidence submitted to the House of Commons Environment Committee the CCPR therefore suggested that it should take over all the executive functions of the Sports Council, including its development work. The rump of the Sports Council would merely advise government on the administration of the grant.

Leaving aside any discussion of the administrative capacity of the CCPR to take over the functions of the Sports Council, the essential choice is not between administration of a policy area by quango or an independent body, but rather which type of quango would be preferable. Although the CCPR is nominally an independent body, it has relied very heavily on government finance and by implication it, like the Sports Council, inhabits that grey area between government and non-government. There is no evidence from within SARD that the government has any intention of restoring to the CCPR its pre-1972 status and functions. In addition the Environment Committee doubted whether the CCPR had any role in public policy towards sport that justified support from public funds.

An alternative vehicle for the promotion of mass participation might be the governing bodies of sport. These were identified by the Sports Council as having an important role to play in this area of policy. The actual and potential role of governing bodies in the 'foundation' and 'participation' levels of sports development varies according to a number of factors, including their traditions, structure, experience and wealth. For example, orienteering receives very little local authority help and therefore has a development policy which covers all four building blocks identified by the Sports Council. By contrast the Amateur Swimming Association tends to concentrate on performance and excellence because by tradition local authorities take responsibility for the foundation and participation aspects of the sport's development. Nevertheless, while the Sports Council referred in 1982 to discussing 'with the governing bodies the role they wish to play in promoting mass participation', by 1988 the Council was admitting that although considerable finance had been provided the contribution of the governing bodies was questionable (Sports Council 1982: 34; 1988: 69). This would seem to support the conclusion of the Association of District Councils (ADC) that 'the tendency among governing bodies is towards excellence . . . [and] we know from experience that [they] are not always helpful in the field which we regard as of paramount importance – the best provision to the largest numbers of people . . .' (House of Commons 1986: 33).

Given the sentiments expressed by the ADC, it is worth considering whether local authorities might not be a successful vehicle for the promotion of mass participation. Not only do local authorities control the bulk of public sector sports facilities, they are also clearly well placed to develop an interest in sport in the young through the school curriculum. However, as was indicated in chapter 3, local authorities vary considerably in the extent to which they give priority to sport and recreation. They also vary in terms of the range of sports they are prepared to foster. It is also highly likely that the advent of compulsory competitive tendering will make local authorities even less willing to promote minority sports.

The Sports Council would still seem to be required to fulfil the function of sports promotion. Its national and regional pattern of organisation enables it to adopt a synoptic view of the service and to use its financial resources for stimulating participation in sport either through the governing bodies or through the local authorities.

Providing a buffer between the government and the policy area was suggested as a second possible function for the newly created Sports Council. To some extent the rhetoric of separation between sport and politics still remains but it is doubtful if the government finds this an inhibiting factor. The strongly interventionist style of the present government and its tendency to use quangos explicitly as a means of achieving its objectives suggests that the government is far less concerned about being seen to be intervening in sport policy. The interventionist attitude of the government towards sport was signalled early on, in 1980, when the government attempted to press the British Olympic Association to withdraw the national team from the Moscow Olympics. Since then the government has also intervened strongly in a range of sports or sport-related issues, including encouraging the selling of surplus school playing fields, the privatisation of local authority sports centre management, drug abuse by athletes and spectator violence. It would therefore seem that this general function of quangos is less appropriate as a justification for the Sports Council in the 1990s.

The third function of quangos appropriate to the Sports Council referred to their capacity to develop a core of expertise which is outside the present range of civil service activities. The Sports Council can claim expertise in two areas in particular, first, regarding technical matters such as design, equipment and materials, and the second regarding the strategic planning of sport. Regarding the first, the rapid expansion of the leisure industry has led to the emergence of a number of specialist architects and designers for the industry. Similarly specialist equipment manufacturing is now far more common than twenty years ago. It is therefore possible to argue that there is sufficient expertise available, albeit highly diffused, outside the Sports Council. Nevertheless the Council frequently finds itself at the centre of innovation in building design, as for example with the development of SASH (Standardised Approach to Sports Halls) and a wide range of research projects covering, for example, artificial cricket pitches, energy saving, the promotion of specialist sports' development, and also coaching support (via the National Coaching Foundation).

Regarding the strategic planning of sport, it is doubtful if any other organisation could fulfil the role performed by the Council. The CCPR and the governing bodies are too concerned with the elite level and local authorities are too preoccupied with mass participation. The Sport and Recreation Division of the DOE is too small and is staffed at the senior level by civil servants who have the expectation of fairly rapid movement to other departments as a normal part of career development and therefore have little incentive to acquire a specialist expertise in sport policy. In addition the Sports Council has, over the years, built up a network of relationships with a wide range of national, regional, local and international organisations involved in sport (see Figure 5). While this in itself does not result in the adoption of a strategic role in a policy community, seeking and holding such a position is a prerequisite of policy leadership.

However, there are constraints on the ability of the Council to develop its strategic role, the most important of which is the generally lower level of influence that the Council has with professional sport. Sports with a long history of professional competition, particularly those with a well established international circuit, have proved less easy for the Council to bring within its ambit for purposes of policy consultation and co-ordination. Boxing, cricket, tennis and football are all

Figure 5 The pattern of contact between the Sports
Council and other organisations

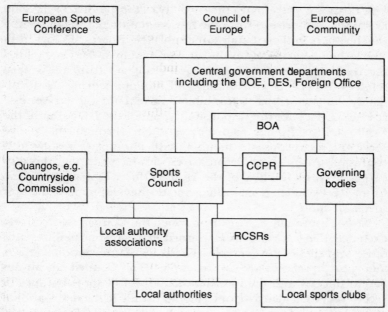

examples of major sports where the professional level is only
peripherally associated with the sports policy community which
has the Council as its focus. Yet there are a number of current or
emerging issues which significantly affect these sports. Drug
abuse control procedures in professional tennis, boxing and
football are thought to be less thorough than in the amateur
sector of the sport. An example of an emerging issue is that of
freedom of contract of professional footballers, which is currently
under debate in the European Community and will need to be
settled by 1992 and the establishment of a single European
market. One way in which the Council seeks to overcome its
limited influence is by continuing to provide small amounts of
grant aid to major spectator sports at the amateur level, for youth
coaching or overseas representation. Although the Environment
Committee felt the 'It seems odd that the big spectator sports
. . . should be getting any grant at all' it did acknowledge that
grants provide 'the Sports Council with a leverage to get things

111

done which ought to be done but would otherwise remain undone' (House of Commons 1986: xxvi, xxvii).

A further constraint on the capacity of the Council to develop its strategic role arises from the fragmentation of the policy area which results in there being some sports or aspects of sport from which the Council feels excluded. For example, the Council has received a number of requests for grant aid from the rescue services associated with sailing and mountaineering. Unfortunately the Council has felt inhibited in making a grant because rescue services are the responsibility, not of the DOE, but of the Home Office (which co-ordinates them through the police service). Discussions are under way to attempt to resolve this confusion. A similar situation arises with horse-racing, this also being the responsibility of the Home Office. Consequently the Council is excluded from influencing the development of a major spectator sport.

Not only are there areas from which the Council is effectively excluded, there are also areas where it shares responsibilities with other branches of government. The areas of international affairs and sport in schools are two examples. The Council has always had a concern with the international aspect of sport but has, in recent years, decided to adopt a higher profile in the international arena as a way of furthering its corporate objectives. For example, through the British International Sports Committee (BISC) the Council will be involved in a programme of funding specific sport development projects overseas in countries such as Indonesia, Zimbabwe and Pakistan, partly as a way of building support for British initiatives in the major international sporting bodies, such as the IOC and the IAAF. At present there seems to be a broadly complementary relationship between the work of the Council in this area and that of the Foreign and Commonwealth Office (FCO), but one wonders whether the BISC would be able to maintain a 'foreign policy' distinct from that of the FCO should a conflict of objectives emerge in the future.[5]

A further area where responsibility is rather uneasily shared relates to the role of sport and physical education in schools. The Council took the initiative in the debate over the development of school sport by establishing a School Sport Forum whose report was published in 1988 with a notable lack of enthusiasm from the Department of Education and Science. The view of the DES is that the Sports Council has little direct interest in the debate over the national curriculum or the selling of school playing fields. At present the relationship is frosty and in stalemate.

In the intervening years since its creation it is possible that the Sports Council has acquired a further function associated with a number of quangos. Some quangos, such as the Gaming Board, the Broadcasting Standards Authority and the British Board of Film Censors, fulfil a regulatory role in their particular policy area. It may be suggested that the Sports Council is acquiring such a role in relation to sport even if only in a peripheral way at present. The Council's regulatory role is most clearly seen in relation to the abuse of drugs by athletes. As will be shown in chapter 8, the Council has played, and continues to play, a central role in the promotion and monitoring of drug testing procedures and is prepared to use its grant control to achieve compliance. The Council is also developing a more interventionist style (regulatory is too strong a word) regarding the plans of governing bodies. Although the Council has required governing bodies to submit plans as the basis of grant allocation from the mid 1980s, from 1990 onwards programme funding will depend on the provision of a more rigorous development plan which will identify objectives, set targets and specify measures of performance. While this may seem a logical extension of the DOE's expectations towards the Council, governing bodies may perceive it as an intervention in their affairs and consequently regulatory in style if not in intention. While the regulatory aspects of the work of the Council are relatively minor, there is the danger that the Council may come to be seen as the policeman of sport rather than the developer of sport.

In summary, the Sports Council retains or has acquired a number of roles which would make it difficult to replace, though by no means indispensable. An important factor in considering the future development of the Council is the progress that has been made in sports development since 1972. In 1972 the Sports Council was created to fill an acknowledged lacuna in the policy area and its activity focused clearly on stimulating the rapid increase in facilities. Over the last eighteen years there has been a rapid growth in local government's capacity to provide for leisure needs as well as a general increase in the facilities available for sport. It is probably fair to say that in the late 1980s the role of the Council is less clearly defined. According to one senior officer of the Council its role for the 1990s is less one of direct intervention and more one of providing advice and strategy development. This shift in emphasis is reflected in a number of developments, including the encouragement to local authorities to develop local strategies for sport and more recently the concern to improve the planning capacity and self-reliance of governing bodies. Additionally, the Council has begun to examine, in conjunction with the Institute of Leisure and Amenity Management, a range of wider management issues associated with competitive tendering and quality measurement.

The movement of the Council towards a more strategic and advisory role is understandable, given the maturation of the policy area. However, it carries with it a high level of risk. Success in fulfilling the early role of the Council was relatively easy to quantify, given that much of its activity produced tangible results, such as more facilities. Success in an advisory or strategy developing role is far less tangible and therefore more difficult for the Council to demonstrate through quantitative performance measures. This does not mean that the Sports Council is more vulnerable to closure or replacement but it does pose the Council with the problem of continuing to demonstrate its worth to government at a time of economic recession.

5

THE GOVERNING BODIES OF SPORT

Each of these Governing Bodies, of whatever size, is recognised as the legislative and disciplinary authority for its particular sport. The autonomy of each, in its own sphere, is almost a sacred principle.

Wolfenden Report (1960: 12)

In this modern world which of us is independent? Not the Sports Council which is dependent on the Government for its grant-in-aid, not the governing bodies of sport, most of whom are increasingly dependent on Government, through the Council, for grant aid . . .

Dick Jeeps, Chairman, Sports Council[1]

This chapter explores the development, organisation and financing of selected governing bodies of sport and also identifies the major issues facing them in the 1990s. In addition the pattern of relations with other sports organisations, including those that are members of the sports policy community, is explored. The brief review of each body will conclude with a consideration of its capacity to influence policy. Apart from domestic governing bodies the chapter will examine the role of international governing and organising bodies and their influence on policy.

The environment that many governing bodies of sport found themselves in during the 1980s was characterised by a pace of change previously experienced towards the end of the last century when many governing bodies were established, and when the concern was to harmonise rules and develop a national pattern of organisation. A number of environmental changes can be identified, although not all will impinge on each body. Of

115

particular importance is the increasing significance of television and sponsorship as sources of income, which has turned a number of sports (such as snooker, badminton, squash and to a degree athletics) from being predominantly voluntary, part-time activities to being businesses with enviable turnovers and well-paid, full-time participants. A related change concerns the greater selectivity, and overall stagnation, of the Sports Council's grant aid. This has forced many governing bodies to look to other sources, for example, commercial sponsorship, for income. These changes have taken place within the context of a broader change in attitudes towards sport and particularly the enthusiasm for newly fashionable sports such as squash, volleyball and hockey. For the governing bodies of the sports growing in popularity there is the challenge of building on this increase in interest and turning it into long-term commitment. For the established sports, such as football, cricket and rugby, the problem is maintaining their market share of new sportsmen and women, and of spectators. Other changes include the decline in school sport, the growing importance of international sports federations, and the slow, but steady, undermining of the amateur basis of many sports.

All governing bodies are having to cope with an increasingly dynamic environment which will put at a premium the ability to anticipate and adapt to change. These new entrepreneurial qualities need to be added to the list of more traditional functions of establishing and enforcing the rules of the sport, stimulating the sport's development, selecting international teams, organising events and representing the interests of the domestic sport in the relevant international federation.

There are well over one hundred governing bodies active in British sport and they range from the large, wealthy bodies with substantial full-time staff such as the Football Association and the Amateur Athletic Association to much smaller bodies which rely heavily on voluntary activity, such as the Tug-of-War Association and the British Bobsleigh Association. Britain's governing bodies, despite a substantial increase in the appointment of paid administrators, are typified by their reliance on voluntary support, their dependence on Sports Council grant and their fierce determination to maintain the lines of demarcation between themselves and other related sports.

While it is not possible to identify a common pattern of

organisation for all governing bodies, certain features are apparent in a substantial number. In general, governing bodies tend to have separate organisations for each of the four home countries, with a significant minority still retaining separate organisations for men and women. Furthermore they frequently have a tiered structure with clubs at the base, affiliated to county or divisional associations, which in turn send representatives to the national body. At national level it is typical to find a core of honorary officers supported by full-time staff, whose number obviously varies considerably, depending on the scale and financial resources of the governing body.

The isolation of sports governing bodies from each other is, to a degree, mitigated by their membership of the Central Council of Physical Recreation and their involvement with the Sports Council. Unfortunately, neither organisation is an effective umbrella organisation for governing bodies. On the one hand the CCPR, owing to its organisational weakness and past poor relationship with the Sports Council, has been for many years an ineffective vehicle for co-ordinating and projecting the interests of sport's governing bodies (see chapter 4). On the other hand the Sports Council, partly owing to its grant aid responsibilities towards governing bodies, does not provide an adequate forum for the development of common interests between individual governing bodies. Don Anthony's comment, made in 1980, that 'the sports governing bodies collectively have not found a contented role *vis-à-vis* the Sports Council' is still broadly applicable today (1980: 11). While there are signs that the CCPR is accepting a more limited role *vis-à-vis* the Sports Council it remains to be seen whether the two organisations can work *together* amicably and productively.

An alternative source of cohesion between governing bodies exists in the British Olympic Association. In many other countries, Italy for example, the national Olympic committee has influence on sport far broader than the selection and management of the Olympic team. However, as will be shown, the BOA has only recently been willing to develop a role beyond that of fund-raising and team management.

Domestic governing bodies and the BOA link British sport into the immensely complex international sporting community. At international level there exists a range of international sports federations (ISFs), most of which are members of the General

117

Assembly of Sports Federations. International governing bodies are primarily concerned with the organising of events, the negotiating of sponsorship and television contracts, and the formulation and amendment of the rules of the sport. Also at international level there are a large number of bodies that exist to organise events. The most important is undoubtedly the International Olympic Committee, but other significant organisations include those responsible for regional, cultural, special interest or political games.

At regional level most continents have their own competitions, and examples include the African, Asian and Caribbean Games. Many of these are run under Olympic rules and provide an opportunity for participants to qualify for Olympic com- petition. The term 'cultural games' is used to refer to organisations such as the Commonwealth Games Federation that organise competitions on the basis of common history or cultural background. French-speaking countries hold similar events to the Commonwealth Games. Among special interest games are those organised for the disabled or for students. The paralympics and the World Student Games are now firm fixtures in the international sporting calender. Finally, in Eastern Europe some international sporting events were organised on the loose political basis of common ideology.

With such a large number of different organisations at both national and international level it is possible to provide an examination of only a selection of the most prominent bodies. Three domestic governing bodies have been chosen, the Amateur Athletic Association, the Hockey Association and the Football Association. The AAA and the Football Association have been selected owing to the prominence of athletics and football, both nationally and internationally, as participation and spectator sports and as such are valuable focuses for exploring a number of issues regarding the organisation of major sports. The Hockey Association was selected as being typical of a group of sports that have experienced rapid growth in their popularity in recent years and consequently raise issues relating to the management of rapid development. The British Olympic Association is also reviewed briefly in its capacity as the national organisation of the International Olympic Committee (IOC). At the international level two international sports federations are examined, the International

Federation of Football Associations (FIFA) and the International Amateur Athletic Federation (IAAF) and also two international event-organising bodies, the IOC and the Commonwealth Games Federation.

NATIONAL GOVERNING BODIES

The Amateur Athletic Association

The Amateur Athletic Association's slow progress towards the formation of a British Athletic Federation has been dogged by regional rivalries and a variety of sectional interests. In many respects it is a reprise of the earlier, equally tortuous, process that eventually resulted in the formation of the AAA in 1880. A principal rivalry was between those who wished athletics to remain a contest between gentlemen and those who preferred to open competition to artisans. This conflict was overlaid with regional divisions between the Midland and Northern clubs and those of London and the universities of Oxford and Cambridge. Overcoming these tensions, the AAA was formed to:

- Improve the management of athletic meetings, and to promote uniformity of rules for the guidance of local committees.
- Deal repressively with any abuses of athletic sport.
- Hold an annual championship meeting.

Athletics grew steadily in popularity throughout the early part of the century and, in the period after the end of the first world war, the organisation of the sport also grew in administrative complexity. The pattern of growth, with separate organisations for Scotland, Wales and Northern Ireland, and for men and women, is typical of many governing bodies. Organised athletics for women began in the early years of the century but it was not until 1920 that the AAA accepted, in principle, responsibility for women's athletics. However, the 'principle' did not hold for long, as the AAA's General Committee refused the application for affiliation of the Women's AAA in 1922 and offered only a 'working agreement'. As Lovesey observes:

> What prompted this volte face we may never know. Whether male chauvinists won the day, or the AAA simply took fright at controlling what was regarded in some quarters as at best

risqué and at worst dangerous to health, the WAAA went its own way, and the working agreement took ten years to emerge.

(1979: 66)

Perhaps the most significant development during the inter-war period was the creation of the British Amateur Athletic Board in 1932. The BAAB grew out of the concern of the AAA to forestall the attempt by the Scottish AAA to affiliate to the International Amateur Athletic Federation. The BAAB consequently replaced the AAA as the organisation linking the domestic athletic bodies to the IAAF.

By 1948, with the establishment of the Welsh AAA, an administrative framework for athletics was in place that was to persist for the next forty years. However, by the 1980s there was increasing concern, both within the governing bodies of athletics and within the Sports Council, at the consequences of administrative fragmentation for the future development of the sport. At the heart of the problem was the existence of nineteen governing organisations and the excessive and unavoidable overlap that resulted in areas such as coaching, the organising of events and sport development. A particularly important issue was the uneven financial relationship between the AAA and the BAAB. During the 1980s the AAA became a wealthy organisation owing its success in gaining sponsorship for events and in selling the television rights. By contrast the BAAB fell seriously into debt despite considerable support from the Sports Council. In a Sports Council inquiry into the financing of athletics requested by the Minister for Sport, Neil Macfarlane, and published in 1983, the Council indicated that unless some rationalisation took place it would review its funding for athletics. This inquiry was part of a continuing debate within athletics which culminated in the proposal, in 1988, to establish a British Athletics Federation which would act as the governing body for athletics throughout Great Britain for both men and women.

Organisation and finance

Decision-making within the AAA lies with the General Committee, which comprises forty-five to fifty members and meets four times a year. Committee members are chosen from

Figure 6 The structure of the Amateur Athletic Association

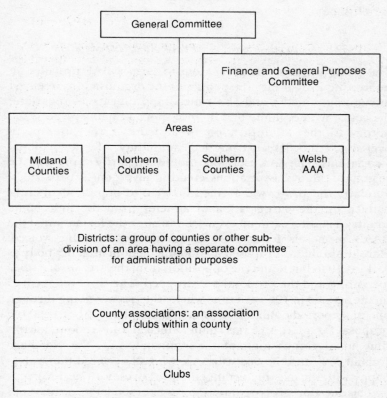

the areas in proportion to the size and number of clubs within their boundaries. Membership of the Committee is also drawn from a number of affiliated organisations, including the English Cross Country Union, the Race Walking Association and the Tug-of-War Association, plus a number of life vice-presidents, who have only limited voting rights. As Figure 6 shows the AAA has a four-tier structure of administration. Day-to-day administration of the AAA is in the hands of a series of sub-committees of the General Committee, with the Finance and General Purposes Committee being particularly important and acting as a *de facto* executive body for the Association. As the Association has grown so too has the size of its full-time staff, adding a necessary layer

121

of professional administration and management on to the large core of voluntary effort that has sustained the AAA since its establishment.

The slow progress towards a British Athletics Federation

The background to the agreement to form a BAF provides an interesting insight into the politics of the organisations involved in running athletics and also raises important issues regarding the best way to organise and finance sport. In many respects the history of the administration of athletics is the attempt to overcome the fiercely guarded autonomy of the regional associations. The AAA itself was established partly to prevent the regional athletics associations creating divergent sets of rules. Similarly the BAAB was formed in 1932 to impose a coherent pattern on the participation of athletes from the four home countries in international events. Soon after the formation of the BAAB proposals for greater integration were being voiced. Harold Abrahams proposed a United Kingdom athletics body as early as 1946 but found the opposition from the area associations too strong and the proposal was dropped. The issue reappeared on the agenda in 1960 at a time when athletics was going through one of its periodic slumps in popularity. At the AGM of 1960 the proposal for a UK AAA was again launched, only to founder this time on the opposition of the Women's AAA, the Northern Ireland AAA and the Scottish AAA, who all declared themselves happy with the existing arrangements (Lovesey 1979: 125).

The question of reorganisation re-emerged later in the 1960s as the financial problems facing athletics deepened. As Lovesey observes, 'The only hope was for a large increase in state aid. To justify that, athletics had to demonstrate to the Government and the Sports Council that it could use the money efficiently' (1979: 131). The response of the AAA and the BAAB was to establish an independent committee of inquiry under the chairmanship of Lord Byers. The Byers Report (1968) was a wide-ranging survey of the state of athletics administration in Britain and among its many recommendations was that a British Athletic Federation be created. The fact that the recommendation came from an independent source did nothing to lessen the critical response from the associations. As a result only slow, though significant, progress was made towards a BAF. In particular, coaching was consolidated under the aegis of the BAAB and, in 1970, the various associations were given clearer representation on the Board.

Some further progress was made during the 1970s, with the BAAB acquiring additional responsibilities concerning the training of officials and liaison with schools. But it was not until the early 1980s that sufficient momentum was gained to raise the proposal as a major item for discussion. The Turner Report 1983, commissioned by the AAA, and the Evans Report 1986, commissioned by the BAAB, reviewed the debate on the creation of a BAF. The accumulated evidence from these, and earlier, reports undoubtedly brought the formation of the BAF closer. An additional reason was the financial crisis that beset athletics in 1987 when the BAAB faced bankruptcy while the AAA ended the year with a healthy financial surplus. The final stimulus to reorganisation was the threat from the Sports Council to end its grant of £187,000 unless there was an administrative reorganisation. John Wheatley, the Sports Council director, warned that 'The Board knows that there can be no further grant, not even against a deficit, while there are so many organisations controlling the sport' (*Guardian* 26 March 1987). A situation where the BAAB provided the most costly services, such as coaching, but where the lion's share of income went to the AAA was bound to lead to a financial crisis eventually.

A working party was established in 1988 by the AAA with the request that it should produce a draft constitution for a BAF. Regional rivalries and control over the income from lucrative events were the themes that underlay the debate on the shape of the new constitution. For example, the Southern Area AAA wanted to keep control over, and the income from, the highly profitable Peugeot Games and consequently produced a draft constitution that made the areas the key units within athletics and marginalised the role of the AAA. In contrast, the initial proposal from the AAA, supported by the Midland and Northern Areas, would have resulted in the AAA retaining a prominent position in the BAF such that it would be in a position to offset the influence of individual area associations. The draft constitution circulated to clubs in June 1989 attempted to reconcile the interests of the areas with those of the AAA. As the chairman of the AAA pointed out in his introduction to the new constitution:

> The advent of the BAF will mean that the Regional Associations [previously referred to as Areas] in England will have an enhanced role in the administration of athletics – equivalent to that of the National Associations in the Celtic countries. . . . The English National Association, formed on the assumption that the AAA and the Women's AAA will amalgamate, will still have important responsibilities. These will include:
>
> 1 Maintain liaison with such bodies as Sports Council, CCPR, Commonwealth Games Council for England.
> 2 Organise national championships.
> 3 Arrange and organise England international matches and the England Team for the Commonwealth Games.
> 4 Produce and execute development plans for English athletics.
>
> (Evans 1989: 5, 6)

The role of the BAF will be to represent British athletics at international level, primarily on the IAAF; to promote sports development in the regions; to establish and maintain rules of competition; and to select teams to represent the UK.

At the heart of the BAF will be a council of forty-four comprised in the main of three or five representatives from each of the national and regional associations plus one or two representatives from a series of special commissions established to promote and develop six specific sports, including cross-country, race walking and tug of war. The effectiveness of the new administrative arrangements has yet to be tested but it does seem that the tensions within athletics so evident during the 1980s have been camouflaged rather than resolved. Given that the constitution is a compromise between regional and national interests, the key test is who controls the income from televised events and whether the BAF has a sufficiently large and secure source of income to allow it to act in an independent manner. Additionally, it remains to be seen whether the BAF council will be capable of evolving a role beyond that of yet another forum for regional squabbling.

The eventual arrival of a BAF reflects an important stage in the maturing of sports organisations so long dogged by a genteel amateurism in administration and management. Although it is too soon to say that the BAF will provide athletics with an organisation capable of building on the success of the 1980s and running and developing a multi-million-pound sport, the creation of the BAF does mark a significant change in the relationship between athletics and the Sports Council. The dependence of athletics on Sports Council grant has steadily declined during the 1980s, the problems of the BAAB notwithstanding. In addition the AAA has been slowly developing its professional capabilities in other management areas such as sports development, marketing, television contract negotiations and promotions. The 1980s have therefore seen the relationship between the AAA and the Sports Council changing from one of dependence of the former on the latter to one of mutual interdependence. The interdependence arises from the AAA's leading role in the anti-doping campaign and its proven ability to negotiate sponsorship and television contracts successfully. However, the AAA and the nascent BAF remain weak in two areas; the first and less important is their capacity to influence government. The AAA is considering attempting to lobby government independently of the Sports Council and the CCPR but, as yet, has not committed any resources to this aim. The second area is much more important and concerns the weakness of the sport's grass-roots development activity. The national picture is one of generally unco-ordinated and widely varying levels of activity. With the decline in school sport the BAF needs to give high priority to ways of capturing the imagination of the school-age population. In both these areas the BAF will rely, to a considerable degree, on the expertise, advice and possibly the finance of the Sports Council.

The Hockey Association

The Hockey Association was founded in 1886 and in its long history can hardly have experienced a more challenging and exciting decade than the 1980s. In the 1960s and 1970s the sport was still characterised by its strong public school roots and was focused on a network of clubs that played primarily on limited county circuits. By the end of the decade the Hockey Association had witnessed the winning of a gold medal at the Seoul Olympics, the successful establishment of a sponsored national hockey league and a mushrooming of interest in the sport among young people from outside the traditional public school/grammar school recruiting grounds. As the president of the Association is quick to point out:

> Our international programmes; competitions and leagues; various sponsorships; our coaching and development activities and almost every single facet of the game are at a new high. Nevertheless, there is still much to do and achieve if we are to exploit our success and yet maintain the integrity of the game.

(Hockey Association 1989)

In other words the key challenge for the Association is to maintain the momentum of development while still retaining control over its direction.

The capacity of the Hockey Association to respond to this challenge depends in part upon the responsiveness of an administrative structure which reflects the strong county base of the sport and the heavy reliance on voluntary effort. The administrative structure of the Association is given in Figure 7.

The administration of the Association is divided between the Management Committee and the Council. The latter meets at least three times per year and has a membership drawn from existing officers and chairmen of the standing committees together with representatives from the various divisions, service associations and counties. The Council has three main functions: first, to select four members of the eight-man Management Committee; second, to appoint a number of selection committees; and third, to consider and approve strategic plans. The Management Committee is responsible for the day-to-day running of the Association. This centralised structure provides a clear focus for the development and organisation of the sport. Unfortunately the Hockey Association is only responsible for men's hockey, and only in England.

Issues facing the Hockey Association

As it enters the 1990s the Hockey Association is in the enviable position of possessing a strong financial base for its activities. From the mid 1980s onwards the Association witnessed a steady

Figure 7 The structure of the Hockey Association

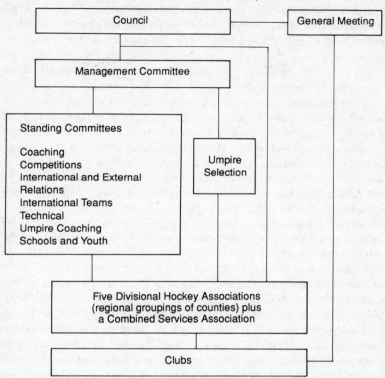

growth in its income from sponsorship that compensated for the levelling off in Sports Council grant. Sponsorship, from banks, insurance companies and the travel industry, now accounts for over one third of the income of the Association. Part of the attraction of hockey to potential sponsors lies in its recent international success. But its 'clean-cut' image and predominantly middle class base are also undoubted advantages in the increasingly fierce competition for sponsorship.

The major issue facing the Association over the coming years is how to capitalise on the recent rapid growth of the sport. At the heart of the Association's strategy is an ambitious five year development scheme aimed primarily at the large number of young people expressing an interest in the sport. The key to the success of the scheme is a national network of development officers liaising with schools, clubs, local authorities and Regional Councils for Sport and Recreation. An important feature of the scheme is that it is a joint enterprise by the Hockey Association and the All England Women's Hockey Association. The success of the scheme depends heavily on the active support of a wide range of public sector and voluntary organisations, and it is in this area that some of the most serious problems may arise.

Traditionally, young people were introduced to hockey at school. Unfortunately the upsurge in interest in hockey in schools, mainly state schools, coincided with the aftermath of the teachers' strikes in the mid 1980s. One consequence of the change in teachers' contracts has been a marked decline in the goodwill necessary to maintain inter-school team sports. The response by the Association has been to encourage clubs to develop links with their local schools in an attempt to fill the gap. The local initiatives underway include the provision of coaching and the running of vacation courses. The Association is also a strong supporter of the dual use of school facilities by pupils and local clubs. This attempt to build stronger club–school links is helped by the long partnership between the Association and its county associations with the local education authority physical education advisers. Hockey clearly appeals to many LEAs and schools because, being a non-contact sport, it is relatively safe. In addition the fact that, up to the age of thirteen or fourteen, hockey can be played in mixed teams makes the sport attractive to those authorities with co-educational schools and strong equal opportunities policies. However, a number of constraints on the development of links between clubs and schools exist; one is that nationally the game is rapidly moving away from the use of grass pitches to playing on artificial surfaces and this may make the sport less attractive to schools. A further constraint lies in the ability of the Hockey Association to persuade clubs to adopt a more proactive role in the development of the sport.

The Association has, over the last few years, demonstrated a strong commitment to the development of the sport and a growing self-sufficiency in terms of management expertise and finance. It is not surprising that its relationship with the Sports Council is a positive one. From the Council's point of view the Association is a model for other governing bodies to follow, particularly concerning its success in attracting sponsorship. The

Association is therefore increasingly independent of the Council and has generated innovative proposals in areas such as marketing and sports development.

However, taking the sport as a whole there is a degree of uneven development that must give cause for concern. Hockey still suffers from the fragmentation that is so typical of the organisation of British sport. Not only is there a geographical division between England and the other home countries, but there is a separate governing body for women's hockey and even an association for mixed hockey. While it is possible to defend such fragmentation on the grounds that it protects and promotes the diversity of participation in hockey it can also be argued that it dilutes and weakens the resource base on which the development of the sport depends.

As regards the relationship between the Association and the CCPR, the Association considers the Central Council as possessing valuable expertise in the more commercial areas of its work such as marketing and support for press officers, but also feels that the CCPR is too small to be an effective pressure group. One of the key problems is obtaining access to the decision processes of the Central Council. The main opportunity for access is through membership of the Council or its sub-committees rather than through any regular consultative or representative medium.

Like many other British sports organizations the Association is keenly aware that the locus of decision-making about the sport is shifting away from domestic to international governing bodies, including the European Hockey Federation (EHF) and the International Hockey Federation (IHF). Within the EHF influence is generally in proportion to the success of the international team and the strength of the domestic game. Consequently the three dominant countries in the EHF are Britain, Holland and West Germany. The roles of the EHF and the IHF are broadly similar, as both are concerned with sport development, TV rights, sponsorship and the organising of events. Traditionally, Pakistan and India have exercised considerable influence within the IHF but in the last ten years or so the EHF members, particularly West Germany, have increased their influence. This shift reflects not only the greater success of the European nations in international competition, but also their greater wealth and consequent capacity to stage competitions. In addition, the acceptance of artificial surfaces for all major matches puts the poorer Third World countries at a distinct disadvantage.

The Football Association

Football, as England's premier sport, has suffered badly during the last ten years. Crumbling stadiums, football hooliganism, exclusion from European competition and numerous professional clubs operating on or below the margins of profitability are the issues that have dominated the sport. Added to this has been the sustained criticism of the administration of the sport coming from government, clubs and the media. If ever a sport needed an effective and imaginative administrative structure to see it through these serious problems football is a prime candidate.

The Football Association (FA), one of the oldest governing bodies in England, was founded in 1863. The FA is at the top of an administrative structure which has over 40,000 clubs at the base and county associations at the intermediate level. The FA is responsible for making the rules governing football in England; it represents England at meetings of the European Association Football Union (UEFA) and the International Federation of Football Associations (FIFA); it hears appeals against decisions taken by county associations, for example over disciplinary matters; it selects teams to represent England and organises a number of competitions, including the Challenge Cup (better known as the FA Cup), the Challenge Trophy (which is open to non-League clubs) plus a number of other competitions at youth and county level.

In 1988 the turnover of the Association was just over £11 million and its profit on the year was £274,401. The income of the FA came from a variety of sources including a profit on matches of £1.2 million (from both domestic Cup competitions and international matches), football pools promoters (£0.3 million), royalties and sales (£1.1 million), and broadcasting fees (£0.5 million). A substantial proportion of the FA's income is spent on administration (£1.6 million in 1988), but £0.46 million was spent on coaching, and £0.7 million distributed as grant aid to a variety of trusts and organisations concerned with the development of football.

A substantial amount of FA income flows through the county associations which are, in many respects, the key administrative units of football in England. The role of the County Associations is similar to that of the FA in that they are responsible for applying FA rules and organising competitions. But they also have responsibility for the selection and training of referees, and monitoring the finances of clubs in their areas.

The central role of the County Associations is clearly evident in the structure of the FA as reflected in the composition of the Council, its main decision-making body. The Council has a membership of ninety-seven, which with some overlap in membership, is composed of a chairman, vice-chairman, eleven life vice-presidents, seven vice-presidents, ten divisional representatives, fifty-nine Association representatives (of which forty-nine are representatives of County Associations), nine representatives of the Football League and four representatives of the British Commonwealth Associations. In common with many other English governing bodies and reflecting the public school and Oxbridge origins of the FA there are places on the Council reserved for representatives of Oxford and Cambridge Universities, the individual armed forces, public schools and the Commonwealth. The FA can be characterised, first of all, by its reliance on the effort of voluntary administrators at county level and their dominance on the FA Council. A second characteristic is the preoccupation of the FA with the amateur game. It is these characteristics which contrast sharply with the world of professional football. Just as Rugby League and northern league cricket represented the working class development of sport so the Football League represents the break between the public school origins and associations of the FA and its rapidly expanding working class following which emerged at the turn of the century. Although the FA and the League have remained close the former has never successfully come to terms with the increasingly commercial and business-oriented clubs affiliated to the Football League.

According to Graham Kelly, the Chief Executive of the FA, 'it is not a case of amateurs governing the professionals. The professionals are well represented on the Council of the FA. It is a democratic organisation and it works pretty well.'[2] However, the professionals, as represented by the Football League, have only nine places allocated to them on the FA Council, although a number of the divisional representatives also have ties with professional football. The dilemma is reflected in the comment of John Davey, the Council member for Sussex, that 'the ruling body [the FA] is not just for the Football League, the ruling body is for all football . . . most football is not the big clubs; most football is outside the Football League'.[3]

The lack of a unified leadership, and the quality of that leadership, at national level has been a source of comment both from politicians and from a variety of reports and enquiries. Despite England winning the World Cup in 1966, the mid 1960s was the period in which the deteriorating financial position of many professional clubs reached crisis point, with both the FA and the League asking for government help. The government substituted an inquiry for financial assistance. The ensuing report of the committee chaired by Sir Norman Chester was published in 1968 (Department of Education and Science 1968). The report highlighted two areas of particular concern: the first related to the policy planning capacity of the FA and the second focused on the relationship between the FA and the Football League. Regarding the first area the question posed by the committee was whether the 'Football Association [has] shown the clarity of purpose and been as forward looking as one has the right to expect in a national governing body. . .' (1968: 105). The answer that the committee provided was not inspiring, for it doubted 'whether many of those intimately concerned with the game would give a firm, positive answer' (1968: 105). In particular it pointed to the absence of 'an effective executive committee' (1968: 105). The committee suggested the establishment of 'a more effective central policy and planning committee' (1968: 106), a widening of Council membership to include representatives of referees, professional footballers and managers (1968: 105) and compulsory retirement at seventy for Council members (1968: 105).

Regarding its relationship with the League the committee referred to its 'over-attention to the affairs of the Football League . . . [and] that it has done too little directly for the amateur game' (1968: 105, 108). In addition the report suggested that the relationship between the FA and the League was muddled and that the FA 'appears to be administering League affairs without being in an effective position to do this' (1968: 109). The committee suggested that there should be a clearer division between the responsibilities of the two bodies and specifically that the FA should 'leave the League more free to administer its own affairs' (1968: 109). This suggestion was in direct contradiction of advice provided two years earlier in a PEP report which suggested that the two organisations should merge (Political and Economic Planning 1966). The absence of consistent external advice is a feature of pronouncements on the management of English football.

One positive outcome of the report was the establishment of an Executive Committee of the Council, although it rejected the widening of its membership and also the suggestion of an age limit to Council membership. There was also little attempt to redefine the relationship between the FA and the League.

These observations on the quality of FA management and strategic planning have been echoed more recently by others, including a number of past Ministers for Sport. Neil Macfarlane (Minister 1981–85) when commenting on the responsibility for the crisis facing football in the early 1980s stated that 'I have no doubt where the accumulative blame lies. It is with the leaders of the professional arm of the sport; at the headquarters of the Football League and Football Association.' Richard Tracey (Minister 1985–87) commented that 'I was always frustrated by a lack of urgency . . . always it seemed to me a problem of delay; no willingness to tackle the problem of the day'.[4] While one must treat the reflections of ex-Ministers with a degree of scepticism there is a degree of consistency which suggests that the FA is perceived as still failing to match the expectations of other key members of the sport policy community.

Many of the concerns voiced about the role and capacity of the FA are repeated with regard to the Football League. A recent report by management consultants concluded that the behaviour of the Management Committee of the League 'was not one of a board devoted to planning and policy setting'. It also observed that 'we would expect the Management Committee to take every opportunity to be seen to be taking a clear lead' but found that major issues such as football hooliganism were only briefly addressed (Arthur Anderson 1989). The Football League's own recently commissioned report on its structure and finance highlighted different problems, although ones that echo the earlier Department of Education and Science report of 1968. The League's report, also chaired by Sir Norman Chester, drew attention, in a more diplomatic way, to the amateurish nature of professional club management, particularly regarding financial matters and the desirability of the League setting higher standards of financial reporting (Football League 1983). But the report also highlighted a fundamental problem facing any attempt to strengthen the role of the League. It pointed out that any change in the relationship between the League and the clubs would require the approval of the clubs themselves and 'That raises very wide issues of policy, for the League is an association of competing clubs and the Management Committee inevitably is drawn from that competitive world' (1983: 41). The present structure of the League is such that change is difficult to achieve, as any major policy change requires a two-thirds majority. In addition the Management Committee has few substantial powers delegated to it. Unlike other industries professional football clubs want both to compete with other clubs and to keep them in business.

Given the present problems of football in Britain the Football Association is in an extremely difficult position. Its competence is judged, by government at least, not in terms of its success in developing the amateur game for the mass of the population but in terms of its capacity to solve the problems of the professional game, over which it has only partial control. Yet for a sport so dependent on voluntarism and composed of fiercely independent clubs it is hardly surprising that the FA has a limited leadership role. Few other governing bodies have resolved successfully the problem of reconciling the needs of amateur and professional involvement in their sport. Most have seen the development of far greater rifts between the amateur and professional, as in boxing, where the professional sport is run by a cartel of managers and promoters, and tennis and snooker, where players exert a dominant influence on the management of the sport.

British Olympic Association

Under the rules of the IOC each country must organise a National Olympic Committee (NOC) which comprises one representative of each governing body recognised by the IOC, plus officers of the British Olympic Association (BOA) and the two IOC members from Britain. The BOA is accountable to the British NOC, which meets four times per year.

The BOA has three primary functions: to organise, and support financially, the preparations by the British team for the Olympic Games; to help national governing bodies in their preparations for the Games; and, finally, to develop interest in the Olympic movement in Britain. A major part of the BOA's activity, at the time of the Olympic Games, is as travel agent, tour manager and medical adviser for British athletes. In 1988 the BOA organised the participation of over 500 athletes and officials: a major undertaking by any standards. In between Olympic Games the BOA spends considerable time and energy raising the finance to enable so many athletes to participate. Its funds, raised through the British Olympic Appeal, come exclusively from private sources, mainly business sponsors and from the general public. For the 1988 Olympics over £4 million was raised, with approximately £2 million coming from the general public and donations from business and the remiaing £2 million coming from commercial sponsorship (for example, for the use of the Olympic logo).

Since 1988 the BOA has widened its range of responsibilities. In particular the Association is now more heavily involved in providing services for Olympic sports, including advice and training on nutrition and sports psychology for Olympic coaches, as well as medical and careers advice for athletes. The BOA funds the British Olympic Medical Centre at Northwick Park hospital in London. The expansion in its role is partly due to requests from governing bodies for specific help, and the greater availability of resources, and partly because it was felt that a gap existed which only a body specifically concerned with the elite end of sport could fill.

The BOA also aims to publicise the aims of the Olympic movement, which it aims to achieve, for example, through liaison work with schools. Other areas of activity include the sponsoring of medical research into fitness and athletic injuries, and the provision of professional services for governing bodies, such as advice on press liaison and public relations. The BOA is at pains to establish and maintain its independence from government, as required by the Olympic Charter, and partly for that reason recently decided that it did not wish to be represented or have members on the Sports Council, the Sports Aid Foundation or the CCPR. Another important part of the explanation lies in the desire of the BOA to establish a more equal relationship with these bodies. The Association argues that its relationship with the Sports Council has improved and that, for example, valuable liaison is now taking place over issues in sports medicine.

One important role of the BOA is to provide a link between national governing bodies and the IOC over issues such as the policy and procedures adopted to combat drug abuse, and the opening up of more events to women competitors. Apart from having members on the IOC the BOA is also involved in the meetings of the Association of National Olympic Committees (ANOC) and the Association of European National Olympic Committees (ENOC). Because not all member countries may have seats on the IOC the meetings of ANOC and ENOC are important forums, not just for the dissemination of information by the IOC but also as a focus of lobbying activity directed at the IOC over issues such as the distribution of income from the sale of television rights.

INTERNATIONAL ORGANISING BODIES AND INTERNATIONAL SPORTS FEDERATIONS

Athletics: The International Amateur Athletic Federation

The formation of the International Amateur Athletic Federation (IAAF) was prompted by the growth of international competition, and the consequent need to codify and harmonise rules of competition and the need to establish and maintain a register of sporting records. In July 1912, a few days after the end of the Stockholm Olympic Games, a meeting of the representatives of seventeen countries took place which resulted in the formation of the IAAF. The close co-operation of the IAAF with the Olympic movement has remained a distinctive feature of the history of the Federation and is enshrined in the constitution of the Federation. Among the other objects of the Federation are those concerned with the organising of competitions, the establishment of rules and the recognition of records. Two more political objectives concern the establishment of 'friendly and loyal co-operation between all members for the benefit of amateur athletics, peace and understanding between nations throughout the world' and ensuring that 'no racial, religious, political or other kind of discrimination be allowed in athletics . . .' (IAAF 1988).

Apart from the South American Confederation, which was established in the early 1920s to support the regional development of athletics, the IAAF remained the only international forum for athletics until the late 1960s. In 1969 the European Athletic Association (EAA) was formed and its constitution was ratified by the IAAF in 1970. Further continental associations followed quickly: the Oceania Regional Group, formed in 1972, with the formation of the African Amateur Athletic Confederation and the Asian Amateur Athletic Association following in 1974. The IAAF provided strong support for the establishment of continental associations as an important basis for the organisation of less expensive competition for many of the poorer countries and as a valuable training for top-level competition.

The Congress of the IAAF meets every two years and makes major decisions, for example concerning the election of committee chairmen, rule changes within track and field, membership of the Federation and the definition of amateur status. Each of the 184 member countries of the Federation has one vote although a member may send up to three delegates to a meeting of the Congress. The body which oversees the day-to-day operation of the Federation is the Council, which comprises twenty-three members elected, for a four year term, by Congress. The rules governing the composition of the Council are such that, as far as is possible, a fair regional representation is achieved. The Council is aided in its supervisory role by a series of committees which include Technical, Women's, Cross-country, Walking, Medical and Veterans. In addition it receives advice from a series of specialist commissions and working groups on subjects including marketing, development and press relations.

The role of the committees is to advise the Council on changes in rules and regulations, disseminate research findings and act as insider pressure groups on behalf of sectional interests in sport. For example, during 1989 the Technical Committee discussed design modifications to the women's 600 gm javelin with a view to improving its landing characteristics. As a result of the committee's work a new javelin design will be permitted from

April 1991. This issue was also the subject of discussion by the Women's Committee, which also fulfils a lobbying role within athletics by constantly reviewing the range of events open to female competitors. During 1989 the committee recommended to the IAAF Congress that member federations hold triple jump events for women at national championships and that the event be open for world record status from 1990. The Women's Committee has the further aim of 'encouraging women not only to take part in the sport as athletes but also as coaches, officials and administrators' (IAAF 1989: 10). As a final example the Federation's Medical Committee is best known for its work on developing anti-doping procedures. However, the committee has a broad range of interests, including the possible harmful effects of long-distance running on young athletes and, in conjunction with the Women's Committee, eating disorders, particularly anorexia nervosa, among female athletes.

The main sources of income of the IAAF are sponsorship and the sale of television rights, with only a nominal income from affiliation fees. The Federation uses the largest share of its considerable income to facilitate the participation of athletes in IAAF competitions. Part of its income is returned to the local organising committee of the event being televised or sponsored, but part is channelled through a network of eight regional development centres strategically located around the world to develop athletics in countries where locally available development funds are likely to be scarce.

The significance of the Federation for athletics and general sport policy both in Britain and world-wide is considerable. There are a number of issues on which the IAAF has adopted a leading role. The most obvious issue concerns drug abuse by athletes and is considered separately in chapter 8, but others include the definition of amateurism and payments to athletes, the eligibility of athletes to compete, the recognition of nations as members of international sports federations, and general sport development policy. An important example of the influence of the Federation concerns the way in which the thorny problem of payments to athletes has been resolved through the establishment of 'athletic funds' managed by the national governing body on behalf of the individual athlete. This solution helped to avoid a damaging fragmentation of athletics into a professional and an amateur circuit. A second example concerns the decision on the eligibility of the South African-born athlete, Zola Budd, to run for Britain. When the issue was discussed by the IAAF Council the recommendation was made to the British Amateur Athletic Board that she be suspended for twelve months.

At the international level the Federation plays a major role over the question of national affiliation. Palestine has already been accepted as a full member of the Federation and Namibia was recently granted provisional membership. It can be only a matter of time before Lithuania and the other Baltic countries make applications for membership.

Not only is the IAAF important in the policy process in its own right, it is also part of an important network of international sports organisations that are exerting increasing influence over national policy communities. The key relationship is between the IAAF and the IOC, though it tends to be mediated by two other bodies, the Association of Summer Olympic International Federations (ASOIF) and the General Association of International Sports Federations (GAISF). International sport development is strongly influenced by these four bodies. For example, the Development Commission of the Federation works closely with Olympic Solidarity (the development body within the IOC) in running joint coach-training sessions through the Regional Development Centres of the IAAF. A further set of examples concern the development of anti-doping policy. For a time the accreditation of drug testing laboratories was a joint IAAF/IOC responsibility. More recently the IOC and ASOIF (of which the IAAF is an influential member) issued a joint declaration of their intention to harmonise their anti-drug rules and regulations. One important consequence of the increase in influence of this cluster of international bodies is their ability to influence the location of prestigious and highly profitable international competitions.

International Federation of Football Associations

In 1904 Belgium, Sweden, Switzerland, Denmark, France, Spain and the Netherlands met to form the Fédération Internationale de Football Association, better known as FIFA. The British Associations, as Tomlinson (1986) points out in his history of the relationship between the FA and FIFA, remained patronisingly and characteristically aloof. By 1989 there were 166 national associations affiliated to FIFA, ranging from the People's Republic of China to San Marino.

As with other international governing bodies the main responsibilities of FIFA are to organise international competition, determine eligibility for participation, and negotiate sponsorship, advertising and television contracts. Apart from the four-yearly World Cup FIFA organises competitions at a variety of age levels, for example an under-twenty competition (the Junior World Cup Finals) in Chile in 1987.

At the heart of the structure of FIFA is the biannual Congress, attended by two representatives from each national football association. The Congress is the decision-making forum for world football. For example, the 1988 Congress approved an age limit of twenty-three years for the members of Olympic teams despite a strongly expressed preference from the IOC for no age limit and only those players who took part in the previous World Cup finals being excluded. At a second tier of administration are the football confederations, organised on a continental basis, which arrange competitions and are responsible for local development activity. UEFA, with thirty-five affiliated national associations, is one such confederation and not only organises a number of major competitions at both club and national level but also determines the eligibility of teams and countries to participate. In this latter capacity UEFA banned English clubs indefinitely from international competitions following the Heysel Stadium disaster.

One key committee of FIFA deals with the negotiation of advertising and television contracts, which, like those for the Olympic Games, are a major and growing source of income, with reputedly £40 million generated from advertising alone for the 1990 World Cup. Other committees cover technical matters, and the organisation of major events, particularly the World Cup. A key body is the International Football Association Board (IFAB), which is responsible for making amendments to the laws of the game. It is not a sub-committee of FIFA but is an independent organisation and comprises eight members, four nominated by FIFA and the remaining four being nominated by the British FAs. Given the general decline of British influence in international sports bodies, the prominence of the British FAs is surprising. The IFAB meets twice a year: once in December as an editorial committee to set the agenda for the second meeting, held in June, when decisions are taken. Recent law changes include those relating to the number of substitutes allowed during matches and the specifications of football boots.

One important issue facing FIFA is its relationship with other major international sports bodies. During the 1980s FIFA lessened the extent of its self-imposed isolation from the other major international sports organisations. In 1988 FIFA joined both the Association of Summer Olympic International Federations and the General Association of International Sports Federations. The entry of FIFA into these organisations reflects the growing involvement of 'professional' football in the Olympic Games. However, the relationship still remains a delicate one, with FIFA wary of promoting football as an Olympic sport to such an extent that it comes to rival its own World Cup. Hence the previously mentioned stipulation by FIFA that Olympic football be limited to an under-twenty-three competition. A further reason for FIFA's improving relations with the Olympic movement is that the former is keen to win the support of the IOC in its attempt to undermine the break-away indoor football federation (Federacion International Futbol Salon). The South American break-away federation has been told by the IOC that FIFA is the only football governing body that it is prepared to recognise.

A second issue facing FIFA concerns the management of the world-wide development of the sport. Although football can lay claim to being the truly major world-wide sport the depth of its roots varies considerably between countries. For example, the World Cup finals have been held only in Europe and South America, the two continents where football has its strongest support. An important part of the development of the sport in other parts of the world is to hold the World Cup finals, which are undeniably the showcase for the marketing of the sport, in parts of the world where the roots of football are shallower but where there is potential for growth. Holding the 1994 finals in the USA is acknowledged as an attempt to break into the richest market in the world and Joao Havelange, the president of FIFA, has encouraged China to bid for the 2002 finals. However, moving the finals away from their traditional locations and the periodic discussions about the number of weaker footballing nations to be allowed access to the finals raises the problem for FIFA of gaining the support of the European and South American football associations for policy developments that break their dominance of international football.

The International Olympic Committee

The International Olympic Committee lies at the centre of the network of international sports organisations. The primary function of the IOC is to oversee Olympic sport and any competitions permitted by the IOC to use the Olympic name, such as the Pan-American Games and the Asian Games. However, given the stature of the Games, the financial resources of the Committee and, not least, the IOC's moral authority, the Committee plays a key role in influencing the direction and pace of development of sport at international and national levels.

The Olympic movement has links with 167 countries, 92 of which, in 1989, had 'members' on the IOC, who reported back to their individual national Olympic committee. The word 'member' is preferred to 'representative' because the IOC charter treats IOC members not as representatives of their respective NOCs to the IOC but rather as members *of the IOC in their country*. The IOC is at the heart of what Scherer refers to as the last empire of this century (quoted in *Sport Intern*, 10 May 1989). He notes that there are thirty ISFs whose sports are part of the Olympic programme, sixteen federations recognised by the IOC and waiting to be included in the Olympic programme, three organising committees for forthcoming Games as well as thirty-six organisations with special objectives recognised by the IOC, such as the World Disabled Sports Federation. In addition to the IOC and the various NOCs there is a World Association of National Olympic Committees and a number of continental Associations of NOCs such as the Pan American Sports Association (PASO). Outside the Olympic structure are the ISFs, which, as the world governing bodies for the separate sports, are responsible at Olympic Games for the technical direction of their sports (equipment and rules) and for the officials, such as referees and judges.

The IOC comprises two organisations: the first is the Session, previously called the General Assembly, which elects the second organisation, the Executive Board. The Session is the parliament of the Olympic movement and consequently makes all the major decisions. The Executive Board is composed of a president, elected for eight years, three vice-presidents, elected for four years, and five further members, also elected for four years. The board is the organisational heart of the Committee. Among its duties are the preparation of IOC agendas, the submission of names of recommended potential new members, the general administration of the IOC and the management of its finances.

The IOC has a large number of commissions to provide advice and to help it run the movement. Among the twenty-three current commissions or working groups are those responsible for developing policy regarding drugs, apartheid, television contract negotiation, and world-wide sport development.

One of the most important sources of IOC influence is its independence from national governments, which is due, in large part, to its considerable financial resources. In recent years the Committee has operated with an annual budget in excess of $15 million and boasts reserves of over $72 million and aims to raise its reserves to over $100 million thus enabling it to meet its annual running costs out of interest. The bulk of IOC income comes from its current 7 per cent share of the television rights in the Games.

The influence of the IOC on the development and organisation of sport is considerable. For example, following a positive decision by the Eligibility Commission of the IOC a sport can receive a major boost to its market. Similarly, a decision by the Medical Commission to alter rules or procedures concerning drug abuse will undoubtedly give a powerful lead to the ISFs and to domestic governing bodies. As such it is the focus of a complex pattern of sophisticated lobbying by ISFs, NOCs and individual governments.

The significance of the IOC is easy to illustrate. In 1989 the IOC Medical Commission initiated a review of boxing to determine the extent to which it is detrimental to health. If the outcome of this review were to be the exclusion of boxing, then it would give a major fillip to the anti-boxing lobbies active in a number of European countries, including Britain. Boxing has already been dropped from the programme of events for the 1991

Afro-Asian Games in the expectation that it will be dropped from the 1992 Olympics. A further example involving the Medical Commission concerns its success in reaching agreement with the Association of Summer Olympic Sports Federations on harmonising their anti-drug abuse strategies.

A contrasting example concerns the campaign to achieve the readmission of golf as an Olympic sport for the 1996 Olympics. Golf was an Olympic sport in the 1900 and 1904 Games but has not been included since. The World Golf Association (WGA) has applied to the IOC for recognition as the sport's international governing body. Resistance to the application comes from those who argue that golf is not a 'world-wide' sport and that the WGA is overshadowed by the professional golf organisations and therefore would not have the authority expected of an international governing body. In terms of developing golf on a global scale Olympic acceptance would obviously be a considerable coup. The WGA is only one on a long list of governing bodies that are pressing the IOC to accept its sport. Other contenders include curling, ski-orienteering, women's softball and a whole range of martial arts. The basic criteria applied by the IOC in determining the eligibility of a sport include that it should be widely practised (by at least fifty countries and in three continents for men's sports); should not involve the use of mechanical means (thereby excluding motor racing); that participation should not be prohibitively expensive (which keeps polo out and may result in the remaining equestrian events being dropped); and finally should be efficiently administered (a serious doubt regarding boxing, following the disputes at the Seoul Olympics).

One problem that the IOC clearly faces is that of balancing the increasingly complex and intense political pressures that confront it. The first problem concerns the difficulties involved in maintaining the independence of the national Olympic committees, while the second concerns preventing the IOC becoming another forum for international politics. As regards the independence of NOCs the IOC is able to insist that it alone can decide who the NOC representative on the IOC will be. But this power must be balanced by a pragmatic recognition that in many, if not most, countries NOCs are heavily dependent on government finance, goodwill and administrative support.

However, IOC delegates jealously guard their independence, as witnessed by the choice of Lillehammer in Norway for the 1994 Winter Olympics. In choosing this small town the IOC rejected Sofia (and the influence of the communist bloc vote), Ostersund in Sweden (even King Carl Gustav lobbied on its behalf) and Anchorage (and the lure of American dollars).

Keeping the IOC free from overt politics is also difficult to achieve. Bearing in mind the recent fragmentation of the communist bloc of countries the dominant political groupings tend to be based upon factors concerned with geography and wealth, although regional conflicts can also impinge on the IOC. The strict rules governing tenure on the various IOC bodies ensure a reasonably regular turnover. However, the IOC is constantly attempting to produce a balanced membership on its key commissions, and especially on the Executive Board, where in 1989 of the ten members three were Europeans, four were Asians, with North America, Africa and Oceania having one member each. One of the objectives of the careful planning of the balance on the IOC's commissions is the need to placate the sectional interests of the rich and poor countries. One illustration of this problem is the recent disagreement between the IOC and the United States Olympic Committee. The source of tension was the division of income from the sale of television rights (Lawrence and Pellegrom 1989). The USOC argued for a greater share of the income from television rights on the grounds that it was the US television companies that made the largest contribution. However, if the USA took a larger share it would mean that there would be less available for the IOC to distribute to poorer countries for sports development activity. Part of the resolution of this conflict involved the establishment of a permanent working group to consider TV contracts and an increase in US representation through the election of the USOC president to the IOC's influential Executive Board.

A further illustration of the use of the Olympic movement as a forum for political conflict concerns the application by Palestine for membership of the IOC and therefore the right to participate in the Games. The Palestine Liberation Organisation is already a member of five ISFs and is supported by a strong Arab lobby within the IOC. However, the memory of the 1972 Munich massacre by Palestinian terrorists is still sharply felt, and there is the strong feeling among IOC members that it is being politically exploited by the PLO.

The Commonwealth Games Federation

After the Olympic Games the Commonwealth Games is the most important multi-sport competition in the world, involving sixty-five countries and a range of over twenty different sports. The role of the Commonwealth Games Federation (CGF) is to promote and organise the four-yearly Games, to establish rules and regulations for the conduct of the Games, and to encourage amateur sport throughout the Commonwealth. As the significance of the Commonwealth has slowly declined in international affairs so the Commonwealth Games have become more significant as the most tangible manifestation of the identity and purpose of the Commonwealth of nations.

The first British Empire Games were held in Hamilton, Ontario in 1930 and in general followed the model of the Olympic Games, particularly in terms of the commitment to amateurism and an explicit commitment to exclude all forms of discrimination. But the Games differ from the Olympics in a number of important ways, for example by the exclusion of team sports. In addition, the Commonwealth Games are limited to only ten sports, of which two must be athletics and swimming, with the other eight selected by the country hosting the Games from a list of approved sports established by the CGF. Thus over the years fencing and rowing have both ceased to be regularly included in the programme and have been replaced by sports such as shooting, weightlifting and gymnastics. For a new sport to be added to the list of approved sports from which the selection is made it must be played in a wide range of countries, have only one ISF, not be solely a team game, not be unduly costly, and not rely on mechanical means. Tennis, table tennis and judo are the most recent sports to be accepted on to the approved list.

The decision-making forum of the CGF is the biannual General Assembly at which each member country has one vote. The main responsibility of the General Assembly is to select the venue for the next Games. Most other matters are delegated to an Executive Committee comprising vice-presidents of the regions (continental groupings) and the officers of the

Federation. The main source of income for the CGF is from the country hosting the next Games and currently amounts to four annual payments of £100,000. To run a major international multi-sport competition with such a fragile financial base is a tribute to the considerable amount of voluntary effort provided. Unfortunately the financial weakness of the CGF, by contrast to the IOC which is aiming to build up a reserve fund of $100 million, is causing some problems. For example, on the question of drug testing the CGF can ensure only limited consistency of procedure from one Games to the next because it is dependent on the host country to finance and provide testing facilities.

However, as the Games have grown in significance, to the Commonwealth as well as to international sport, there has been growing concern to provide the Games with a more secure financial base. At the meeting of Commonwealth Heads of Government in 1989 a Canadian proposal to examine the finances of the Games was accepted and is currently the subject of discussion by a working party.

Not only is the CGF important as a symbol of the political aims of the Commonwealth, it is also important as a major international sports body. For example, it is the focus of considerable lobbying by international sports federations seeking not only acceptance of their sport in major competitions such as the Commonwealth Games but, more importantly, eligibility as an Olympic sport. Thus karate, handball, triathlon and netball have all attempted to gain acceptance in recent years. There is also increasing pressure on the CGF to admit popular team games such as volleyball and basketball, and also to allow competitions, particularly regional competitions, outside the Games themselves but under the aegis of the CGF.

In addition to the common concern of the CGF and the IOC over the eligibility of sports for their respective competitions the two organisations share other common interests. In particular they have a mutual commitment to the development of sport world-wide and there are a number of countries, for example the smaller islands in the Caribbean and Oceania, that are members of the CGF but are not members of the IOC. Consequently there is scope for close liaison between the CGF and Olympic Solidarity, the development commission of the IOC.

Finally, it is worth noting that the CGF is one of the few

remaining international sport bodies which retains a strong British influence. As a result the British International Sports Committee (BISC), which has a broad concern to enhance the influence of Britain in international sport, sees the CGF as an important focus for its activities. Thus the small grant from the Sports Council to the CGF from 1990 is most likely the result of BISC lobbying.

CONCLUSION

During the post-war period there has been a steady internationalisation of the government of sport. The rapid expansion in the calendar of international competitions and the growth in prestige of these events has had the consequence of forcing many domestic governing bodies to adjust their rules and schedule of competitions to fit in with the international calendar of their sport. For example, most top-class athletes gear their personal calendar to major international meetings, while the membership of the England football team is strongly influenced by the need to build a team for the next European Championships or World Cup.

The consequences of this trend can be seen at two levels: first at the level of ISFs and international organising bodies and second, in terms of the implications of internationalisation for domestic governing bodies in Britain.

Looking first at the international organisations, it is undoubtedly the case that they are becoming the focus of increasingly sophisticated lobbying from a number of sporting and non-sporting interests. Acceptance by the IOC or the Commonwealth Games Federation as a recognised sport not only opens the door to competition at the highest international level but also makes sports much more attractive to sponsors. Similarly the acceptance by the IOC of applications for membership, from countries such as Namibia and Palestine, is frequently seen as an important step in the international relations strategies of some countries.

The relationship between the IOC and the major ISFs is a further issue which will occupy the main international sports organisations during the 1990s. Primo Nebiolo, the president of the IAAF, has recently proposed that the presidents of the Olympic ISFs should be ex-officio members of the IOC. The rationale for the proposal is that the IOC should be the pre-eminent voice of international sport, but at present only four Olympic sports are represented on the IOC by their presidents. However, there are a number of ISFs that view such an arrangement as undesirable and would prefer to remain independent of the IOC, thereby leaving themselves in a better position from which to lobby the Committee.

What Nebiolo's proposal does highlight is the extent to which sport is dominated at the international level by a small number of extremely influential organisations. It is not surprising that the membership and constitutions of these bodies are becoming the subject of intense scrutiny by Third World countries in particular. For example, Eichberg refers to the IOC as an 'oligarchic, self-coopting organisation with worldwide monopolistic tendencies lack[ing] a democratic structure, legitimation, and control from below' (1984: 97). Eichberg also notes the tension between Unesco, which has a broad sport/culture responsibility on behalf of the United Nations and where the non-European and non-Western countries have a solid majority, and the IOC, in which 'Western and European functionaries still dominate' (1984: 97).

This geopolitical tension is also reflected in the debate about the acceptance of sports for international-level competition, especially at the Olympic Games. The Olympic Council of Asia has already made it clear that it feels that it is not getting its fair share of IOC development money and has expressed its concern that while Asia has 72 per cent of the world's population, Asian athletes only won 10.2 per cent of the medals. One explanation for this is that sport is less developed than in other parts of the world, hence the request for more development funds from Olympic Solidarity. An alternative explanation is that the mix of sports at Olympic (and Commonwealth Games) level is culturally biased against Asian countries. With a few exceptions, such as judo, the overwhelming majority of Olympic sports are of Western origin. The extensive sporting heritage of Asian countries that includes a wide range of martial arts is virtually ignored (Eichberg 1981; Johnson 1980; Brohm 1979).

Moving from these major international issues to the domestic level, the first question that arises is the extent to which British governing bodies and their representatives on international

149

bodies are prepared to respond to these issues. While an orchestrated response might seem unduly manipulative it is clear that the resolution of many of these issues will have consequences for sport in Britain. For many British governing bodies the choice is between having to adapt to decisions they have not helped to make or being consciously a part of the decision-making process. Unfortunately for many governing bodies in Britain the maintenance of boundaries in relation to other governing bodies is a dominant concern and such a high degree of factionalism makes a concerted voice difficult to achieve. Against this background the establishment of the British International Sports Committee jointly by the Sports Council, the BOA and the CCPR is a small but important step towards an acceptance that the policy community of sport is no longer confined to national boundaries. A key question therefore is the extent to which major domestic policy objectives, concerning football hooliganism and drug abuse for example, can be achieved without the co-operation and positive support of a number of international sports organisations. This forms one of the central questions in the case studies in chapters 7 and 8.

6

THE POLICY PROCESS FOR SPORT

The great mass of government today is the work of an able but secretive bureaucracy, tempered by the ever-present apprehension of revolt of sectional interests, and mitigated by the spasmodic interventions of imperfectly comprehending Ministers.

Sidney and Beatrice Webb[1]

While housing, transport, education and other areas of public policy can point to a healthy literature concerning the process by which policy is made, a similar literature for sport is, at best, sparse. Part of the explanation lies in the relatively recent identification of sport (and recreation and leisure) as a legitimate interest of government, the fragmentation of the policy area and its status in relation to the core concerns of government. However, in recent years there has been a noticeable increase in the interest and involvement of government in issues relating to sport and it is therefore appropriate that closer consideration be given to the way in which policy for sport and recreation is made and the consequences that greater government involvement has for policy development.

There is an unfortunately large number of different approaches to the study of policy-making. Some focus on the way actors in the process make their decisions while others focus on the structures within which decision-makers operate; some seek explanation at the macro level of wider society while others, more modestly, seek to explain how small groups make decisions; some aim to be descriptive where others aim at prescription. The proliferation of approaches indicates the difficulty of finding a model or framework which is able to encompass the heterogeneity of behaviour, methods, strategies and outcomes involved in policy-making. The field of study abounds with models, concepts and theories with partial explanatory value. A detailed review of the range of approaches to policy-making is outside the remit of this book and consequently only a brief survey is given before the preferred approach is outlined and examined. For those wishing to explore the variety of approaches to policy-making more thoroughly there are a number of general reviews available which provide points of entry to the literature.[2]

THE POLICY PROCESS

The student of the public policy process faces considerable problems in conceptualising the focus of study. Developing an agreed definition of policy and identifying the process by which it is made are both major problems. Concerning the question of defining policy, Brian Smith (1979) has identified a number of differing uses of the term, from policy as 'the structure or confluence of values and behaviour involving a governmental prescription' (Morton Kroll 1969) to policy as 'general directives on the main lines of action to be followed' (Dror 1968: 14). The term 'policy', then, may be used quite loosely to include what Hogwood refers to as 'policy as aspiration' (1987: 4) as well as more precisely to describe the 'deliberate choice of action or inaction' (Smith 1979: 13). It is therefore important to accept that a considerable degree of ambiguity surrounds the use of the term 'policy'. For the political scientist the consequences of this ambiguity are that care needs to be taken in distinguishing policy from political goals while also acknowledging that policy may become a goal in itself.

If policy is difficult to define, then identifying a theoretical framework and a conceptual language which illuminate the process by which it is made is equally problematic. An ideal theoretical framework should enhance description by exposing underlying social processes and thereby help the researcher to look beyond the surface appearance of social phenomena. As Ranson (1980) observes, 'central to such activity is abstract, conceptual analysis isolating the dimensions and constituents of the social arrangements that we wish to explain'. An adequate theory for the study of public policy would be one that provides illumination at three levels of analysis: first at the micro level of the individual actors that comprise organisations, where theory is concerned to uncover the interests, ideologies, expectations and values that they either bring with them into the organisation or else develop while part of the organisation. The main concern here is with questions of 'meaning' which involve an attempt to understand how actors make sense of their world and the consequences that this has for the policy process.

Theory should also illuminate at a second, middle or meso level where the focus is on organisations and institutions in the policy arena. Here the aim is to uncover the characteristics of the pattern of inter-organisational relationships, how the relationships are articulated and which strategies are adopted to pursue policy objectives. The focus of research may be on the resources possessed by individual organisations and the pattern of resource dependences that are found within a policy network. Finally, theory should illuminate at the macro level of the wider social structure within which organisations and institutions operate and it should direct our attention to the structure of power in society and the ideology that supports it. It should also focus on the ways in which the power of the dominant groups, classes or coalitions is articulated and the consequences that this has for the role ascribed or permitted to organisations.

The present study takes the second level, that of the organisation and the inter-organisational network of which it is a part, as the primary focus for analysis. However, this is not to deny the importance of research at the micro and macro levels; rather it reflects the need to be selective in a book of this type. Consequently there follows a brief review of the major macro social theories and some concepts of particular value in policy analysis. These are followed by a more detailed discussion of the concepts of 'policy community' and 'policy network', which are seen as particularly useful tools for analysing the way policy is developed as part of a pattern of inter-organisational relations.

THEORIES OF SOCIETY

Neo-Marxism is a convenient shorthand for a series of overlapping theoretical frameworks derived from the work of Marx. Two distinct strands can be identified, the first the instrumentalist model, and the second the structuralist model. The instrumentalist model views the state and the policy it develops as controlled by the capitalist class, which does not rule directly, but rather controls the government, which rules on its behalf and in its interests. As Dunleavy and O'Leary point out, an important element in the instrumentalist model is that 'capitalists, state bureaucrats and political leaders are unified into a single cohesive group by their common social origin, similar lifestyles and values, and by the existence of numerous networks and forums where co-ordinated strategies for public policy are hammered out' (1987: 237). Public policy, whatever its superficial intention, is designed to maintain the capitalist economy. Thus current sport policy may be seen as, on the one hand, designed to create opportunities for profit through, for example, the imposition of compulsory competitive tendering on local authorities. On the other hand it may be seen as a means of exercising social control over the working class in general and over young males in particular. (See Miliband 1969 for a fuller outline of the instrumentalist position.) The instrumentalist analysis has been strongly criticised, specifically for lacking the necessary subtlety to accommodate the variety of policy outputs from modern capitalist states and the varying fortunes of capitalism in the post-war period (Saunders 1980).

The structuralist model seeks to overcome some of the weaknesses encountered in the instrumentalist approach. Poulantzas (1978) made the most sophisticated statement of the structuralist position and centred his argument on the assertion that the state is relatively autonomous from the ruling class rather than simply being its tool. The state's key function is to maintain the political unity of the ruling class and to ensure its position as the politically dominant class. This role can, however, be fulfilled only if the state is in a position of relative autonomy from the bourgeoisie and consequently able to negotiate/mediate between the various class factions. Policy may not always be in the direct interests of the ruling class, as it is the product of the specific balance of class forces at any one particular time. However, in the last instance the state will always act in the interests of capitalism. This argument introduces an unavoidable tautology whereby the state is seen as being in the long-term interests of the ruling class, though in the short term its policy may reflect the more immediate pressures of class conflict.[3]

A more promising approach to understanding the macro-level context of the policy process is based on a pluralist analysis of society. According to pluralism, power in society is dispersed among a politically active citizenry and among a multiplicity of elites, institutions and organisations. The underlying assumption is that policy is the outcome of a process of competition between these interests. Access to the policy process is relatively open and it is assumed that no particular interest will be excluded permanently, and that all issues will find a place on the political agenda. The state in the pluralist model is neutral and fulfils the function of adjudicating between interests and has no inherent bias towards one set of interests.

Early empirical studies seemed to confirm the pluralist thesis (Dahl 1961; Polsby 1963). More recently a number of serious challenges have been made to the pre-eminent position of pluralism in British and North American political science. Among the criticisms directed at pluralism is that citizens are far from being the politically aware and active actors that pluralists would have us believe (Bogdanor 1981). A further criticism is directed at the supposed 'openness' of the political agenda. Bachrach and Baratz (1970) argued that some interests are sufficiently powerful that they can prevent issues coming on to the agenda for public debate and can consequently confine political debate to 'safe' issues which do not threaten their fundamental interests. A final criticism comes from Lindblom (1977), who argues that business cannot be treated as just one of a number of interests competing for influence over policy. According to Lindblom pluralists must recognise that business is a privileged participant in the policy process. At the core of his analysis is the argument that government is heavily dependent on businesses for certain key functions, relating for example to employment and growth. The picture that Lindblom paints is of a state formally independent of business but heavily reliant upon it for achieving publicly accepted objectives. It is the scale of the dependence and the normally high correlation between business interests and social values that give business its pre-eminent position in democracy.

Lindblom's analysis is a long way from the model of pluralism presented by Dahl or indeed in Lindblom's early writing. It is therefore increasingly common to refer to analysis such as this as neo-pluralist. The neo-pluralist analysis still exhibits the attachment to pluralist values and specifically the belief that 'contemporary liberal democracies remain basically, if inadequately, directed towards the satisfaction of ordinary people's wants' (Dunleavy and O'Leary 1987: 284). The distinctive feature of neo-pluralism is a concern to describe political processes more accurately and to take account of the ambiguities and paradoxes in the policy-making process. A good example of this is Lindblom's theory of incrementalism.

Incrementalism was a reaction to the rational comprehensive model of the policy process and was based on the identification of a series of clearly defined stages.[4] According to the rational model, objectives are identified and agreed; priorities are set; all alternative means of achieving the objectives are identified (policies); the consequences of all the policies are exposed; policy consequences are compared to objectives and priorities and the policy whose consequences most closely match the objectives is selected and implemented. Lindblom's essential criticism of this model was that it bore little relation to reality. Rather than behaving in such a comprehensive and synoptic way policy-makers adopt a more modest and pragmatic approach whereby only a limited range of policies is considered. Change is small scale and root-and-branch change is avoided. Essentially it is suggested that in practice policy-makers will prefer piecemeal change in existing policy in preference to the search for an optimal solution. It is further suggested that bargaining, compromise and negotiation are integral to policy formation and that maximising agreement may be more important than the quality of the decision. Incrementalism fits in well with the pluralist model of political behaviour and directs attention away from constructing theoretical models of the policy process towards an empirical analysis of the pattern of relationships between actors, the strategies adopted to influence policy and the resources available to those in the policy arena.

To complement the discussion of pluralism and increment-alism it is important to explore more explicitly the role of government in the policy-making and implementation process. It is central to the pluralist model that the rationalist assumptions of government homogeneity are challenged and that its fragmentation is acknowledged. Pluralists challenge the notion that government bodies are instruments designed for the purpose of goal attainment, with their structures and processes functioning in such a way as to enhance this attainment process. According to Barret and Fudge (1981):

> Such a policy centred or 'top–down' view of the process treats implementors as mere agents for policy-makers and tends to play down issues such as power relations, conflicting interests and value systems between individuals and agencies responsible for making policy and those responsible for taking action.

It is important to acknowledge that the institutions, such as local authorities, quangos and central government departments, that make up the state have interests and objectives of their own which frequently lead to competition between state institutions for access to and influence over the policy process. One must also go a stage further and accept that tensions and conflicts exist within state institutions. This takes the focus of research down to the behavioural level, where the concern is with how people act in organisations. On closer examination of organisations, including state organisations, one finds not a cohesive collection of individuals, conscious of externally defined goals and working towards their achievement, but rather a collection of sub-groups frequently exhibiting different perceptions of the organisation's purpose, committed to the goals to varying degrees and, most importantly, often vying with one another for dominance within the organisation and the right to define the goals (Jenkins and Gray 1983; Perrow 1979; Barret and Fudge 1981; Strauss *et al.* 1963; Strauss 1978).

The pluralist analysis of political processes coupled with insights derived from organisational sociology form the broad context for this study of the policy process for sport. From a review of the literature of policy-making there are two concepts which are particularly valuable when exploring public policy. The first is the notion of a policy cycle and the second is that of the policy community. The concept of the policy cycle was developed partly as a response to the view of policy-making derived from the systems model (Burch and Wood 1983; Easton 1965), which suggests a linear process where the political system receives inputs in the form of demands, resources or supports and converts them into outputs which may take a variety of forms such as

157

legislation, goods and services. While this may be a useful starting point for analysis it suggests a rather static role for government and is probably too rigid a framework to cope with the variety of policy areas and issues that need to be examined.

THE POLICY CYCLE

Refinements on this approach break the process down into a series of stages in the life cycle of a policy issue. The process may therefore be seen as starting with issue articulation/agenda setting, through issue processing and option selection, to implementation and impact evaluation. Hogwood and Gunn (1984) have made the most comprehensive exposition of the policy cycle. For them the process can be analysed most successfully when the following stages are considered:

1 *Deciding to decide (issue search or agenda setting)*. At the heart of this stage is the question of how certain problems become transformed into public issues. One might ask, for example, how the problems associated with drug abuse by athletes, spectator violence or competitive sport in school got on to the political agenda.
2 *Deciding how to decide (or issue filtration)*. In essence this involves deciding the route that a policy will take through the political system and the scarce resources of government that will be invested in its resolution and management.
3 *Issue definition*. In the life cycle of an issue there usually comes a stage when the issue has to be clarified and/or redefined. This is frequently done so that an issue which might cut across a series of related policy areas can be defined as the property of one particular policy community. Thus it might be argued that spectator violence has been defined as a law and order issue rather than as a sports issue. By contrast, violence on the field of play is still, with some notable exceptions, treated as a matter for the sport policy community and not the law and order policy community.
4 *Forecasting*. An important part of responding to a problem is making attempts to anticipate how the issue will develop.
5 *Setting objectives and priorities*. As Hogwood and Gunn admit the setting of explicit objectives is part of the rhetoric of

administration rather than the reality of policy-making and 'the explicit setting of objectives is often avoided or at least "fudged" in policy-making' (1984: 8). Yet there is frequently a need to articulate objectives and priorities at some stage in the process.

6 *Option analysis*. The questions to be addressed at this stage concern the extent to which options are evaluated and the techniques of evaluation adopted.

7 *Policy implementation, monitoring and control*. Policy implementation is a key stage in the policy process and may well be highly contentious. A number of decisions may have to be made at this stage concerning who is to be responsible for implementation (for example, local government or a quango), or what methods, techniques and technologies will be adopted and utilised. Decisions have also to be made regarding how progress in implementation will be monitored.

8 *Evaluation and review*. Evaluation refers to major periodic examinations of policy which involve assessing whether policy is achieving the intended outcomes.

9 *Policy maintenance, succession or termination*. In the life cycle of most policies there will come a time when they need to be abandoned, either because objectives have been achieved or because they have changed, or possibly replaced by new policies. The focus of interest here is how policies are modified or abandoned.

Not all issues will exhibit all nine stages and Hogwood and Gunn are keen to stress that the stages provide a framework for organising and analysing what happens in the policy process and do not comprise a prescriptive model and should not therefore be seen as comparable to the rational comprehensive model. They stress that their conception of the policy cycle is 'a contingent approach, which recognises both the resource limitations which preclude in-depth analysis on all issues, and [the] political factors which sometimes make attempts at "objective" analysis irrelevant' (1984: 5). The framework can be used, therefore, within a broader pluralist analysis of society and sits comfortably alongside an incrementalist description of the policy process. The policy cycle approach has a number of advantages, first, that it draws attention to the interaction between the policy process and the context it takes place within, second that it captures the dynamic interrelationship between politics and administration (Hogwood 1987).

POLICY COMMUNITIES AND POLICY NETWORKS

In recent years considerable attention has focused on the suggestion that the concept of a policy community also has particular value in exploring the way in which policy is made. It is suggested that by applying the policy cycle framework against the background of a policy community it is possible to generate important insights into the way in which policy is made for sport and leisure in Britain.

The notion of the policy community is the product of a number of different strands of research. From the sociology of organisations comes the idea that members of organisations display a primary concern with 'the requirements of organisational maintenance and enhancement' (Wilson 1973), rather than simply being concerned to achieve the public goals of the government of the day. Downs (1967) developed this view and suggested that organisations occupy 'policy space', which Jordan and Richardson (1987: 166–7) likened to the concept of 'territory' where 'each organisation or bureau has a notion of its own "territory", rather as an animal or bird in the wild has its own territory, and it will resist invasion of this territory by other agencies'. Building on this conception, it is possible to speculate about the policy heartland of an agency as well as its policy periphery or those issues which it considers to be alien.

Developments in the study of the role of pressure groups in policy-making have also contributed to the growth of interest in policy communities. For group theorists, public policy is the product of the interaction of a cluster of interest groups and reflects the balance of influence at any particular time (Richardson and Jordan 1979). Part of the conceptual language of the group theorists is that clusters of interest groups can be identified with particular policy areas and exhibit a degree of stability over time.

Combining the two notions of interest group clusters and the concern of the members of organisations with the maintenance of their policy space it is possible to conceptualise the policy process as taking place within a sectorised arena. Sectorisation reflects the 'strong political and psychological pressures causing the policy-making system to disintegrate into relatively autonomous sectors or segments' (Richardson and Jordan 1979). In attempting to isolate the characteristics of policy sectors the term 'policy community' has increasingly been used.

The concept of a policy community is one of a number of related concepts which take the span and intensity of issue interest/control as being defining characteristics. At one extreme there will be a number of potential policy actors with a direct or indirect interest in a particular policy area. Thus for sport this would include those who own, manage or work for organisations in the general sports industry. It would also include voluntary and governmental organisations as well as government departments, local authorities, political parties, pressure groups and international organisations. The range of actual and potential actors with an interest in the policy area is obviously enormous, but it is important to acknowledge that from time to time they may become involved in a particular sports issue. Following Wilks and Wright (1987: 296) an appropriate description of this level of interest and involvement is a policy universe.

The policy community exists within a policy universe. Unfortunately, as with many relatively new concepts, there is considerable definitional confusion about the appropriate use of the term 'policy community'. Disagreement arises over a number of aspects of communities, including the nature of the membership, the capacity of the community to exclude actors, the extent of organisation and structure, the sources of cohesion, and the issue scope of communities.

Starting with the question of membership, Wright (1988: 606) sees a policy community as comprising 'those actors and potential actors drawn from the policy universe who share a common identity or interest'. In contrast to most other writers Wright sees community membership as suggesting potential involvement in responding to issues rather than actual involvement. Other writers view membership as indicating actual involvement. Laffin, for example, following Friend *et al.* (1974), defines a policy community as 'a relatively small group of participants in the policy process which has emerged to deal with some identifiable class of problems that have or could become the concern of central government' (1986: 110). Hogwood broadly agrees and suggests that such a group may be widely drawn and also that a 'crucial feature of policy communities is that the community consists not only of civil servants and ministers but of relevant "recognized" interest groups and other governmental bodies, both appointed and elected local authorities' (1987: 18).

One aspect of membership on which there is a high degree of agreement is the centrality of professions. Rhodes and Wistow (1988) and Sharpe (1985) among others identify professional communities as important elements within policy communities. Professional communities 'comprise governmental specialist functionaries who operate at the different levels of government, and share a common interest which is strengthened by membership of a professional association' (Sharpe 1985: 367). The significance of professionals is that they constitute a potentially cohesive and influential lobby within a policy community. Laffin acknowledges that professions vary in terms of their cohesion and value consensus but argues that professions 'within a community take a common policy line on a wider range of issues and customarily act in concert to influence policy' (1986: 109).

While many policy areas have strong professions active within the policy community, sport would seem to be an anomaly. Professionalisation is a slow and highly contested process, particularly within local authority sports administration, hence a central role for a sports management profession is a claim which is difficult to sustain (Houlihan 1988). Thus, while there is an occupational group of sports managers in local authorities, the Sports Council and the governing bodies, their perspectives on problems and solutions are still influenced to a greater extent by their association with their employing organisation than by their shared service focus.

Having considered the nature of the membership of a policy community, the question arises of the capacity of the community to restrict entry. Rhodes sees this capacity as a key characteristic which he describes as a compartmentalised horizontal structure where there is a high degree of insulation from, and often conflict with, other policy communities. For Rhodes the community is 'substantially closed to other communities and invariably to the general public (including Parliament)' (1986: 23). Thus with regard to the sport policy community one would expect to find organisations representing football spectators excluded from membership.

The third issue concerning communities is the extent of organisation and structure within them. The stability of membership and the pattern of resource dependence in communities will both affect the character and extent of integration. For Jordan and Richardson policy communities are typified by their continuity and 'implicit authority structures' (1982: 94). In some communities authority structures may simply reflect the pattern of financial resource dependence and be focused, most frequently, on the government department. In others there may be actors in the policy process that possess authority based on their control over other resources such as knowledge, manpower or physical facilities. However, while the potential for authority structures to develop must be recognised it must also be acknowledged that the extent to which they persist varies considerably.

The fourth issue, sources of cohesion within the policy community, has generated extensive discussion and tends to focus on the importance of shared perceptions of problems and solutions as well as common attitudes and values. Hogwood (1979), for example, refers to the existence of a common technical language, while Dunleavy (1981) identifies the key characteristics as 'the acceptance or dominance of an effectively unified view of the world across different sectors and institutions'. This value consensus may derive from the fact that while the membership of a community may be widely drawn it is essentially a producer-oriented group (Millward: 1982) with clear functional interests focused on a particular service or department of central government (Rhodes 1986). Rhodes develops this point and refers to the high degree of vertical interdependence found in communities, in other words 'a non-executant role for central departments which are dependent on other organisations for the implementation of policies' (1986: 23). The relationship of the Minister for Sport and SARD with the Sports Council illustrates this observation.

From this description it would seem that the source of stability of the community is to be found primarily in a strong value consensus. In other words co-operative action between organis-ations is the outcome of sharing some or all of the following: interests, attitudes and objectives. Benson develops this theme by suggesting that it is necessary to locate the pattern of relationships between organisations and actors within a 'deep structure' of power relations found in wider society (Benson: 1979). Benson argues that the nature and character of network configurations and the distribution of power within communities and networks is not just the outcome of effective strategy development in the competition for resources, but is also explained by biases fundamental to the social structure. These biases are manifest not simply as power constellations (classes, interest groups, etc.) with vested interests in the stability or otherwise of the network or social structure, but also in the taken-for-granted rules of structure formation. In other words there is acceptance within the community and network that solutions to problems must be consistent with the 'fundamental features of the total social formation' (Benson 1979). This analysis has many echoes of Lindblom's conceptualisation of the relationship between business and government under neo-pluralism.

In practice therefore value consensus derived from a acceptance of a 'deep structure' of power relations is the foundation upon which community relationships develop. However, the day-to-day character of the relationships is likely to be based upon a more pragmatic source such as resource dependence. Benson (1982) and Rhodes (1985, 1986) both draw attention to the importance of resource dependence as the basis for the pattern and intensity of relations within a policy community. Resources may be of a variety of types and refer to any tangible or intangible product or activity which policy actors require in order to further their interests. Resources may therefore include, *inter alia*, finance, control over legislation, specialist knowledge, legitimacy, manpower and equipment. Resource dependence occurs when resources required by one organisation are controlled by another. The result of resource dependence is a pattern of bargaining and negotiation. Within any community the degree of dependence and the extent of resource control exercised by individual actors will vary and it is common for one actor to hold a central position within the community based on its resource control and the consequent dependence of others. In summary, while a value consensus may be a powerful spur to co-operation it is suggested that it is rarely sufficient to sustain a policy community through the tensions inherent in policy-making and that consequently it is frequently augmented by patterns of resource need and control.

The final problem in refining the definition of policy communities is to consider the range of issues that they can legitimately deal with. In general policy communities deal with routine or normal issues, for, by their very nature, they function effectively only so long as issues can be resolved satisfactorily using the pool of resources available to the community. However, there will be issues that will by-pass communities, possibly as a consequence of lack of interest or neglect by the community or because the issue has been redefined as the property of another (more powerful) policy community or where there is a dispute between communities over the 'ownership' of an issue (Hogwood 1987: 46–54).

As is implied in the discussion of a policy community, not all its members will be active in considering or resolving every issue. It is therefore necessary to define a further concept, a policy network which describes those actors involved with specific issues, such as drug abuse by athletes, or a particular process, such as planning sports development. In summary a policy community contains those actors with a general concern for the sport policy, while the policy network contains those actors involved in developing policy responses to a particular issue or problem. Distinguishing between the concepts of a policy community and a policy network has three important advantages (Wright 1988: 606). First it enables a distinction to be drawn between those actors within the community who are none the less excluded from policy networks. Second, it enables us to identify those actors that are regularly involved across a number of policy networks. As Figure 8 suggests, not all members of the policy community will be involved in dealing with every issue, nor will the membership of a particular network come exclusively from within the policy community. In particular it enables us to identify policy networks where membership is drawn from two different communities. For example the issue of sport in schools involves actors from the sport policy community and from the education policy community. Finally, one needs to acknowledge that while every policy sector will generate a policy community this is no guarantee that a policy network will emerge to deal with particular issues. Some communities may lack the necessary value consensus or strength of mutual interests to provide the basis for the formation of a network. The relationship between the concepts of policy

Figure 8 The context of the policy community

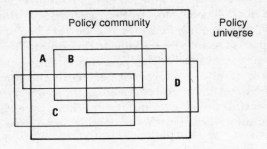

universe, policy community and policy network is shown in Figure 8, where A, B, C and D represent policy networks.

Part of the value of using the concept of a policy community, and the related concepts of policy universe and policy network, to study the process of policy-making is derived from its appeal as a descriptive device which takes account of the conventional wisdom concerning the negotiated nature of policy-making and avoids the rigidities of other, for example corporatist, metaphors. More significantly it provides a set of concepts that enables 'detailed case studies and still [facilitates] the comparative analysis of several policy areas' (Wistow and Rhodes 1987). It enables a focus on the pattern of recurring relations between members, the nature, extent and source of value consensus and the degree to which issues are the property of identifiable groups of actors in the policy process.

There is much in the literature of policy-making to suggest that the development of a policy community, and a sub-set of policy networks, is a sign of a mature policy area where boundaries are acknowledged and the expertise of the community members is respected, thus providing a disincentive to intervention by (more powerful) outsiders. This description would seem more appropriate to policy areas such as housing, education and defence than to leisure and recreation. Indeed Wistow and Rhodes (1987: 8) describe leisure and recreation as an 'issue network', which, according to their use of the term, is less integrated and has a larger number of participants with a lower degree of interdependence, stability and continuity than a policy commun- ity. Accepting the issue that networks and policy communities represent different positions on a continuum of metaphors of the policy process, a number of important questions arise for the student of public policy for sport and leisure. First there is the question of whether Wistow and Rhodes are accurate in their description. Second the question of whether there are any signs of change and development in the sport and leisure policy area which would suggest that the characteristics associated with a policy community are emerging. Third, are there good prospects for the development of a mature policy community for sport and leisure?

A POLICY COMMUNITY FOR SPORT

It has been suggested that policy communities often develop around government departments (Rhodes 1986) and also that government departments or agencies often fulfil a pre-eminent role, that of an 'authoritative regulator' in dealing with conflicts within the community (Theonig 1978). The basis of this suggested role is the resource position of government. While it does not control all resources, it generally exercises significant control over some, such as finance, and may well possess a near monopoly over others, such as political authority. In examining sport policy the non-executive role of the Minister for Sport and the SARD suggests that the Sports Council is a better starting point for plotting the pattern of relationships. Figure 9 identifies the key relationships that focus on the Sports Council.

One way of attempting to plot the character and contours of the policy community for sport is to begin by identifying the pattern of major resource dependences. The aim is therefore to identify which organisations are involved, the resource depend- ences that link them together, the level of dependence, and the extent of common interests/shared values.

Within any policy community significant resources will include finance, information, constitutional–legal (i.e. the ability to make or change laws, regulations, etc.), organisation (including manpower, facilities, equipment and land) and political legitimacy (Rhodes 1988: 110–17). The primary resources possessed by the Sports Council are financial, informational and

167

Figure 9 Key relationships in the sports policy community

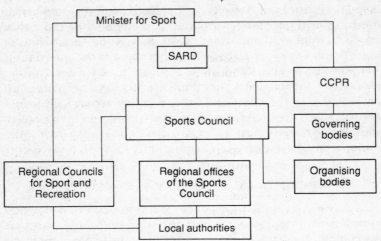

political. The key dependence relationship for the Sports Council is with governing bodies, many of whom rely heavily on the Council's grant for the growth and often the survival of their sport. Similarly many governing bodies look to the Council for the provision of technical information and expertise (regarding playing surfaces, drug testing and marketing, for example). However, the degree of dependence varies considerably, with the larger governing bodies such as the Amateur Athletic Association and the Football Association being of sufficient size to function comfortably without Sports Council resources. Indeed one of the reasons that the Council continues to grant-aid the larger governing bodies is precisely in order to maintain what is essentially a consultative link rather than a dependence relationship. It would be fair to argue that the Sports Council's continued influence in the policy community derives as much from its privileged political access as from its control over financial and informational resources. The close links between the Council and SARD and the Minister are essential in maintaining its influence in the community. Finally, one must add that the centrality of the Sports Council also reflects the absence of any alternative organisation, including the CCPR, that has a realistic capacity to fulfil a co-ordinating and integrating role, and which possesses a comparable degree of political access.

Generally, the larger governing bodies possess sufficient financial, informational and organisational resources to enable them to act independently of both the Sports Council and the CCPR, should they so wish. Bodies such as the Hockey Association, the Football Association and the AAA receive only a small proportion of their income in the form of grant from the Sports Council, are sufficiently large and wealthy to be able to employ or purchase technical and professional expertise (in marketing and public relations, for example) and also have a well developed organisational infrastructure which would enable them to pursue modest sports development policies relatively independent of local authorities. For the smaller governing bodies the picture is very different, with many run on very limited budgets, heavily dependent on Sports Council grant and on the voluntary effort of a dedicated few.

Table 7 summarises the main types of linking relationships found within the policy community. The table is a snapshot of the

Table 7 Linkages within the policy community

Form of relationship	Basis of the relationship	Character of the relationship
Bureaucratic	Convention legislation	Relatively clearly defined; predictable; regular; frequent
Formal professional	Shared expertise and ideology	Continuous; narrowly based
Technical	Requirements of plan	Periodic: cyclical; often strong financial element
Informal professional	Shared interests and problems	Irregular; frequent; personal
Informal consultative	Information transmission	Irregular; infrequent; often strongly political
Formal consultative	Information exchange	Regular; often overtly political
Party political	Broadly common ideology	Infrequent; not always consensual

characteristics of the relationship at a particular time, and it is important to emphasise that the links that bind organisations are not fixed but evolve in terms of their intensity and nature. The relationship between the Sports Council and the SARD and the Minister for Sport is the best example of a bureaucratic relationship. At the heart of the relationship is the Minister's oversight of the grant-aiding activity of the Council. However, the relationship is augmented by a technical linkage focused on the Council's annual strategic and financial planning exercise, which has been strengthened recently at the insistence of the National Audit Office and the Public Accounts Committee of the House of Commons.

The key relationship between the Council and the governing bodies of sport is in a period of change. Until the late 1980s the relationship was a mix of the informal professional and the technical. The focus of the relationship was financial (grant distribution) and in that sense had a strong technical element, but the method of monitoring the use of the grant reflected a relaxed bond that one would expect to find within a professional community rather than existing between grant provider and grant applicant. More recently, and following sustained criticism of the Council's methods of financial control, the technical and professional linkages have become more distinct. The Council is requiring governing bodies to produce an acceptable corporate plan for the development of their sport as a condition of grant aid. The plan is to become the basis of a more effective and rigorous performance monitoring process. One consequence of the strengthening of the technical relationship is that the relationship may well become more overtly political as governing bodies are obliged to engage in more intensive lobbying to maximise their grant. One would therefore expect that consultative links would become more important as both organisations sought to increase the quantity and quality of information that is received about each other's plans.

The link between the Sports Council and the governing bodies is a good illustration of the role and level of significance of professionals within a policy community. At the formal level sports administrators from the Council and from the governing bodies will meet to discuss strategic planning, either for a particular sport or for some issue of common interest, such as sport for the disabled or British influence in international sports federations. This type of link is supported by a continuous pattern of informal personal professional links which greatly enhance the sense of community among professionals. This day-to-day contact may arise over problems associated with a particular scheme or aspect of sport development and results in both the establishment and the dissemination of 'best practice' and the development and reinforcement of that sense of common identity and purpose which is an essential element in the establishment of a profession.

One would expect the same technical and professional relationship to exist between the Sports Council and the CCPR. Unfortunately the relationship between these two organisations is generally poor and consequently it is the more formal links which predominate. The technical link is important and is based on the fulfilment of the contractual arrangement between the Sports Council and the CCPR concerning the annual funding of the latter's activities. What seems to be lacking is a relaxed and informal professional officer link. Contact is more akin to the formal consultative linkage which tends to involve the political leaders of organisations rather than their professional staff. In this case the contact is between the politically appointed members of the Sports Council and the members of the CCPR and takes place at the meetings of the Sports Council and its sub-committees. Consequently it is less likely to involve professional officers and is closer to the process of consultation between two interest groups.

The relationship between the Sports Council and the Regional Councils for Sport and Recreation is best seen as an example of a consultative link. The relative autonomy of the Regional Councils from the Sports Council is based on the appointment of regional chairmen by the Minister and their direct accountability and access to him. However, the two levels work closely together through a pattern of informal and, more importantly, formal consultative links. The most important formal link is the quarterly meeting between the Sports Council chairman and the Regional chairmen. Although these meetings take place within a broad consensus regarding sport development priorities they must be seen as comprising a political linkage, as it is here that negotiations over the content of regional strategies and their relationship to the national strategy take place. Supporting this formal contact is a continuous pattern of informal consultation between Sports Council professional staff and those in the regional offices, often focused on more routine matters as well as the preparation and implementation of regional strategies and the distribution of grant aid.

A further example of a consultative linkage exists between the Regional Councils for Sport and Recreation and the local authorities that nominate members to it. The sports development activity of the Sports Council, bearing in mind its limited finances, relies very heavily on the co-operation of the local authorities. Consultation of both a formal type, through membership of the regional council, and informally, through rounds of visits and delegations, is a major feature of the relationship.

In order to complete the picture of the sport policy community it is important to identify those other policy communities that are most likely to impinge upon it, whether as a result of a specific challenge for control of an issue or simply because an issue is accepted as of legitimate interest to two or more communities. Figure 10 suggests that three related policy communities regularly impinge on the sports community, namely that for law and order, focused on the Home Office, that for foreign affairs, focused on the Foreign Office and that for medicine, focused on the medical profession. In Figure 10 the issue of drug abuse clearly involves not just the sport policy community but also the medical and law and order communities, as questions regarding clinical judgement and drug control legislation are prominent. As the Council of Europe is an important forum for discussion of anti-doping policy, the foreign policy community has also been

Figure 10 Sport and related policy communities

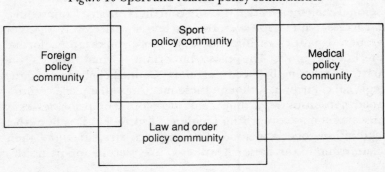

involved. Similarly policy towards football hooliganism concerns both the law and order and the foreign policy communities in addition to that of sport. The significance of the surrounding policy communities is not simply that they affect the range of actors and organisations that comprise specific policy networks. They are also significant in affecting the way in which the sport policy community views problems and the range of policy options that are considered. This is a particularly important point given the fact that the three communities mentioned in Figure 10 are more powerful within the political system than that for sport. Consequently maintaining the integrity of the sport policy community boundary might prove difficult were it to be subject to a challenge for control over an issue. One way in which challenges can be forestalled is for the sport community to take account of the priorities of other communities when devising its policy response.

The case studies which follow explore the response of the putative sport policy community to three contrasting issues: football hooliganism, drug abuse by athletes and sport for school-age children. The case studies are intended to illuminate the pattern of interaction on particular issues and the degree of influence of individual policy actors. They are also intended to provide the basis on which conclusions about the nature and characteristics of the policy process for sport may be drawn.

7

THE DEVELOPMENT OF POLICY FOR FOOTBALL HOOLIGANISM

A hooligan is a hooligan no matter where he operates and the fact that his behaviour is conspicuous at a football match has very often nothing to do with the game itself.

McElhone Report (1977: 1)

I hope that last Wednesday's sickening events will unite all decent people in helping to eradicate hooliganism. . . . If English clubs are to play football in Europe again, they can do so only when their good name and that of their followers and supporters has been restored.

Margaret Thatcher, 3 June 1985[1]

In June 1985 sport reached the top of the agenda of British politics. Meetings were held at Downing Street which involved senior Ministers, the Prime Minister and the leaders of the Sports Council, Football Association and Football League. However, far from this being a reflection of the growing maturity of the sport policy community it is best seen as an attempt by the government to force the creation of a policy community to tackle the problem of spectator violence. The cause of the unusual prominence of sport policy was the death of thirty-nine people at the European Cup Final between Liverpool and Juventus at the Heysel Stadium in Brussels.

For the previous twenty years or so the problem of football spectator violence had hovered on the edges of the national political agenda. The incident at the Heysel Stadium contained many of the ingredients identified by Hogwood and Gunn (1984) as important for an issue to claim the attention and resources of national decision-makers. Hogwood and Gunn suggest that one

174

or more of the following circumstances will normally force an issue on to the political agenda: that it has reached crisis level; that it has achieved particularity and is clearly defined as a specific type of problem in the public mind; that the issue is emotive; that it has an actual or potentially wide impact; that the issue raises questions of power and legitimacy in society; and finally that it is fashionable. The nature of the disaster at Heysel fulfilled many of these criteria.

That thirty-nine deaths, in the context of a football match, may be considered a problem of crisis proportions hardly needs stating. However, it was not simply the scale of the loss of life that was crucial but also that the incident took place abroad and that the behaviour of British football fans was broadcast to well over 100 million television viewers world-wide as part of one of the world's most important sporting events. In addition, 'the football hooligan', like 'the mugger' and 'the Teddy boy' before him, was rapidly becoming an identifiable stereotype in the public consciousness. The issue was certainly emotive and was seen, by politicians in particular, as an issue of respect for the law and thus raised questions of power and legitimacy. This is not to suggest that governments had not previously taken notice of the problems associated with crowd behaviour. As will be shown, there is a long history of government-sponsored enquiries and reports. However, they generally had a limited impact, possibly because they were frequently set limited terms of reference and partly because the initial event that had prompted the inquiry had been overtaken by more pressing political problems by the time of publication.

For Downs (1972) issues move through an 'issue attention cycle' where, following a period when the issue exists but is not recognised, the issue is subject to 'alarmed discovery and euphoric enthusiasm'. This is followed by a growing realisation of the cost of any solution, which leads to a gradual cooling of enthusiasm and the quiet transfer of the issue to the 'back burner' of political debate, where the issue is often forgotten. The government had shown some awareness of the problem of hooliganism in the early 1980s. For example, the Prime Minister was in Italy in 1980 during the European Championships when outbreaks of violence involving British supporters occurred and the DOE's working group on football spectator violence reported in 1984. In addition the British media continued to give outbreaks of hooliganism extensive coverage during much of the 1980s. Thus Heysel caused, if not the discovery of hooliganism as an issue, then certainly the sharp movement of the issue up the political agenda. The subsequent disaster at Hillsborough helped to keep the issue of crowd control from drifting too rapidly to the back burner of politics.[2]

The institutional context into which the issue emerged has been explored in chapter 5 and consequently only the most significant features will be repeated here. The Football Association as the sport's governing body was bound to be strongly involved in any attempt to devise a policy to combat hooliganism. However, as has been shown, its influence over the professional game is limited and its relationship with the Football League's Management Committee and with individual clubs is both vague and at times brittle. The Football League's relationship with the league clubs is based on the determined independence of individual clubs and their reluctance to transfer too much control to the League. The organisation of the Football League therefore militates against change and makes a strong leadership role for the League difficult to imagine.

The emergence in the late 1960s of football hooliganism as a fairly constant feature of the English football season prompted a number of studies of its causes (Marsh *et al.* 1978; Ingham 1978; Taylor 1982; Dunning *et al.* 1982, 1986) and strategies for containment (Popplewell 1986; DOE 1984). The combined effect of these studies was to demonstrate that the phenomenon of spectator violence was far from new and not confined to football.[3] The inquiry chaired by Justice Popplewell best summarises the extent and history of concern with the problem of soccer violence:

> When my Interim Report was published, it might have been thought by some that the suggestions which I set out had only recently been considered. . . . The problem of crowd control and safety had, so it was said, suddenly arisen. I have to say that almost all the matters into which I have been asked to inquire and almost all the solutions I have proposed, have been previously considered in detail by many distinguished Inquiries over a period of 60 years.
>
> (Popplewell 1986: 10)

Starting with the Shorrt Report in 1924, which was established to consider the question of crowd control following the first FA Cup Final, there have been at least seven further reports or inquiries into aspects of spectator violence or crowd control.

In reading these reports one becomes quickly aware that football spectator violence was treated in a largely *ad hoc* fashion. Spectator violence was seen as a local, rather than a national, problem; it was also seen as spasmodic group violence and not as a definable category of violence which was later to be labelled as 'football hooliganism'. In general the issue was seen as being a series of localised problems of crowd management and therefore the preserve of the local police force, local clubs and the governing bodies of football, with the Home Office or other departments of central government rarely becoming involved.

Yet it is in the early discussion of football hooliganism that the contours of the present debate may clearly be seen. The initial debate about spectator violence was couched in terms of crowd management and it was only gradually that the problem became defined as one of law and order. Part of the explanation for this change was undoubtedly the commonsense one that the incidence of violence at sporting events steadily increased, but it is also due to the failure of the Football Association, the Football League, and individual clubs to accept the problem as their responsibility. In 1924 the Shorrt Report observed that:

> we are assured that [the] governing bodies are only too anxious to secure that their sport is carried on under conditions which will promote the public safety, and we feel at this stage it is safe to leave the matter to them.
>
> (para. 67)

However, in 1946 the Moelwyn-Hughes Report, which was established following the collapse of safety barriers at Bolton Wanderers' ground, was highly critical of the decision by the Shorrt Committee to leave the responsibility for action with the governing bodies. '[Shorrt] anaemically recommended that adequate provision for safety be left to the pressure of the governing bodies in sport. The most important of these was the FA which has not deigned to appear before the Committee ...' The Moelwyn-Hughes Report made a series of recommendations and argued that there was a clear need for legislation in the area of crowd control. However, no legislation emerged, as the government was still intent on keeping the issue as one of management of a private function rather than as one of public order.

By the time spectator violence emerged in the late 1960s as an increasingly regular feature of the football season the general importance of sport in British political life had increased, as indicated by the appointment of a Minister for Sport. Denis Howell, the Minister from 1964 and one of the first holders of the post, gave his support to a major inquiry into the causes of football hooliganism. The Harrington Report published in 1968 highlighted the extent of inaction following the Shorrt and Moelwyn-Hughes Reports and confirmed the mix of apathy and disdain with which the football clubs viewed the problem. The report noted that:

> clubs often seem keener to spend money on the purchase of new players than to undertake any major spending on ground improvements which would increase safety and make hooligan control easier. One gets the impression that some clubs disclaim any responsibility for the behaviour of their supporters.

(pp. 33, 35)

During the early and mid 1970s hooliganism continued as an annual accompaniment to the football season, but as more pressing economic and social problems dominated the political agenda the problems associated with hooliganism remained peripheral to political debate. Such concern as there was among senior politicians tended to focus on the behaviour of British fans abroad and the harm that this was doing, internationally, to the image of Britain. During this time the clubs did make some progress in segregating fans from players and from their rivals, but this was more in response to a spate of pitch invasions which interrupted play rather than to the desire to maintain public order.

By the late 1970s national media and political attention was again being focused on crowd behaviour at matches but the lack of action by clubs in general in earlier years meant that discussion of solutions to the problems focused less on the action that clubs might take and more on the action that other organisations, previously only marginally involved in the issue, might take. This

178

discussion increasingly centred on the role of police at grounds (for example, the development of crowd control techniques and consideration of the question of who should pay for policing), the powers of magistrates to deal with football hooliganism and the scope for legislation to coerce recalcitrant clubs to act.

The McElhone Report (1977) on the crowd behaviour of Scottish supporters, although briefed to 'make recommendations to the Scottish Football Association and other organizations concerned', made it clear that the, by now, conventional exhortations to clubs to introduce more sophisticated crowd control measures were no longer sufficient. In addition the report recommended that 'Courts should make use of higher fining powers under the Criminal Law Act 1977' and that 'the police should have statutory powers to search'.

The tone and thrust of the McElhone Report were repeated in the report of the DOE working party on football spectator violence (DOE 1984). The brief of the working party was to 'review what *further* options were available to tackle the problem'. In one of the most direct criticisms of the Football Association the report argued that the Association's rules were unclear regarding its capacity to sanction clubs for inadequate crowd control precautions and that urgent steps should be taken to clarify the rules governing the relationship of individual clubs to the FA. Generally speaking the Football Association has been reluctant to test the extent of its control over clubs. The course of action preferred by the FA has been to look to government to give a lead.

> The football authorities, that is the FA and the Football League, have been deeply worried about the rise and persistence of football hooliganism, but maintain that its causes and cure lie outside their control. They have urged tougher action by the courts and that new harsher penalties to be made law.
>
> (SSRC/SC 1978)

Four years later Bert Millichip, the chairman of the FA and past chairman of the FA's disciplinary committee, repeated this view. 'The only way we shall find the cure is by the co-operation of all parties, and perhaps in the first instance we need a lead from the Government' (1982). It was clear that the FA did not see itself as the focal point or catalyst for the development of a policy.

The attitude of the FA was in direct contradiction to the view of the government as expressed by the DOE working party, which stated that 'The Football Association therefore has the primary responsibility for ensuring order within grounds (DOE 1984: 17). Given that all clubs are subject to the rules of the FA, which include a specific requirement that clubs take all reasonable precautions against crowd disorder, the view of the DOE seems valid. Indeed the FA has a well established procedure for determining whether disciplinary action should be taken against a club where crowd misbehaviour has occurred. As the DOE report states:

> Following any violence in the stadium, the Football Association considers whether there is *prima facie* evidence of misconduct by either club. It bases this judgement largely on the referee's report but also on reports from the clubs themselves. If evidence of misconduct is established, the FA holds a Commission of Inquiry into the incident.
>
> (1984: 17)

However, instances of the FA taking firm action against clubs following commissions of inquiry, such as banning Birmingham City fans from away games following violence at the last match of the 1988–89 season, are rare. In a number of cases where firm action has been attempted the FA has had to retreat in the face of legal challenges from clubs. For example, in 1983 Chelsea FC were required not to take supporters to away matches and to compensate the opposing team for the loss of revenue. However, the requirement was dropped when Chelsea threatened legal action.

It is possible to argue that UEFA has imposed the sterner punishments on British clubs associated with crowd misbehaviour. There is a long history of punishments preceding the ban following the Heysel disaster. During the 1970s UEFA imposed bans of two and four years respectively on the participation of Glasgow Rangers (1972) and Leeds United (1975) in European competition. Tottenham Hotspur and Manchester United were also given less severe punishments following incidents of crowd violence.

Although the disciplinary action of the FA can, with justification, be seen as weak it, together with the Football

League, did provide some, largely verbal, encouragement to clubs to develop policies to improve crowd behaviour and to improve the relationship between the club and the community within which it was set. During the 1980s a number of clubs have attempted to develop what are generally referred to as 'Football in the Community' schemes and now involve well over half the ninety-two League clubs. But these schemes were stimulated more by the government than by the football authorities. In 1978, following a serious incident of crowd violence at the Norwich City ground, Denis Howell, then Minister for Sport, allocated £1.6 million, through the Sports Council, for schemes aimed at making clubs more responsive to communities. More recently the Football Trust has provided money for the development of 'Football in the Community' schemes.

Most of the more successful schemes are based on the model developed by the Professional Footballers' Association, which receives finance from the Training Agency and relies on the development of close links with local authorities (Sutherland and Stewart 1989). Calderdale District Council has probably developed the most significant relationship with its local team through the council's ownership of Halifax Town Football Club. Calderdale have modernised the ground in return for the expansion of community use of the pitch. They are also exploring the possibility of renegotiating players' contracts to include an obligation to work in the community, for example in a coaching capacity (Whannel 1989). Preston North End FC has a similarly close relationship with its local authority and has developed an extensive community scheme, aimed primarily at children and adolescents.

As a final example Lewisham Council sponsors Millwall FC at the rate of £70,000 a year. The club has appointed a community officer who has developed contacts with schools, youth clubs and other community groups, and has organised a local football festival and has sponsored a women's team. Millwall FC's ambitious scheme involved not only Lewisham Council but also the now defunct Greater London Council and Inner London Education Authority, and the Sports Council, who all provided support of one kind or another. A key test for this scheme and the others like it is whether they will survive the inevitable scaling down of finance from public bodies and the Football Trust and, in Millwall's case, relegation to Division II at the end of the 1989–90 season (Lightbown and Schwartz 1988). More importantly, although the FA and the Football League are both strongly supportive of the community initiatives much of the initial drive came from public bodies (local authorities and the Training Agency), from individual clubs and from the Professional Footballers' Association. Finally, for a number of the largest clubs their support is no longer geographically concentrated close to their ground. Many now have a regional, and in some cases national, basis for support. Also many clubs are much more commercial organisations and are consequently more likely to judge community schemes in terms of the opportunity cost incurred and whether it is likely to attract more supporters.

The 1984 DOE working party report is important, not only for its forceful attempt to highlight the central responsibility of the FA for crowd safety and behaviour, but also because it marks a broadening in the range of organisations actively addressing the problem of football hooliganism. In particular the mid 1980s saw a clear determination by the police to develop a more consistent national approach to football-related violence, while the courts were encouraged to adopt a more severe attitude towards hooliganism. However, the courts were reluctant to be seen as the prime 'solution' to the problem, and resisted Neil Macfarlane's attempt to encourage magistrates to 'exercise their sentencing power to the full' (Macfarlane 1986: 31–2). As Douglas Acres, Chairman of the Sentencing of Offenders Committee of the Magistrates' Association, observed, 'It is easy to say football hooligans should be dealt with in this or that fashion. I want to emphasize that it is not justice to deal with people in a uniform way' (1982: 19). However, the Court of Appeal gave a clear lead to magistrates, with Lord Justice Lawton recommending custodial sentences and suggesting that 'the time has come for the courts to impose sentences to deter those minded to use violence at or near football matches' (*Times Law Report*, 17 January 1984). In consequence many local benches were quite willing to use their powers of sentencing to make an example of those convicted of offences associated with sporting events (DOE 1984).

The 1980s also marked the greater involvement of local government. The interest of local authorities was stimulated by a number of factors: first their general concern for the quality of life of those who live near the football grounds, second their responsibility for funding the police, and thirdly the duties imposed on county councils by the Safety of Sports Grounds Act 1975. Both the Association of County Councils and the Association of Metropolitan Authorities submitted evidence to the Popplewell Inquiry. The latter Association provided not only a list of technical recommendations on ground safety but also a series of broader strategic policy suggestions aimed at combating hooliganism. However, as the AMA noted, the 'Technical recommendations were incorporated [but] the social policy recommendations were largely ignored' (quoted in House of Commons Library Research Division 1989).

The 1980s have thus seen the issue of football hooliganism move up the political agenda but with a marked reluctance on the part of the key actors involved to take a clear policy lead. The government, the clubs, the FA, the police and the courts have all exhibited a reluctance to adopt the role of policy leader. The main consequence is that the problem has been addressed through a series of half-measures, frequently short-term and unco-ordinated. This vacuum within the policy arena has tended to result in central government adopting a leading role more by default than by conscious choice. In the post-Heysel period it is the government which has attempted to inject a sense of urgency and a degree of co-ordination among English clubs. The series of meetings called by Mrs Thatcher with Ministers and representatives of the FA and the Football League seemed to confirm the impression that the governing bodies and most clubs lacked the will and possibly the capacity to initiate a positive response to the crisis. As Macfarlane noted:

Ingham [Mrs Thatcher's press secretary] had formed the view that England's football authorities were probably less inclined to do anything after the ninety-four deaths [from the fire at Bradford City Football ground and the collapsed wall at the Heysel Stadium] than before.

(1986: 10)

The Heysel disaster was important both in terms of the development of policy towards hooliganism and also in terms of its impact on the context of policy development. From the government's point of view Heysel forced the issue firmly on to

183

the political agenda and was consequently seen by the government both as an opportunity to give direction to policy development and, more importantly, as the catalyst which should provoke the long-awaited commitment to action from the clubs and the FA. However, as Macfarlane's account makes clear, the commitment was slow in developing. In the immediate aftermath of the disaster the decision by the FA (made under considerable government pressure) to withdraw English clubs from the next season's European competitions in anticipation of a UEFA ban was challenged by the four clubs affected, who went to the High Court to have the FA's decision reversed, claiming that it was 'ill-judged, arbitrary and unlawful' (*Guardian*, 29 June 1985). This 'damaging conflict over sectional interest and public responsibilities' (Dunning *et al.* 1988) did little to inspire the confidence of the government.

The government's approach to policy-making for hooliganism is based partly on frustration with the perceived inertia of the football authorities, but also on an assessment of the problem which suggests that hooliganism is amenable to quick policy solutions. Canter *et al.* (1989) describe the approach of successive governments to problems associated with football as 'legislation by disaster'. The implication being that on the one hand government is reluctant to take a long-term view of the sport and its problems, and on the other that it is solving the last problem rather than anticipating the next.

The accumulation of research into the causes of football hooliganism is now extensive, yet little seems to have penetrated the thinking of governments. The explanations of hooliganism are varied and include predominantly psychological explanations in terms of 'male bonding' (Tiger 1969) and the ritualisation of male aggression (Marsh *et al.* 1978); predominantly historical explanations which refer to working class traditions of loyalty to the local club (Clarke 1978); and sociological explanations which draw attention to the socialisation of young working class males into a sub-culture that emphasises toughness as a virtue (Dunning *et al.* 1986).[4] Much of the research into football hooliganism is aimed more at explaining its persistence than at proposing policy action. But a number of policy suggestions have emerged directly or indirectly from this research effort, including building closer links between the club and the community, taking steps to upgrade the facilities for spectators at stadiums, and making stadiums more attractive to women and families. Unfortunately most of the proposed solutions possess one or more of the following characteristics, namely that they are long-term, low-key, expensive and complex to administer. By contrast the government has, for much of the 1970s and 1980s, generally seemed to prefer solutions that would seem to promise an immediate effect, have a high public profile, are cheap, and are either simple to administer or can be administered by a non-government body. This approach is illustrated in the debate over the introduction of a compulsory membership scheme.

THE FOOTBALL SPECTATORS ACT 1989

The government, in a statement by the Prime Minister to the House of Commons in the week following Heysel, made clear the direction in which it wished policy to develop. A five point plan was outlined which included the banning of alcohol in football grounds, the strengthening and clarification of police powers, stricter control of safety procedures at grounds and 'the introduction of membership schemes, far more all-ticket matches and stricter controls or, in some cases, a ban on visiting spectators' (House of Commons, *Debates*, vol. 80, 21–3, 1985). Legislation followed quickly with the Bill to ban alcohol in trains and coaches travelling to matches, and also inside sports grounds, introduced within weeks of the Prime Minister's statement of intent. The Act, modelled on the legislation already in operation in Scotland for nearly five years, was controversial, as the evidence linking categorically the sale of alcohol *in* sports grounds to spectator violence is difficult to find. On the one hand there is strong support for the ban in Scotland both from administrators and from the police (House of Commons Library 1985: 29–30). On the other hand Tom Pendry, chairman of the All Party Football Committee of the House of Commons, has argued that:

> There is little evidence to support the view that the sale of alcohol at matches increases the level of violence. When drink is not available inside the ground, supporters either arrive 'tanked up' or else attempt to bring in their own supplies.

> (House of Commons Library 1985: 29)

More recently David Phillips, at the time Assistant Chief Constable of Greater Manchester, expressed a similar view, suggesting that the ban simply encourages supporters to drink beforehand and arrive late for the kick-off (Whannel 1989). Lord Justice Taylor, in his final report on the Hillsborough disaster, acknowledged both that alcohol abuse was a problem but also that the ban on alcohol had little discernible effect on the consumption of alcohol.

> Drinking before matches increased in parallel with the growth of hooliganism . . . a cult of drinking to excess . . . certainly is [a major factor] and it remains so despite legislation banning sales or possession of alcohol in football grounds and the carrying of alcohol on public service and hired vehicles bound for such grounds.
>
> (Lord Justice Taylor 1990)

The ban on alcohol was followed by a series of measures designed to clarify the law with regard to crowd behaviour. In particular, Part IV of the Public Order Act 1986 gave the courts new powers to issue an exclusion order against any person convicted of a football related offence. An exclusion order prohibited a person from attending specified football matches for a period determined by magistrates.

By far the most controversial proposal from the government was to introduce a membership scheme. In Lord Justice Taylor's final report he noted that 'membership cards' had been one of the most frequently mentioned recommendations of previous reports and studies (1990: 104). The DOE working party, while acknowledging the problems of practicability, recommended that 'the FA should re-examine quickly and in detail a [membership] scheme . . .' (DOE 1984: 21). The interim report of Justice Popplewell, while also acknowledging the practical problems, added weight to the DOE recommendation by suggesting that 'consideration should continue to be given to some form of membership scheme for Football League clubs in England and Wales' (1986). In his final report Justice Popplewell was much more appreciative of the problems involved in making a national scheme work.

While the football authorities were willing to review the suggestion, there was a marked lack of enthusiasm for the idea.

However, the League established a working party which, in its report of September 1985, proposed a limited membership scheme to cover families, children and accredited supporters. The League's approach was to use a membership scheme as a way of attracting desirable groups to attend matches. This was in sharp contrast to the government's perception of the scheme, which was as a means of excluding troublemakers. Thus despite claims from clubs and the FA that a new determination now existed to tackle hooliganism it was not long before the government was once more expressing its dissatisfaction. In October 1986 Richard Tracey, appointed Sports Minister in late 1985, gave the Football League six weeks in which to report on progress in introducing membership schemes, which the government had suggested more than a year earlier. He commented that 'only a few clubs have introduced schemes. . . . We believe urgent action is now needed' (DOE press release, 9 October 1986).

In the subsequent report the League maintained its strategy of attempting to minimise the effect of a membership scheme on access to grounds. 'The League do not feel that a comprehensive national scheme covering all spectators is either a practical or desirable solution' (1986: 2). The report also rehearsed many of the arguments that would recur during the passage of the Bill through Parliament. In particular the League argued that many crowd problems occur outside the ground; that clubs already work closely with their local police forces and have 'generally dealt with large crowds perfectly adequately'; and finally that the introduction of a national membership scheme 'could well have a serious effect on Association Football as a spectator sport' (1986: 2–3). The League offered to pursue the development of existing schemes to achieve 'controlled access', aiming to include 70 per cent of attenders though 'this may take some considerable time to achieve'.

The government interpreted these words as signifying complacency and a deplorable lack of commitment and as such seeming to confirm the government's view that the football authorities were incapable of the kind of decisive action the Prime Minister desired. Four months after the League's report a meeting was called by the Minister for Sport with the representatives of the League, the FA, the Home Office and the police which produced an eight point plan reflecting 'the government's and the football authorities' continuing commitment to tackle hooliganism in partnership' (DOE press notice, 23 February 1987). The plan again emphasised the importance of a membership scheme and included the request to all clubs 'to develop and introduce membership schemes for specific areas of their grounds by the beginning of the 1987–88 season' (DOE press release, 23 February 1987).

However, the 'partnership' between the government and the football authorities was not a mutual one, as the Minister was forcing the issue of membership against a background of limited enthusiasm from the clubs. As a result, in early 1988, the Minister announced that he intended to meet the six clubs who had failed to make any progress in establishing schemes. By the middle of 1988 the new Minister, Colin Moynihan, was still expressing disappointment with the efforts of the League clubs.[5] But his audience for these expressions was no longer a purely domestic one but was the international governing bodies of football and UEFA in particular. As was soon to become apparent, a key lever in the hands of the government was its ability to influence, if not control, the return of English clubs to European competition. If persuasion and exhortation were having only a limited impact on the co-operation of the clubs and football authorities, then the financial consequences of continuing exclusion from Europe were a valuable additional tool. Moynihan, in writing to Jacques Georges, president of UEFA, reported that progress towards a voluntary scheme had been slow. 'Sixteen clubs have met the 50 per cent ground capacity provision of the February 1987 agreement. Eighteen clubs have achieved between 40–50 per cent, 21 between 30–40 per cent, 20 between 20–30 per cent, 9 between 10–20 per cent, and 8 with less than 10 per cent' (Moynihan 1988). Most notably Moynihan drew attention to the failure of the League to make progress with the proposals to introduce a reciprocal membership scheme which was initially intended to be partially in place for the 1988–89 season.

Despite some progress in improving crowd control at grounds (though possibly at the cost of displacing the violence to areas outside the grounds) the level of hooliganism following Heysel did not decline as rapidly as the government wished, and the government's perception was that a considerable portion of the blame lay with the football authorities. The government's view was that it had fulfilled its part of the partnership by altering the law regarding crowd safety and hooliganism, encouraging the police to adopt a more determined and concerted approach to prosecuting the instigators of violence, and providing the courts with a wider range of sentencing options. The government's dissatisfaction surfaced as a result of the approach by the FA to UEFA with the request that the ban be lifted for the 1988–89 season. Colin Moynihan made it clear that while the decision on the date of English clubs' return to European competition lay in the hands of UEFA the government would see it as its duty to express an opinion as to the appropriateness of any proposed date for readmission. Indeed, in January 1988 UEFA postponed a decision on English clubs owing to the doubts expressed by Moynihan. Jacques Georges, the UEFA president, confirmed that no objection had been raised by the UEFA members to the readmission of English clubs.

The slow pace of action by the League and the outbreak of further incidents of hooliganism in June 1988 during the European Championships in West Germany prompted the government to announce its intention to introduce a membership scheme through legislation. An undoubted cause of the League's lack of progress in introducing a voluntary membership scheme was the difficulty in achieving the agreement of individual clubs, highlighting once more the ambiguous relationship between the FA, the League and individual clubs. A working party, chaired by Moynihan and with representatives of the football authorities, produced a report which became the basis of the Football Spectators Bill, introduced into the House of Lords in January 1989. The Bill was drafted to provide a framework that would allow the football authorities to work out the details of the scheme. 'Enabling legislation' as it is called is frequently criticised for failing to provide sufficient detail for Parliament to debate and also for simply reflecting hasty government action. While these criticisms may apply here it is plausible that the government was keeping the legislation deliberately vague in order to force the football authorities to adopt a more active role in the policy to combat hooliganism.

Part One of the Bill gave the Secretary of State the power to 'designate' certain matches, mainly matches between League clubs. Once a match has been designated attendance would be open only to 'authorised spectators', predominantly members of the football membership scheme. Some exemptions were allowed, for the disabled and those under ten years of age, but suggested exemptions for other groups such as women and pensioners were rejected by the government. However, the government did accept that there was a need for some form of temporary membership to cover foreign visitors, school parties and guests of members. The Bill made it an offence for persons to enter a designated match if they were not a member or included in an exempted category. Administration of the scheme was to be the responsibility of a Football Membership Authority (FMA), to be approved by the Secretary of State. The hope was that the FMA would be run by the FA and the League and would set up and run the membership scheme, once the Secretary of State's approval had been received. The Bill also outlined the respective roles of the clubs and of the FMA as well as specifying the conditions under which a member might be disqualified. Finally, the Bill made it clear that the cost of introducing and running the scheme would fall on the football authorities and clubs. Part Two of the Bill was designed to address the problem of violence by English football supporters abroad and enabled the courts to require individuals convicted of offences associated with football hooliganism to report to an agency at times when the England team or English clubs were involved in matches abroad.

The debate on the Bill, which carried on for much of 1989, not only tested the lobbying capacity of the football authorities, supporters and clubs, but also illustrated how numerous and diverse the actors in the policy process were becoming. The football authorities provided comprehensive briefings for MPs and attacked the Bill from a number of different points of view. At the heart of their objections was the view that the Bill did not tackle the root cause of the problem and would simply displace the problem to outside the ground. This was a view strongly supported by the police, with the chairman of the Police Federation arguing that:

> It's likely to create more trouble and problems than it's trying to solve, and in particular it would require more police on duty outside the ground than at present. It's a threat to safety and public tranquillity.
>
> (*Guardian*, 9 January 1989)

The chairman of the Police Federation, while opposing the membership scheme, was also severely critical of the football authorities, arguing that 'football has been badly served by its own leaders' and that football as an industry had given the impression that it would 'only do what it had to to comply with statutory safety requirements' (*The Independent*, 18 May 1989). The Federation also expressed support for the Luton Town experiment of banning visiting supporters.

In addition the football authorities argued that the measures currently in operation, such as closed circuit television at grounds and the 'Football in the Community' initiatives, were already showing results in the form of a decline in violence. Furthermore, the authorities stressed the great inconvenience caused to the majority of fans owing to the actions of a tiny minority, and pointed to the likely loss of revenue for clubs consequent upon the decline in casual attendance at matches. The financial impact of the scheme caused the clubs and the League great concern. In a study commissioned jointly by the League and the FA the gross cost of the scheme was estimated at between £25 million and £38 million over a five year period, with a possible net effect somewhere between break-even and a cost of £12 million. The authorities were also concerned that if the membership register was subject to the 1984 Data Protection Act it would limit the opportunities to exploit the membership list for commercial purposes. A related concern was expressed by the National Council for Civil Liberties, which claimed that the Bill gave a degree of discretionary power to withdraw membership without appeal which constituted an infringement of civil liberties. Finally, the football authorities stressed the problems of developing and installing the necessary technology to make a computer-based scheme work.

The government was unsympathetic to many of these objections. Colin Moynihan argued that the Bill would not displace violence to outside the ground.

> [the] Bill, in disqualifying troublemakers from attending designated matches, will be effective in reducing misbehaviour inside grounds and, since those disqualified will be deterred from travelling to matches, outside and on journeys to and from matches as well.
>
> (House of Commons, 20 March 1989)

The Minister also referred to the experience of Luton Town FC in support of his opinion. Luton's experience was much debated in the House of Commons during the passage of the Bill. For David Evans, MP for Welwyn and Hatfield and, in 1989, chairman of Luton Town, the experience of his club's experiment with a membership scheme which banned away fans was conclusive. He pointed out that 'three seasons ago there were 115 arrests and seven stabbings. Over the past two seasons and eighty League games there has not been one arrest or stabbing at the ground' (House of Commons, *Debates*, vol. 135, cols. 565–6, 16 June 1988). However, while the Minister saw Luton Town FC as evidence in support of the Bill, Tom Pendry, chairman of the All Party Football Committee, interpreted the evidence quite differently. He agreed that the scheme had resulted in a decline in violent incidents inside the ground but added:

> In 1987 violent offences in Britain rose by 12 per cent. In Bedfordshire (excluding police division 'C' which contains Luton) violent offences rose by just 9.6 per cent. In the Luton area violent offences rose by 14 per cent. The identity card scheme in place at Luton Town not only caused attendances to fall dramatically last season by 27 per cent, it also displaced rather than removed violence.
>
> (Quoted in House of Commons Research Division 1989: 31)

THE TAYLOR REPORT

During the passage of the Bill, on 15 April 1989, ninety-five people died and 174 were injured as a result of being crushed against the perimeter fence and at the back of the terrace at the FA Cup semi-final between Liverpool and Nottingham Forest, held at Sheffield Wednesday's Hillsborough ground. An inquiry was established under Lord Justice Taylor and the Home Secretary announced that there might be amendments to the Bill, depending on the inquiry's conclusions. But more significantly the Home Secretary saw the events at Hillsborough as providing further evidence of the necessity of the Bill. However, the Home Office was also at pains to stress that the Bill provided an enabling framework and was not a detailed set of proposals. As Lord Hesketh pointed out in the House of Lords:

I invite your Lordships to recall that Part 1 of the Bill does not itself implement the national membership scheme. It provides the framework within which the Football Membership Authority will draw up the scheme.

(House of Lords, *Debates*, vol. 508, cols. 1651–3, 16 June 1989)

The government was now in an extremely difficult position. On the one hand the membership scheme was the main plank of its anti-hooligan strategy and was also its most effective means of forcing the pace of FA, League and club activity on hooliganism. On the other hand the government was initially forced to acknowledge that it could not proceed with the implementation of the scheme until after the Taylor Report. As time went on it became clear that the future of the scheme rather than simply its implementation depended on the outcome of the report. When the report was published in January 1990 its rejection of the government's membership scheme was clear. Taylor agreed with many of the objections raised by the football authorities and the police but in particular expressed scepticism regarding the capacity of current computer systems to cope with the demands that would be made on them. His report also supported those who felt that the membership proposal would intensify problems outside the ground. Taylor's worries were confirmed by the experience of the Dutch at the start of their season in August 1989. The Dutch authorities had imposed a similar computer-based membership scheme on five clubs but were forced to abandon the scheme indefinitely after only one week's experience owing to supporters ignoring the requirement to obtain a card and turning up in such large numbers at the grounds that the police felt that public order could be maintained only by abandoning the scheme.

Following the publication of the Taylor Report the government announced that the membership scheme would not be implemented, although the enabling framework would remain on the statute book. Although the report was an undoubted setback for the government, especially since the Prime Minister had invested so much personal prestige in the scheme, it was far from being a victory for the football clubs and authorities. Since the Heysel Stadium disaster the FA, the League and the clubs had all been progressively marginalised in the ensuing debate on anti-hooligan policy, though it must be acknowledged that they were reluctant to adopt the forceful role that the government expected. The Taylor Report, far from returning the policy initiative to the football authorities and the clubs confirmed their marginal, and essentially reactive role. Lord Justice Taylor seemed to have the same lack of confidence in the management capacity of the football authorities as did Mrs Thatcher. In one important respect Taylor was a much more formidable participant in the policy network, for his report effectively depoliticised the issue.

During the debate on the membership scheme the issue had become overlaid with party political divisions which blurred the problem being addressed. As the debate progressed the issue of hooliganism was often redefined as one of commitment to the national game of football or antipathy to a predominantly working class sport. The Taylor Report returned the spotlight to the kernel of the problem and made it much more difficult for the other participants in the network to redefine the issue and thereby obscure the focus. In consequence it might be argued that while the report was undoubtedly embarrassing to the government in the short term, in the longer term it may prove to be a much more effective source of pressure for policy innovation regarding hooliganism.

Apart from his rejection of the membership scheme Lord Justice Taylor made one proposal which will have significant consequences for the clubs. He recommended that all Football League grounds should become all-seated by August 1999, with first and second division clubs converting their grounds by August 1994. In making this recommendation he was adding weight to FIFA's policy and following the same strategy as the Dutch, who in the wake of the collapse of their attempt to introduce a membership scheme have opted for all-seat stadiums as an alternative policy to combat hooliganism.[6] The financial implications of this proposal are more serious than those of the membership scheme but, although there were some objections to the proposal, criticism from the football authorities was generally muted. The effect of Lord Justice Taylor within the policy network can be seen, first, in the general acceptance of the proposal by the authorities and, second, in the response of the government. The initial reaction of the government to the cost implications of the proposal came from the Home Secretary, who insisted that there would be no government contribution to the estimated £130 million cost. This initial reaction was in keeping with the confrontational atmosphere which surrounded so much of the debate on the Football Spectators Act. However, in the 1990 budget the government did alter the regulations on pools duty to make more money available to the Football Trust to aid clubs in meeting the costs. It is possible to argue that the 'mellowing' of the government's attitude to helping clubs financially was aided by the depoliticising of the issue by Taylor.

Taylor, like the government before him, firmly identified the clubs as having the prime responsibility for the safety and comfort of spectators. He also intensified the pressure on the football authorities by strongly criticising the quality of management in football. He pointed to the poor leadership given by the FA and Football League and specifically pointed to their failure to accept that they were primarily responsible for giving clubs advice on matters of crowd safety. His criticisms were unquestionably intensified by the apparent disarray among the football authorities over the appropriate response to an outbreak of hooliganism in May 1989. Bert Millichip, the chairman of the FA, outlined a set of proposals to the FA Council which included the selective banning of visiting supporters and implied some form of identification card for supporters. Not only did his proposals result in criticism from many club administrators, it prompted the Football League to issue an immediate rejection of the proposals as impracticable (*The Times*, 19 May 1989). The impression of disarray was compounded by the announcement of a different set of proposals from Graham Kelly, the chief executive of the FA. While the FA was right to point out that the Millichip and Kelly proposals were discussion papers for an FA Council meeting and not policy pronouncements, the episode was interpreted by the press and by members of the policy network as further confirmation of their impression of poor leadership and disunity among the football authorities (*The Times*, 19 May 1989; *The Independent*, 19 May 1989).

While it is too soon to say that the membership scheme has been shelved indefinitely it is likely that the focus of policy development regarding hooliganism will move elsewhere. Yet it would be wrong to see the debate on the membership scheme as representing the only areas where policy innovation was taking place. Although it did dominate debate for the later part of the 1980s the intensity of debate masks other areas of progress in policy development and other arenas of policy debate and determination. In one sense the threat of a statutory membership scheme did have the desired effect of keeping the issue of hooliganism at the top of the agendas of the FA, the Football League and individual clubs, and resulted in a number of policy innovations such as the variety of community liaison schemes, experiments with all-seat stadiums and experiments with a variety of club-initiated membership arrangements. It would be wrong to see the period as a stand-off between the government and the football authorities, with the latter frozen into inaction.

Howell, commenting in his autobiography on problems within football, noted the importance of the Chester Report. In particular, he noted its long-term value as a source of ideas when new problems arose. The same comment may well be made of the Taylor Report in the years to come. Having dealt with many of the issues specific to the Hillsborough disaster in his interim report, Taylor devoted the bulk of his final report to a wide-ranging review of the state of football and made a total of seventy-six recommendations and observations for the short, medium and long term. Short-term recommendations included improvement of first aid facilities and ease of movement through gangways; medium-term proposals included the creation of new offences concerning, for example, pitch invasion and the chanting of racialist abuse; long-term proposals included the establishment of all-seat stadiums.

UEFA AND THE COUNCIL OF EUROPE

Of equal importance was the activity taking place in other forums of policy debate. In particular, while the domestic political debate was dominated by the issue of membership and identity cards, debates on hooliganism were taking place in two important international arenas, the Council of Europe and UEFA. Part of the government's response to the Heysel disaster was to encourage UEFA and other governments to examine the arrangements made to cope with an influx of visiting supporters. A key forum for this debate was the Council of Europe, which has a strong tradition of concern with sport and leisure policy. In August 1985, within three months of the deaths at the Heysel stadium, the Council had agreed a convention which aimed to achieve a degree of uniformity between member states in their approach to hooliganism (Council of Europe 1985). It especially aimed to improve the exchange of information between police forces and domestic football authorities, and to encourage the development of measures designed to identify offenders and ensure that fewer went unpunished for incidents of hooliganism. A committee of officials was established to monitor the implementation of the convention which produced a further set of proposals in 1989. The British Minister for Sport took a leading role in the debates in the Council and saw the convention as a complement to his attempts to develop an anti-hooligan policy at home.

In his relationship with UEFA the Minister was less concerned to encourage the development of a complementary policy. His main objective was rather to influence the deliberations of UEFA as a means of adding weight to the pressure that the British government was putting on the FA and Football League to adopt a policy stance which was both more vigorous and more to the government's liking. In the wake of the deaths at Heysel UEFA imposed an indefinite ban on the participation of English clubs in European competitions. One obvious problem with an indefinite ban is to determine the criteria by which the ban might be lifted. By late 1987 there was growing feeling among other UEFA members that English clubs should be readmitted. However, Colin Moynihan saw the UEFA ban as an important incentive for the football authorities to take action on hooliganism – an incentive that would be lost should English clubs be readmitted too soon. As a result Moynihan made it his business to make the government's views known to UEFA and found a generally sympathetic ear in Jacques Georges, UEFA's president. Georges was quoted as declaring, 'if [Moynihan] says no, that is likely to be it . . . the support of the British Government . . . is a condition' (*The Independent*, 4 May 1988). It would therefore seem that despite assertions to the contrary Moynihan and the British government effectively controlled access by English clubs to European football. This was one of the government's strongest cards in its attempts to force the pace of policy implementation regarding hooliganism at domestic matches. This position confirmed the full implications of the final sentence of Mrs Thatcher's statement in the wake of the Heysel disaster that 'If English clubs are to play football in Europe again, they can do so only when their good name, and that of their followers and supporters, has been restored' (House of Commons, *Debates*, vol. 80, cols. 21–3).

The FA renewed its application for readmission in early 1989 for the following season, only to be rebuffed by Georges who again based his rejection on the lack of support from the British government. He summed up UEFA's position in the following terms. 'If the government says no, UEFA cannot say something else. We cannot run European competitions without government participation in security. Then the responsibility would be ours, which is too great a risk' (*The Independent*, 2 February 1989). Part of UEFA's hesitance was undeniably owing to the fact that there were still a number of claims by relatives of the Heysel victims still waiting to come to court. However, it was clear that the FA would have little success if the government remained unsupportive. Moynihan's attitude was uncompromising. 'I cannot believe that they [UEFA] would be wise to admit English clubs at this stage. No new measures have been introduced by football authorities since the disgraceful scenes in West Germany last June' (*The Independent*, 27 February 1989).

UEFA's position became unquestionably more difficult as the 1980s came to an end. First there was the growing conviction among UEFA members that English clubs had suffered enough, that no useful purpose was being served by excluding them any longer, and that European competitions were weaker through their continued absence. The new president of UEFA, Lennart Johansson, who replaced Jacques Georges in 1989, was also more sympathetic to an early return for English clubs. In addition football hooliganism was becoming a serious problem in other European countries. This had the effect of altering the perspective of some UEFA representatives, especially those from Holland and West Germany, on English hooliganism, as it was now a shared experience for many administrators. It also made a policy response of excluding the offending country less acceptable. Second, UEFA was coming under increasing pressure from the European Community Parliament, where a motion was passed calling for court action against UEFA on the grounds that its ban was against the Treaty of Rome. The net effect of these pressures was that, in April 1989, UEFA compromised by deciding to readmit English clubs for the 1990–91 season, subject to two conditions, the first of which was the support of the British government. Whether that support is forthcoming or not depends on the football authorities maintaining the momentum generated by the Taylor Report. The second condition was that English supporters were well behaved at the 1990 World Cup finals in Italy.

Unfortunately a number of incidents occurred at the World Cup that involved English supporters, one of which resulted in the deportation of over 230 supporters by Italian military air transport after an outbreak of rioting in Rimini. In all, nearly 300 English football supporters were deported and a further sixty-six were charged with offences during the tournament, out of a total of 129 charges. At some matches involving the English team over 7,000 police were on duty.

However, in July 1990 UEFA decided unanimously to lift the ban on English clubs unconditionally. The only qualification was that the ban on the participation of Liverpool should continue for at least another year. The justification for the readmission of English teams given by UEFA's president was that 'English supporters are no worse than those in other countries'. Moynihan rationalised his, and the government's, support for readmission on the basis that:

> I have been heartened by the exemplary behaviour of the English players and those thousands of followers who contributed to a relatively peaceful World Cup. Without doubt the relative peace was only achieved by the firm application of predetermined measures and at considerable cost.

> (*The Times*, 11 July 1990)

Both these statements are curious, to say the least. For UEFA the fact that fans in West Germany and Holland now have as poor a record as English fans seemed to be a strange basis for its decision. Equally obscure is the assumption that the good behaviour of the English football team is an indicator of the likely good behaviour of the supporters of English league teams. However, it is

Moynihan's last comment which is the most significant. The price of a 'relatively peaceful' tournament was extremely high and it is debatable how many countries will be willing to have their cities turned into alcohol-free police camps just for the sake of a football match against an English team.

The readmission of English clubs and the less antagonistic attitude of the government reflect not simply the degree of action taken by the football authorities, but also probably reflect the problems facing the government in maintaining its own momentum on the issue. The football authorities have undoubtedly done much over the last five years to adopt a more positive and proactive approach to the problem of hooliganism. In addition, and potentially of greater significance, there is discussion between the FA and the Football League on a possible merger of the two organisations which would do much to placate the critics of the management and leadership provided for football at national level.

Unfortunately there is little evidence that the problem of football hooliganism has been solved. Many of the policy proposals are only in their early days, for example the 'Football in the Community' schemes, while other proposals, such as all-seat stadiums, are many years away. It is therefore likely that part of the explanation of the government's lessening of involvement in the issue is that of 'issue fatigue'. Downs's notion of the issue attention cycle was mentioned at the beginning of this chapter, where it was suggested that the series of disasters associated with football prevented hooliganism moving to the political 'back burner'. The gradual shift of an issue out of the political focus is often caused by the realisation of the costs, and not just the financial costs, of the solution. The Taylor Report not only rejected the government's primary policy response to the problem, the membership scheme, it also made it clear that complex social problems rarely have simple solutions. Faced with the prospect of a much more complex process of issue analysis and policy review, the government has sought to distance itself from the deliberations of the policy network at least until the next crisis.

8

THE DEVELOPMENT OF POLICY TO COMBAT DRUG ABUSE BY ATHLETES

The axiom with track and field athletes was, 'if you don't take it, you don't make it'.

Dr Mario Astaphan[1]

We are getting tired of continued drug abuse. . . . We plan to eradicate this cancer from our midst.

John Smith, Chairman of the Sports Council[2]

In April 1987 Birgit Dressel, the West German heptathlete, died from what a report in *Athletics Weekly* described as 'long term drug abuse'. Dressel had allegedly been taking and mixing over 100 different substances, ranging from harmless homoeopathic remedies to anabolic steroids. The magazine quoted from the report of the West German prosecutor that it was

impossible to retrace the therapy administered by medical experts as it was so diverse and variable. It also included so many mixed drugs and foreign proteins which, taken together, have an inestimable effect on the human body.

(*Athletics Weekly*, 10 October 1987)

The history of drug abuse in sport stretches as far back as the history of sport itself. Hanley (1979) recounts how Greek athletes were thought to have used stimulants to improve their performance as early as the third century BC. More recently, in 1865, canal swimmers in Amsterdam used caffeine-based drugs, while boxers in the late nineteenth century preferred mixtures of brandy and cocaine (Woolley 1987). The first sign that the use of drugs to enhance sporting performance was systematic and regular among athletes rather than exceptional emerged in the

1960s. Unfortunately much of the evidence concerning the scale of drug abuse was and remains anecdotal. Allegations that 30 per cent or even 50 per cent of Olympic athletes have used drugs to enhance their performance are simply allegations. However, what little research there is (mainly North American) does suggest that drug abuse is more than a peripheral issue in sport (Williams 1974; Cooter 1980; Clements 1983; see Ljungqvist 1975 for European data).

The incident which brought drug abuse by athletes to the top of the sports agenda was undoubtedly the discovery that the anabolic steroid, stanozolol, was present in Ben Johnson's urine sample when he won the Olympic 100 metres at the 1988 Olympic Games in a world record time. The subsequent inquiry by the Canadian government made it clear that Johnson's abuse of drugs was not an isolated case and that his doctor and coach were also deeply involved. The reputation of British athletes also was tarnished by the disclosure that traces of frusemide were found in the urine sample of Kerrith Brown, who won a bronze medal in judo at the Seoul Olympics.

In Britain the modern history of drug abuse begins with the death of the ex-world professional road-racing champion Tom Simpson, who died during the 1967 Tour de France. Traces of stimulants were found in his body. More recently, in 1988, Britain's international pole-vaulter Jeff Gutteridge was tested positive for anabolic steroids in out-of-competition testing.

The realisation that drug abuse was a serious problem over a range of sports prompted action both internationally and domestically. At the international level the IOC, in 1962, passed a resolution against 'doping'. In 1967 the IOC Medical Commission was established, one of its aims being to produce a plan to combat drug abuse in sport. Drug testing at the Olympic Games took place, for the first time, at the 1968 winter Games in Grenoble, although on a modest scale. Tests were carried out only for narcotic analgesics and stimulants, as a detection method for anabolic steroids had not yet been developed. Drug testing was also introduced at other major international sporting events at about the same time (the World Cup in 1966 and the Commonwealth Games in 1970).

Parallel to the activity of the IOC, the IAAF was also discussing how to tackle the problem of drug abuse. In 1972 the IAAF formed its Medical Committee and began testing for anabolic steroids at the 1974 European Athletics Championships in Rome. By 1976 the IAAF Medical Committee had established a clear agenda for its anti-doping activities which included refining testing procedures, updating doping regulations, and an education programme. Yet it was not until the late 1970s that testing became systematic and also more professional. In 1978 the Federation introduced a minimum eighteen-month suspension for doping cases and by 1979 it had agreed standardised testing procedures and also the criteria for accreditation of laboratories undertaking tests. In 1980 these guidelines were adopted by the IOC, which also took over the responsibility for accreditation and, since 1988, the annual reaccreditation of laboratories, and also for the updating of the drug testing procedures.

The most important non-sports international body to adopt a prominent role in the campaign against drug abuse was the Council of Europe, which in 1963 published a clear definition of doping. Later, in 1979, the Council adopted a recommendation urging member states to combat drugs in sport and followed this, in 1984, with a European anti-doping charter for sport, which outlined in considerable detail the steps that members should take. More recently the Council of Europe has published an international anti-doping convention designed to reinforce the action by the IOC and calling on governments to take steps to provide legislative support for the anti-drug campaign in sport.

In Britain the Sports Council formed a working party to examine drug abuse in sport in 1965 and a few years later, in 1969, provided support for research, at St Thomas's Hospital, into testing techniques. Although some governing bodies, such as the British Cycling Federation,[3] had become involved in drug testing in the 1960s it was in the 1970s that they became more heavily involved, with, for example, the British Amateur Athletics Board (BAAB) introducing testing at international events in 1975. A major step forward for the British anti-drug campaign was the decision in 1978, by the Sports Council, to fund the research and testing activities of the Chelsea College Drug Control and Teaching Centre, which is the only British testing laboratory accredited by the IOC. During the 1980s the Sports Council refined its guidelines regarding testing and also increased the pressure on governing bodies to introduce anti-doping measures.

THE POLICY CONTEXT

As with many issues in sport the development of a domestic policy towards drug abuse by athletes needs to be examined in the context of a broader international debate and policy process. Indeed, the development of policy at the international level was, and still is, crucial for the achievement of domestic policy objectives regarding drug abuse. Consequently, an important aspect of the examination of the policy process is the establishment and fostering of a pattern of international links between domestic organisations and a variety of international governmental and non-governmental bodies (see Figure 11).

Policy to combat drug abuse by athletes depends not simply on the determination and resources of individual nations or individual sports bodies but on the systematic development of policy and procedures across a range of disparate organisations at the national and international level. The way in which the policy

Figure 11 The institutional context of anti-doping policy

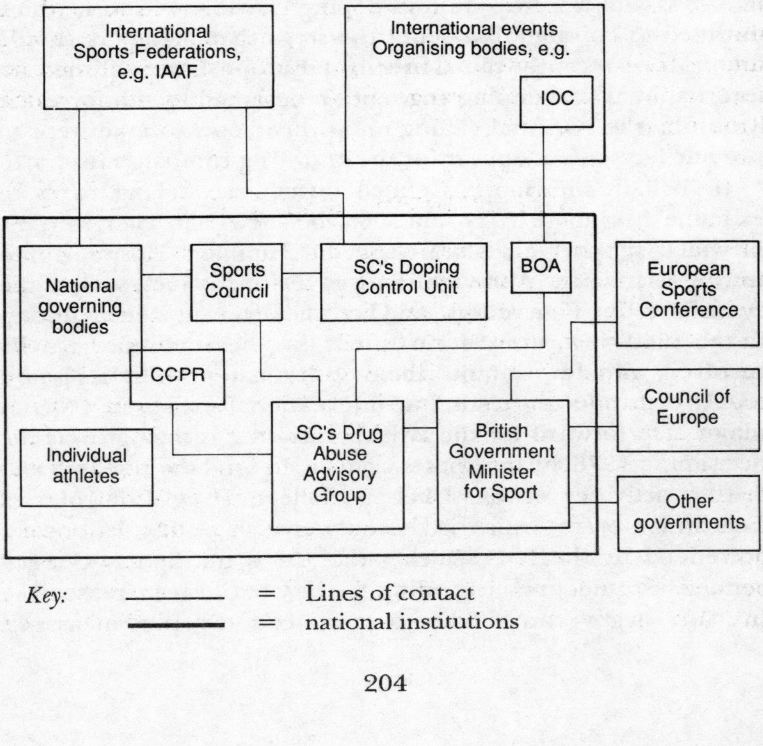

Key:

——————— = Lines of contact

━━━━━━━ = national institutions

initiative moves between organisations and levels, the way in which influence is manifested in the policy arena and the way in which policy choice at one level constrains or stimulates choice at other levels are important elements in the study of the policy process regarding drug abuse. A study of anti-doping policy therefore involves not only the examination of the activities of British institutions and key policy actors, but also an understanding of the way in which actors and organisations in Britain manage the network of international relations essential for the success of domestic policy objectives.

However, care must be taken not to assume that international relations were, and are, being developed in order to provide a vehicle for securing support for domestic objectives regarding drug abuse. International contacts are fostered in order to achieve a wide range of policy goals, for example to affect the location of major international sporting events. Consequently it might be possible to argue, somewhat cynically, that by adopting the moral high ground over an issue such as drug abuse Britain gains an opportunity to influence other policy decisions in sport such as where the 1996 or 2000 Olympic Games will be held. In short, the development of a policy towards drug abuse is not simply a domestic issue, and in the international arena it must be seen in the context of a range of international issues in which Britain has an interest.

ATTITUDES AND VALUES

The focus of this study is on the practical problems of developing and putting into operation a policy designed to eliminate drug abuse by athletes. There is, though, an important debate about the moral basis of prohibiting drug use that needs to be explored briefly, as the questions raised by the debate help to illustrate why the condemnation of drugs in sport has been less than unanimous and why progress, both nationally and internationally, has been uneven.

At first sight the consensus within sport condemning the use of drugs to enhance performance is firm. There are numerous examples of high-minded statements by administrators, politicians and many athletes pointing out the incompatibility between the use of drugs and the ideals on which sport is based. In 1976 Lord Killanin wrote in the foreword to the booklet outlining the IOC's medical controls for the Montreal Olympics that 'Our ideal is the complete and harmonious human being which is the essence of the Olympic movement. We must therefore prevent the creation of artificial men and women' (IOC 1976). Sebastian Coe, speaking on behalf of Olympic athletes in 1981, stated that 'we consider [doping] to be the most shameful abuse of the Olympic idea . . .'.

The early rhetoric regarding drug abuse was full of the high moral tone evident in these quotations, but more recent statements on the abuse of drugs in sport adopt a slightly more pragmatic argument reflecting some of the hesitation and ambiguity apparent within the sporting community. Arguments relying on the moral sensitivity and rectitude of athletes and administrators are coupled with warnings about the health risks of drug abuse or the bad example being set to children. In 1985 Sir Arthur Gold asserted that 'Sport is about health and honesty and the illicit use of drugs is unhealthy and dishonest' (Gold 1985). Sebastian Coe, in launching the Sports Council's leaflet 'Dying to Win' in 1987 emphasised that:

it is vital that we provide better information and education about drugs and their dangers. *Dying to Win* gets the message across very bluntly that it is simply not worth anyone risking their life to win at sport.

(Sports Council 1987)

Colin Moynihan, arguing for a strong anti-doping stand by the governing bodies, notes that 'Abuse can lead to serious physical consequences. . . . Moreover, there are urgent ethical considerations: drug abuse contravenes what is meant by sport. It is a form of cheating.' Finally, in the DOE report Moynihan and Coe argue that:

The problem is no longer simply an ethical one for sport. There are broader considerations especially as regards youngsters keen to emulate their sporting heroes . . . [It] is patently wrong for the misuse of drugs in any context to be given the slightest measure of acceptability.

(Moynihan and Coe 1987: 1)

The Dubin Inquiry in Canada (where a major focus was Ben Johnson's drug abuse) and the Coni Report in Britain (on allegations of drug abuse by British athletes) both suggest that deeply ambivalent attitudes towards the use of drugs in sport exist and that the early consensus on opposition to drug use was more apparent than real. Few sportsmen would publicly support the sensational assertion by the American field athlete Harold Connolly that 'The overwhelming majority of athletes I know would do anything and take anything, short of killing themselves, to improve athletic performance',[4] but there are suggestions that many accept that drug taking is increasingly a part of preparation and training in a wide range of sports. In the wake of the Johnson scandal Philip Halpern, who prosecuted the British Olympic medallist, David Jenkins, remarked that 'Throughout late September, October and November I would say that 70 per cent or more of the drugs we have confiscated have been Winstrol V'.[5] Winstrol V is a brand name of the veterinary form of stanozolol, which Johnson used and which, according to the IOC's own tests, is one of the most difficult steroids to detect (Donike 1987).

Not only is there growing acceptance that the extent of drug use has probably been seriously underestimated but there are also signs that the fundamental objection to the use of drugs, that it is unethical and a form of cheating, is being challenged at both the amateur and the professional levels of sport and among administrators as well as athletes. For example, Steven Baddeley, one of Britain's leading badminton players, argues for a more selective approach to controlling drug abuse. He dismisses many of the arguments regarding drug abuse in sport as 'paternalistic' and as based on 'an outdated hang-over from the days of amateurism' (Baddeley 1988). R. H. Nicholson, deputy director of the Institute of Medical Ethics and life member of the National Rifle Association, suggests that there 'are no overriding ethical reasons that force one to conclude either that drug taking by an individual sportsman is necessarily unethical, or that the governing bodies of sport must have rules to prevent and punish drug taking' (1987: 29). He argues that sport is inherently unfair and that the use of drugs is simply one dimension of unfairness. This is a view that has received a measure of sympathy if not direct support. A number of sports writers and athletes have highlighted the advantages accruing to athletes from rich countries who have access to computer-aided training programmes and the latest equipment. Formula One motor racing, pole-vaulting, swimming, tennis and cycle racing are only a few of the sports in which wealth and the consequent access that it gives to high-technology research constitute serious barriers to 'fair' competition.

Nicholson also suggests that in professional sport the aim is to make money and that the way this is achieved is by the production of a spectacle for the audience and for the sponsors. 'If the organisers of professional sport do not consider that drug use spoils the spectacle, then – provided the sportsman is fully aware of the drug's effects – there seems to be little objection to drug use' (1986: 2). This would certainly seem to be the case in professional cycling, where, when Pedro Delgado narrowly avoided charges of drug abuse during the 1988 Tour de France, not one of his fellow riders voiced any objection to his continued participation in the race.[6] (See also Brown 1984, Woodland 1980 and Simon 1984 for further discussion of the ethical basis for the condemnation of drug use.)

Developing Nicholson's argument, one might suggest that the notion of 'the sporting ideal' is largely a modern-day myth and that in the late twentieth century professional sport has much more in common with other forms of professional entertainment such as music, acting and dance and should abide by a different set of ethical values.

AGREEING A LIST OF PROSCRIBED DRUGS

The ambiguous response from sportsmen and women and the debate over the ethical basis for denying drug use have both affected progress in developing an effective policy towards the issue. Although policy statements have been published, progress in agreeing a core list of proscribed drugs, testing procedures and sanctions has been much slower. Of the three problems, that of developing a core list of proscribed drugs has probably been the easiest to achieve.[7] In this, as in many other aspects of policy development, the Sports Council has taken a leading role, backed by the strong political support from the Minister. The 1987 DOE publication on the misuse of drugs in sport was a joint report by the Minister, Colin Moynihan and the then vice-chairman of the Sports Council, Sebastian Coe. The report includes the list of proscribed drugs and procedures prepared by the International

Olympic Committee's Medical Commission in 1986 (Moynihan and Coe 1987). This list identifies the classes of drugs prohibited and covers stimulants such as amphetamine and the more common stimulants, including caffeine (present in coffee), and many proprietary cold and hay fever preparations; narcotics, most commonly used as painkillers, including morphine and more common drugs such as codeine which are used in many cough and cold preparations; anabolic steroids, which can increase muscle bulk and may also be used to enable more intensive training, including stanozolol, which Ben Johnson was alleged to have used in the 1988 Olympics; beta-blockers, designed to relax muscles and reduce tension; diuretics, used to flush drugs out of the body or to reduce weight quickly in weight-related events, including frusemide, which was found in the urine sample of the Briton, Kerrith Brown, after he had won the bronze medal at the 1988 Olympics; and finally some hormones which can be used to increase tissue growth. The list also covers banned practices such as blood doping and urine substitution.

The range of drugs included on the IOC list, the basis for Sports Council policy and that of most countries, is dependent upon technology and money. In general the IOC will, logically enough, only include a new drug on its list when satisfactory testing methods have been developed. For example, anabolic steroids were known to be used by athletes for many years (possibly since the 1964 Olympic Games) before Professor Raymond Brooks and his colleagues, in Britain in 1973, announced that they had developed an effective test for anabolic steroids. Scientists are currently refining an effective test for a new drug, erythroproetin (referred to as EPO), which speeds up the body's production of red blood cells, which in turn enables the athlete to absorb more oxygen. Surprisingly EPO was added to the list of IOC doping classes in April 1990 even though there is still no unequivocal detection method. A similar problem arises with hGH, a growth hormone, which, though detectable, poses the problem for scientists of deciding what level of hGH is 'normal'.

The adequacy of the IOC list is highly dependent on the outcome of a process of technological competition between the pharmaceutical industry and the research funded by the IOC and, in Britain, the Sports Council. The mismatch in resources is such that a number of sports administrators are questioning whether sport has the resources to keep up with the development of new drugs. Manfred Donike, a leading researcher on drug abuse in sport and member of the IOC Medical Commission, argues that research to counter drug abuse in sport is not moving fast enough to keep up with pharmaceutical advances (*The Independent*, 7 February 1989). In a similar vein Arne Ljungqvist, chairman of the IAAF's medical committee, was recently reported as predicting a time when the cost of policing drug abuse would become too high for sport (ibid., 7 June 1989). About 40,000 tests are conducted each year throughout the world at a cost of approximately £90 per test. Further evidence of the scale of the resource problem comes from the most recent IOC exercise in laboratory reaccreditation in 1989. Of the twenty-two laboratories tested, only fifteen remain on the IOC's approved list. Of the seven not on the revised list, five were dropped because they could not meet the standards required by the IOC while the other two withdrew because of the expense involved in maintaining the laboratory to IOC standards. As a result there are no accredited laboratories in any Third World country and only five outside Europe.[8]

Criticism of the list of proscribed drugs has been slight and has mainly concerned the inclusion of specific drugs, such as beta-blockers. For example, the World Professional Billiards and Snooker Association was not enthusiastic about adding beta-blockers to its own list of banned drugs in early 1988. A number of professional snooker players argued that the ban was inappropriate because snooker is not an Olympic sport and that its participants play longer. Nicholson is also less than enthusiastic about the ban on beta-blockers applying to full-bore target rifle shooting, which is an Olympic sport. He argues that the evidence suggests that expert shots gain little from the use of beta-blockers and that 'It is arguable that beta-blockers would make the sport fairer [because] it produces most enhancement of performance in the less skilled marksman . . . [and would therefore make] the competition more equal' (1987: 35). The debate over the use of beta-blockers was brought into sharp relief during the modern pentathlon events of the 1984 Olympics. The modern pentathlon involves a mix of sports, one of which is shooting, where beta-blockers are alleged to give an advantage. While beta-blockers were not banned by the IOC in 1984 team doctors had to certify that an athlete needed the drug for health reasons. After the physically exhausting events such as swimming and cross-country running, but before the shooting event, Donohoe and Johnson report, 'To the amazement of officials, managers came forward with doctor's certificates covering whole teams' (1986: 85).

Where broader criticisms are made of the list of proscribed drugs the disagreement tends to focus on a distinction between performance-enhancing and restorative drugs. Examples of restorative drugs include those used to control an illness such as asthma (many anti-asthmatic preparations contain ephedrine, which is banned), and also those used to reduce pain (such as the mild narcotic analgesics like codeine). At present the IOC will not accept a doctor's opinion that an athlete needs to take a particular drug, such as ephedrine, simply to allow him or her to compete on equal terms with other athletes. Malcolm Bottomley, a member of the BAAB's Medical Committee, expressed concern 'about the present list of banned drugs and the sometimes apparently unnecessary restrictions that the regulations place on therapeutic options' (1987: 210). He argues for a quantitative analysis which enables small doses of certain drugs, for which there are no permitted alternatives, to be used for therapeutic purposes. His concluding comments highlight the potential ethical dilemmas facing doctors. 'There is, in our view, a possibility that over-enthusiastic inclusion of drugs in the banned list without a careful and reasoned analysis could constitute interference with the patients' right to satisfactory medical care' (1987: 211).[9]

The debate regarding the use of drugs to control pain is more complex and raises wider ethical issues. At the 1988 Olympics Peter Elliot, who won a silver medal, was in such pain that he had to have five injections to enable him to run seven races in nine days. Elliot returned home on crutches and needed a considerable period of physiotherapy. It is a fine ethical distinction between the use of drugs to suppress pain and their use to improve muscle strength. Both alter the body's natural state and both enhance performance.

Part of the explanation of the inflexibility of the IOC's list is that many drugs perform more than one function, for example frusemide, which Kerrith Brown was alleged to have used, kills pain by reducing swelling, but may also be used to flush out the traces of other drugs. However, the IOC's attitude in allowing local painkillers is more difficult to explain and must pose sports doctors with a serious ethical dilemma of prescribing drugs not to cure an injury but to suppress its symptoms so that athletes can compete and possibly inflict more injury on themselves.

In general, snooker and shooting apart, there has been little public disagreement over the list of banned drugs. At national level most governing bodies of sport have, as recommended by the Sports Council, adopted the IOC's guidelines or those of their international sports federation/governing body (ISF) and incorporated them into their own regulations and codes of conduct. Increasingly the IOC list is being seen as the international standard and there are only relatively minor differences between the lists produced by the IOC, the ISFs and British governing bodies. For example, the IAAF permits the therapeutic use of codeine where the IOC does not; the modern pentathlon has added sedatives, such as valium, to its list; the International Rugby Board has added lignocaine, a local anaesthetic, to its list; the World Professional Billiards and Snooker Association (WPBSA) allows selective use of cardio-beta blockers if permission is applied for in advance. Cycling, through the International Federation of Professional Cycling, bans a broader range of steroids than other sports but also wants a revision of the list to allow some mild pain killers such as codeine on the grounds that 'It's unjust that in the anti-doping battle there is no difference in [the] manner that the amateurs and professionals are treated' (*The Independent*, 23 August 1988). The International Cycling Union has recently removed beta-blockers from its list of proscribed drugs.

The role of the Sports Council is of central importance in explaining the general consensus among British governing bodies against drug abuse. The Council is also important in stimulating policy activity at the international level. At the domestic level it must be acknowledged that linking the continuation of Sports Council grant with compliance has encouraged a number of otherwise reluctant governing bodies to toe the line. In addition the Council has initiated a number of specific inquiries into drug abuse in particular sports. The latest is an inquiry into power- and weight-lifting under the chairmanship of

Norman Jacobs following the positive drug tests on Dean Wiley, a double Commonwealth champion, and two Welsh lifters at the 1990 Auckland Commonwealth Games. The unequivocal lead from the Council has received strong and sustained support from the Minister. As Moynihan and Coe make clear:

> the Government and the Sports Council have to be concerned that their investment of taxpayers' money in sports' governing bodies is not even remotely or indirectly linked to any unsatisfactory arrangements those bodies have for dealing with drug abuse.

(1987: 2)

At the national level the Minister has not only been important in reinforcing the Sports Council's resolve on the issue, but he has also been important in placing the issue on the agendas of other departments in government for whom it is a peripheral issue. For example, Moynihan has pushed the issue on to the agenda of the Foreign Office, through his role in the Council of Europe, and that of the Home Office, by encouraging the Home Secretary's Ministerial Group on the Misuse of Drugs to consider making the possession of anabolic steroids without a prescription an offence under the Misuse of Drugs Act 1971.[10]

The Minister's strong support is crucial to the long-term success of the campaign if it is accepted that an anti-drug policy can be successful at national level only if it is complemented at international level by a similar enthusiasm and commitment. Colin Moynihan has taken a clear lead at international level, specifically through the Council of Europe, to build up and then to maintain the momentum of the campaign. For example, the Minister was a prime mover in encouraging the Council of Europe to prepare a European Anti-doping Convention in 1989, and he was the first Minister to sign it.

Given the significance of the international context for the success of domestic policy towards drug abuse it is not surprising that the Sports Council has, in recent years, refined its capacity to participate at international level. Two organisations are of particular importance, the Council of Europe (particularly its Expert Group on Doping) and the European Sports Conference (ESC). The Council of Europe has been involved in discussing doping policy since the late 1970s, with the passing of the

European Charter on Doping in 1984 a significant landmark in the development of an international policy. The ESC, because its membership includes East European countries, is a valuable vehicle for extending debate on sports issues beyond the membership of the Council of Europe. The Conference's Anti-doping Working Group, established in 1985, has been particularly important in debating and harmonising national anti-drug regulations and campaigns and thereby complementing the work of the Council of Europe, the IAAF and the IOC. The ESC is likely to become even more important following the collapse of the communist governments in Eastern Europe and the strong allegations of systematic official drug abuse by athletes in countries such as East Germany. Of particular importance for Britain's contribution to policy discussion is the role of the Sports Council in providing the secretariat of the Anti-doping Working Group.

Progress towards an agreed list of proscribed drugs, involving as it does the co-ordination of the pace and content of policy processes at a number of levels and among a diverse set of institutions, has been steady, if somewhat slow. Unfortunately there has been much greater difficulty in getting agreement on testing procedures and their effective implementation.

TESTING PROCEDURES

Despite six years of pressure from the Sports Council on governing bodies to introduce rigorous testing procedures there is still a considerable lack of standardisation in the ways that sportsmen are selected for testing, the frequency of testing and the circumstances under which tests are administered.

In determining its policy on the list of proscribed drugs the Sports Council follows the lead given by the IAAF and the IOC and, as was shown, there are only minor variations between the lists of the major governing bodies. With regard to testing procedures the situation is not so clear-cut. The main concern of the IOC is to establish a rigorous programme of testing during the Olympic Games. By contrast the Sports Council and domestic and international governing bodies are concerned that athletes remain drug-free at all phases of their career, not just during events.

Among the international governing bodies the IAAF has been one of the most prominent, often working closely with the IOC. During a season the IAAF would expect to carry out tests at all world and area (continental) championships, including the Grand Prix series of meetings. In total this amounts to some twenty meetings per year plus another forty evening meetings. At the last World Championships, which involved about 1,600 athletes, the Federation carried out approximately 200 tests. Tests were carried out on the basis of testing all athletes in the first three places plus a random selection. For an evening meeting the IAAF carries out, on average, eight to twelve tests. The number of athletes tested is limited, in general, by the high cost of testing, but more specifically by the type of meeting, the number of athletes participating and the history of drug abuse in the sport. As well as policing its own events the Federation monitors the administration of its anti-drug policy in member countries. Monitoring takes the form of an annual questionnaire and is supplemented by the provision of training courses, often in conjunction with the IOC Medical Commission. Financial assistance is also made available to members that lack the money to mount their own anti-drug programme.

The Sports Council has also devoted considerable resources, both financial and political, to devising a regime of testing which encompasses a broad range of sports and covers the peak years of an athlete's competitive career. This has proved, and continues to prove, to be a particularly difficult objective to achieve. Guidance from the Sports Council is clearest with regard to the conduct of the actual test, the involvement of the governing body, the right of appeal, etc. (see, for example, Sports Council for Wales 1988; Hoppner 1987; Ljungqvist 1987). There is less guidance, and consequently considerable variation between governing bodies, concerning the frequency of tests, the proportion of athletes to be tested in any given period and the level of competition at which testing should start. The Sports Council is well aware of these problems, but faces the difficulty that a standard set of guidelines is not the answer, as virtually each sport needs a testing regime tailored to its own particular character and organisation.

The implementation of policy regarding procedures for testing can be divided into two phases. The first phase, from 1984 to 1987, was characterised by a strong lead by the Minister for Sport, the Sports Council and major British governing bodies such as the British Amateur Athletics Board and was generally targeted at the sports community as a whole. In 1984 the Sports Council announced that governing bodies were to be required to introduce drug tests. The Council used a number of tactics in order to achieve compliance, the most significant of which was making compliance a condition of continued grant aid to governing bodies. In addition the Council offered to provide a 100 per cent subsidy to cover the testing costs incurred by governing bodies. The Council has also invested heavily in the research and development of scientific methods necessary for effective testing (£500,000 over the last ten years or so). In the financial year 1989–90 the Council expected to spend £500,000 on all aspects of its anti-drug campaign, which included money for an educational programme, the subsidy to cover the cost of testing and its investment in scientific research.

However, in 1985 Dick Jeeps, then chairman of the Sports Council, reported that 'even with 100 per cent subsidies from the Sports Council to meet the testing costs only twenty-five sports have carried out testing since 1979 and some of those on a very, very limited scale' (Sports Council 1986: 1). The limited success of the Council's 1984 initiative is also reflected in the DOE/Sports Council paper (Moynihan and Coe 1987), which acknowledges that too many loopholes exist and that the potential for evasion and manipulation is great. The paper makes a series of recommendations about the need for tighter procedures which would make evasion more difficult. Part of the problem facing the Council in implementing its policy is that a number of the most recalcitrant sports share one or more of the following characteristics: they have weak governing bodies, they are professional sports and they have strong international governing bodies which eclipse the national bodies.

Tennis is an example of a sport which exhibits the first two characteristics and, to a degree, the third as well. The sport is dominated, at the international circuit level, by the Association of Tennis Professionals (ATP) and the Women's International Tennis Association (WITA), the men's and women's players' unions, which agreed to limited testing only in 1989. There has been testing on the men's professional circuit, but not the women's, for 'recreational' drugs (a euphemism for marijuana and cocaine) since 1986, but the ATP and the WITA agreed to test for steroids only in 1989. Part of the motivation for accepting a degree of testing was the decision to include tennis in the 1988 Olympics. Regarding the domestic game, as recently as 1986 the All England Lawn Tennis and Croquet Club, which organises the Wimbledon competition, was heavily criticised for its 'relaxed' approach to drug testing. It agreed that tests would be carried out, but after discussion with the men's professional organisation it was agreed that tests would be for drugs of addiction only and that any positive results would not be reported, rather the individual concerned would be required to seek medical advice. However, the amateur game in Britain, controlled by the Lawn Tennis Association (LTA), has been subject to more rigorous testing through the IOC-approved laboratories since 1988. The All England Lawn Tennis and Croquet Club, and the Wimbledon competition, do not come under the jurisdiction of the LTA.

There are a number of other examples of the problems faced in achieving a consistent approach to testing procedures from governing bodies. For example, the International Weightlifting Federation, prompted by a series of positive drug tests, has introduced a testing procedure. However, the particular procedure adopted, known as 'the steroid profile procedure', is highly controversial and is not approved by the IOC. A rather different situation exists in professional football, although it too is a cause of concern. In England the FA has been conducting tests for over ten years but only 700 tests had been carried out between 1979 and 1988, which is an extremely small sample. The Scottish FA agreed to introduce testing only recently, in 1989.

The second phase of the Council's strategy dates from 1988 and is marked by a greater emphasis on negotiating a testing regime with individual governing bodies and refining existing procedures. This shift in emphasis is partly a result of a recognition that testing regimes must be tailored to the characteristics of each sport. Consequently the Sports Council will expect each governing body to provide both a competition calendar and a training calendar (to be updated every six months). The Council will also expect the governing body to provide details of its proposed testing regime as a basis for discussion. The testing regime for a particular sport will cover the

THE GOVERNMENT AND POLITICS OF SPORT

level or ranking at which testing should start, for example club, county or national team level. The nature of the regime will also be affected by the organisation of the sport, for example whether it has a squad system of training, such as in football, or whether training is largely an individual activity as in most athletics. Regular squad training provides the Sports Council's sampling officers with a number of opportunities to carry out tests. However, where training is organised on an individual basis the problems of testing are much greater and a detailed calendar of each athlete's training routine is required.

Against this background of negotiation with individual governing bodies the Sports Council is also monitoring developments in, and of, sports which are currently subject only to limited testing or are not required to carry out tests to determine whether they should be included. For example, as volleyball has grown steadily in popularity the question of whether it should be subject to more extensive testing is raised. Testing might become more extensive if the British team were to qualify for the Olympic Games. Similarly, the growing success of rugby union leagues may lead to the introduction of testing at club level in the next two or three years (there is already testing at international level).

In both phases of policy implementation the Sports Council has been strongly supported by the Minister, who has used his position to draw attention to those sports that have proved dilatory in compliance. For example, while the Sports Council offered to assist with testing at Wimbledon the Minister was also drawing public attention to the poor record on testing at this major event. Colin Moynihan has made similar public statements about weight lifting, professional football and snooker (*Observer*, 7 July 1989; *The Times*, 23 November 1989; *The Independent*, 3 December 1989; *The Independent*, 8 January 1988).

The most recent initiative from the Council is the introduction, from April 1988, of random out-of-season drug testing. The tests will cover the sports (approximately thirty) considered to be most prone to drug abuse. This decision follows a pilot scheme carried out in 1985 by the BAAB, with the aid of Council funds, which led in April 1986 to the introduction of out-of-season testing in athletics. Within athletics the scheme is designed to cover the top ten men and women in each event, approximately 650 athletes in all. It is a condition of eligibility for selection for international competition that an athlete agrees to participate in the scheme. A random selection of athletes is made each month and about 150 test were carried out in the first full year of operation. The scheme is designed to cover athletes who are training abroad and the Sports Council is aiming to establish a series of reciprocal agreements with the drug testing bodies abroad. So far agreements have been reached with a number of Scandinavian countries.

For random out-of-season testing to be successful and to spread to other sports it is essential that the policy and procedure are adopted as widely as possible within the sporting world. To this end the General Association of International Sports Federations lent its weight to the extension of testing at its 1988 conference, as did the European Sports Conference when it met in Sofia in 1989. Later, in April 1989, the IAAF council decided to impose random testing on all international athletes, thereby by-passing those remaining countries where random out-of-season testing does not take place. In May 1990, in one of the first examples of random testing by an international governing body, an IAAF 'flying squad' of drug testers visited the Soviet Union and tested sixteen athletes; all tests were negative. Similar 'flying squad' teams were subsequently sent to Italy and France.

In assessing the success of the policy a number of questions need to be considered: first, are governing bodies and individual athletes obliged to take part; second, how will the implementation be monitored, and third, how are positive results dealt with? On the admission of John Smith, the then chairman of the Council, there is no legal obligation to participate either on the individual sportsmen or women or on their governing body. Smith 'anticipated the full co-operation from the governing bodies, and hoped they would penalise individual members' (*The Independent*, 3 November 1987). However, as has been shown, not all governing bodies are as committed as the BAAB or have as much authority over their members. Equally important other countries may be less willing or financially able to undertake reciprocal arrangements covering out-of-season testing. Richard Pound, a vice-president of the IOC, has even suggested that the IAAF itself was guilty of suppressing positive drug tests at the 1983 World Championships (*The Independent*, 10 May 1989). It must be remembered that in order for punitive action to be taken against athletes caught using drugs there must be strict adherence to the IOC procedures. There must be doubts about the technical capacity of drug testing authorities in those countries (the vast majority) that do not have an accredited IOC laboratory.

It is not only abroad that the capacity of the testing authority must be questioned. The Sports Council, which trains and provides most sampling officers (testers), is finding them difficult to recruit and train fast enough to meet demand, despite conducting almost 3,500 tests in 1989 across the range of sports. The question needs to be asked as to what the optimum number of tests is per year to make the taking of some of the steroids in the 17-alphamethyl group, which can allegedly be taken as close as fifteen days before a test and not be detected, an unacceptable risk for athletes. It must also be remembered that Ben Johnson admitted taking drugs during 1986 and 1987, when he was tested a total of seventeen times without being caught. Obviously the effectiveness of the policy depends on the human resources and finance available to the Sports Council and also to the only IOC-accredited testing centre in Britain, at King's College (previously Chelsea College).

A further problem concerns the growing likelihood of legal challenge to the results of tests. Legal challenges are likely to focus on the procedure followed as well as the conduct of the 'hearing' by the governing body. The experience of the four British competitors charged with drug abuse in Seoul has prompted the BOA to include lawyers as part of their staff for the 1992 Olympics. It is suggested that three of the four accused athletes were able to clear their name of 'dishonest intent' by having access to appropriate advice (*The Independent*, 20 June 1989). Both Sandra Gasser and Jeff Gutteridge took their cases, unsuccessfully, to the High Court to challenge the decision of the governing body. In order to make such a challenge difficult to sustain governing bodies must ensure that their procedures are beyond reproach. As Michael Beloff QC is reported as observing, 'Natural justice and its twin pillars – the rule against bias and the right to be heard – certainly apply to the proceedings of sporting bodies. [Yet fair play was] often conspicuously absent from the procedures of governing bodies' (*The Independent*, 3 October 1988). In a number of countries there have already been legal challenges to governing bodies who have banned or suspended athletes found to have used drugs.[11]

Of all the problems facing the effective implementation of the anti-doping policy it is in this area of sanctions that the greatest ambiguity still remains. Within the Sports Council Sebastian Coe (then vice-chairman), on the one hand, advocated a 'life ban' for those found guilty of drug abuse while on the other, John Smith (then chairman of the Sports Council) talked merely of hoping that governing bodies might refuse to select the guilty for major events. John Smith subsequently went on record as recommending a life ban for athletes found guilty of serious misuse of drugs. Within athletics there also seems to be a degree of uncertainty concerning the appropriate response to a positive drug test. Sir Arthur Gold, vice-chairman of the British Olympic Association, wants suspension for life while Nigel Cooper, until recently the BAAB's secretary, wants each case dealt with on its merits. This confusion is not helped by the willingness of the International Amateur Athletics Federation to settle for a two year suspension for a first offence. Similar problems arise concerning the different penalties dealt out to amateurs and to professionals. In cycling, for example, an amateur caught taking drugs will be expelled from the race, but a professional rider will be fined, relegated to the back of the race and receive a suspended suspension!

PENALTIES

It is confusion like this that fuels the suspicion that when positive results are found the governing bodies will lack the resolve to take exemplary action. There are, as yet, few reports of the actions of disciplinary committees in dealing with drug abusers and it is therefore unwise to predict how they will react. However, recent examples show some of the difficulties.

In April 1988, in a random out-of-competition test, Jeff Gutteridge became the first amateur in athletics to be tested positive for drugs in British history. In July the same year he was effectively banned for life. The standard penalty imposed by the IAAF is a two year ban, after which the athlete's national governing body may apply for his or her reinstatement. The BAAB made it clear to Gutteridge that no such application would be made on his behalf. Given the strong statements by many leading actors in the anti-drug policy process, the penalty imposed on Gutteridge is not surprising. However, the penalty is exceptional when comparisons are made with other countries, where few athletes have received a life ban for a first offence. The norm is still a six to twelve month ban for a first offence and one to three years for a second offence. Such exemplary action by the British authorities is understandable but might be difficult to sustain if their lead is not followed by other countries, the ISFs and particularly by the IOC. In 1988 the IOC considered the issue of penalties and attempted to link the severity of the penalty to the gravity of the offence. It suggested that a distinction should be made between serious drug offences, such as the use of amphetamines, and minor offences, such as the use of ephedrine. For the serious drug abuse the recommended penalty was a two year ban for the first offence and a life ban for a subsequent offence. For the less serious abuse of drugs the penalty for a first offence should be a three month ban, two years for a second offence, and a life ban for a third offence. In the next few years it is likely that domestic and international governing bodies will have to follow the lead of the IOC and devise a tariff of penalties to cover the possible permutations of extent and circumstances relating to individual offences.

The case of Ben Johnson highlights many of the underlying tensions involved in punishing drug abuse. In accordance with IAAF rules Johnson was suspended for two years following his positive drug test in Seoul. The ban would therefore expire in September 1990 and he would be eligible to compete in international events again. The two year ban, recently increased from eighteen months, has been criticised by a number of athletes who suspect that many banned athletes can use the time during which they are suspended to train, using drugs, without any chance of being tested, and then return to competition stronger than ever. The IAAF, however, requires suspended athletes to submit to regular testing during their period of suspension. The Canadian Olympic Association, the Canadian government and the Canadian Track and Field Association have all stated that Johnson will not represent Canada at the 1992 Olympics, and that he may never represent Canada again. However, this is not as clear-cut as it may sound, as Johnson has a number of ways of continuing his career. First, Juan Samaranch, president of the

IOC, commented that Johnson should not be treated more severely than any other athlete. He has also gone on record as stating that he would like to see Johnson participate in the 1992 Barcelona Olympics. In this situation Johnson could apply to participate as an individual rather than as a representative of Canada. A second option is to represent Jamaica, his country of birth. Jamaica's Prime Minister has reportedly made this suggestion to Johnson. A third possibility is that Johnson competes outside the IAAF and Olympic circuit. Johnson has received a number of offers involving a rematch against Carl Lewis.

Not only does the Johnson episode highlight the difficulty of making a life ban effective but it also raises a further issue of the status of his previous victories and medals. Johnson has, for example, admitted that he took drugs prior to his record-breaking World Championship victory in Rome in 1987. Because IAAF rules did not allow the retrospective removal of records or medals the result must stand. In September 1989 the IAAF partially closed this gap and amended its rules to allow it to remove the recognition of records retrospectively from athletes found guilty of drug abuse. In addition the IAAF has also suggested that every sponsorship contract should include a clause that allows the sponsor to withdraw from the contract if the athlete is found to be using drugs. Nevertheless Johnson will still keep his title of world champion owing to doubts within the IAAF about the legality of the retrospective removal of titles.

CONCLUSION

At the beginning of this chapter it was suggested that the development of a co-ordinated policy to combat drug abuse was intimately linked to an examination of the establishment and fostering of a pattern of international links between domestic organisations and a variety of international governmental and non-governmental bodies. In Britain the lead within the policy community has been relatively clear, authoritative and consistent. The Sports Council has used its financial power (and the financial dependence of most governing bodies), its technical resources and its political authority to give a powerful lead within the domestic arena. It has done much to persuade domestic governing bodies to develop a policy towards the problem. If a criticism can be levelled at the Sports Council it is that by fulfilling such a central role in the testing procedures it runs the risk of failing to enable governing bodies to build up expertise. There can be few British governing bodies that would have the expertise to implement a similar anti-doping policy should the Sports Council for some reason have to withdraw its resources and support.

The Sports Council has also, through the active involvement of the Minister, been able to give a strong lead at international level through such bodies as the Council of Europe, the European Sports Conference, GAISF, the IAAF and the IOC. In the short history of the campaign against drug abuse by athletes there are clear achievements to be noted, many of which owe much to the persistence of the Sports Council and other British sports organisations. However, it is undoubtedly early days yet in the attempt to rid sport of drugs.

Progress towards a uniform international and comprehensive anti-doping policy is similar to the progress of a wartime convoy. The rapidity of progress is dictated by the speed of the slowest ship; attempts, by the faster ships, to steam ahead only leave gaps to be exploited by the enemy; during the journey the resolve of the convoy is being challenged by constant probing of its defences. While considerable progress has been made, policy formation and implementation are still in their early days.

Undoubtedly the test for the international sports community is whether it has the capacity to deal with drug abuse by wealthy athletes at the peak of their career. While the major international sports bodies have altered their rules to make them more consistent there are still probably enough loopholes to make cheating through the use of drugs attractive. This poses a particular problem for the Sports Council and for British governing bodies such as the BAAB. As sport becomes more professionalised and international in character it may well be that not only will athletes be able to move outside the scope of national organisations but also the organisation and administration of sporting events will move from control by governing bodies towards control by professional players, agents and managers, as has been the case to a noticeable extent in tennis, boxing and snooker. It is therefore possible that the campaign to combat drug abuse may be overtaken by longer-term changes in the way sport is organised and financed.

9

SPORT POLICY FOR SCHOOL-AGE CHILDREN

Sport can help man make the best use of all that education has to offer him: it is life as it could and should be.

Philip Noel-Baker[1]

It is *not* the responsibility of PE teachers to produce the elite young sportspersons of national standard within school time and at the expense of the rest of the pupils in their school.

M. Skinsley (1987: 58)

The school years are an obviously important period in introducing children to the enjoyment and satisfaction to be gained from active participation in sport. The profits of many leisure centres and the fortunes of many clubs rest on the steady flow of enthusiastic older pupils and school leavers. The school-age group has the highest level of participation of any age group. Yet where does the strategic planning to meet the needs of this group take place? Which organisation sees itself as having the prime responsibility for fostering the clear enthusiasm for sport that exists among schoolchildren?

The purpose of this chapter is to examine the extent to which a policy for the sporting needs of this age group exists and who is involved in forming the policy. At first glance the picture regarding overall responsibility is unclear, as a number of organisations can claim an interest in the sporting and recreational development of the young, including the Sports Council, the Department of Education and Science, local authority recreation and education departments, the CCPR, governing bodies of sport, the youth service and the National Children's Play and Recreation Unit. Each of these organisations brings a different set of attitudes and values into the policy arena and consequently has its own definitions of the issues involved and its own set of preferred solutions. The chapter examines first of all the recent attempts to raise the profile of the issue; secondly it examines the range of organisations with an interest in children's sport and the factors that affect their approach to the issue; and finally the chapter evaluates the attempts by the Sports Council to provide a focus for policy development and the difficulties it faces in terms of policy implementation.

THE EMERGENCE OF THE ISSUE OF SPORT FOR SCHOOL-AGE CHILDREN

The growing concern with the provision of sporting opportunities for young people can be traced to a number of organisations and can also be seen as a subsidiary element to a number of wider debates.[2] Of particular importance has been the Central Council of Physical Recreation. The prime role of the Council is to act as the representative voice of sport and as such it is able to speak on behalf of the major governing bodies and organisations with an interest in school sport, including teaching unions and youth work bodies. Bringing the issue of school sport on to the agenda of the Sports Council is due, at least in part, to the persistence of the Central Council. As early as 1980 Peter Lawson, the CCPR's General Secretary, called for a public inquiry into sport in schools. The Council reflected a range of concerns evident among governing bodies of sport and other interested organisations, which included the decline in team sport, the pressure to reduce the timetable allocation to PE, and the use of non-specialist PE staff to supervise physical education classes.

The question of sport in school became more urgent for governing bodies owing to the coincidence of three unrelated factors. First, the governing bodies of the major sports began to realise that the sport interests of young people were steadily broadening both within the physical education curriculum and outside school time. The traditional post-war diet of football, hockey and rugby in the winter and cricket, netball and athletics in the summer began to be significantly modified in schools in the early 1970s. Only swimming retained its traditional prominence in the curriculum. Athletics and the traditional team sports slowly began to appreciate that they were having to compete with other, newer sports for the pool of talented youngsters. The second factor concerned demographic change and the decline in the number of young people which began to make itself felt in secondary schools in the mid 1980s. This factor compounded the first, as not only were more sports competing for the pool of talented young sportsmen and women, but the size of the pool was also contracting.

The final factor concerns developments within schools in the 1980s. At the most general level physical educationists were, once more, redefining the role of the subject in the education process and, in the eyes of some governing bodies, reducing the amount of sport within the PE curriculum (HMI 1978). Other specific concerns related to decline in extra-curricular sport following the protracted teachers' dispute in 1985 and the subsequent introduction of more clearly defined teachers' contracts (SHA 1987). The details of the new contract, and the method by which it was introduced, combined to reduce the number of staff hours available for organising and supervising out-of- school sport. The contract specified *inter alia* the number of hours that staff were expected to teach and also specified a number of hours for additional activities, for example staff training and meetings. A common consequence was that staff training and meetings were often organised in the hour following the end of the school day, thus making team training more difficult to organise. Probably of greater significance was the loss of goodwill among staff, particularly among the non-PE staff, and a consequent decline in their willingness to run school teams. Indeed one important and worrying trend identified by those involved in school athletics is the decline in athletic success among inner city schools, in Birmingham for example, and their replacement by suburban schools. One suggested explanation was that inner city schools relied more heavily on the organisational capacity and resources of teachers than the suburban schools, where parents are more likely to have the money, time and transport needed for the athletic development of their children.

One further development in schools needs to be mentioned and relates to the regulations issued by the DES in 1981 encouraging education authorities to sell surplus playing fields (DES 1981). The justification given by the DES was that many of the playing fields allocated to schools were being under-used, partly as a result of the decline in the number of school-age children but also, it was claimed, because the use of playing fields featured less prominently in the PE curriculum.

The combination of these factors led to growing expressions of unease among governing bodies and, on their behalf, by the Central Council of Physical Recreation.[3] Other organisations to express their concern included the National Playing Fields Association (1989), the Physical Education Association (1987) and the Secondary Heads' Association (1987).

The Sports Council was also giving the issue of sport for school-age children greater consideration in its strategic planning process. Although the charter of the Sports Council does not specifically preclude a focus on school-age children there has always been a tacit acceptance that the primary responsibility lay with local education authorities, schools and teachers. Indeed until the 1980s there was little evidence to suggest that schools and PE teachers were not continuing to fulfil their traditional role of introducing children to sport and nurturing young talent. In addition, the Council had identified other target groups and objectives as having greater priority. In the 1982 strategy document (Sports Council 1982) the Sports Council focused on the uneven participation between men and women, the high drop-out rate in the late teenage years, and the low level of participation among the middle-aged. Accordingly targets were set for an increase in men's and particularly women's participation in indoor and outdoor sport. In the new strategy document, *Into the 90s*, the Council renewed 'the emphasis on those 1982 priorities where progress has been slow' (Sports Council 1988: 58) and identified women and young people as its principal targets for extending participation.

In *Into the 90s* the Sports Council noted that with the school population set to rise by 800,000 between 1993 and 2003 the schools and the youth service would be faced with a considerable challenge in providing sporting opportunities. Regarding schoolchildren below the age of thirteen the document said little or nothing. The thirteen to twenty-four age group is the first to be discussed in detail in the document. Given that the Council's strategic planning relates only partially to the school-age population the question of who plans the sporting provision of those between five and eighteen remains.

The importance of this age group for the success of its policy of raising general participation levels is clearly appreciated by the Sports Council, which notes that:

> The Council increasingly takes the view that sporting attitudes and habits formed before the age of 16 are the major determinant of adult sporting and leisure lifestyles. It has given insufficient attention to this area in the past, and will seek to increase its involvement in the next five years.
>
> (Sports Council 1988: 67–8)

The Council also notes that nearly three-quarters of school-children intend to participate in sport after leaving school. However, the Council also provides evidence which shows that despite these good intentions the level of participation among the thirteen to twenty-four age group declined in percentage terms between 1983 and 1988 despite it being an important focus of two of the Council's recent campaigns, 'Ever Thought of Sport?' and 'What's your Sport?'. Consequently, in *Into the 90s* the Sports Council identifies the thirteen to twenty-four age group as one of its target groups.

The research and discussion that preceded the 1988 strategic plan were supported by the Council's experience from the national demonstration project 'Active Lifestyles' and from a number of regional projects. The net effect was to raise the profile of sport and children within the Council and consequently render the Council more receptive to the representations made to it by governing bodies and the CCPR. The problem facing the Council was in part a procedural one. As previously mentioned, the Council had generally tended to restrict its responsibilities for sport to the post-school years. Although the Council argued that the primary reason for this was that there were other, more pressing, priorities it is also the case that any extension of policy planning to cover the school years and pre-school years would involve closer links with a number of organisations, including the Department of Education and Science and the Home Office respectively. Policy initiatives requiring the co-operation of two or more central government departments have a mixed history and rarely generate enthusiasm from either civil servants or their Ministers.

This difficulty notwithstanding, a seminar was organised in

November 1986 under a joint initiative by the DOE and the DES. The seminar brought together a range of representatives of the governing bodies and of educational interests. A broad range of issues were raised, including the contrasting perspectives on the role of sport in school held by educationists and the governing bodies. While the civil servant from the DES talked of the need for balance within the PE curriculum and warned against a narrow focus on a limited number of sports, the chairman of the CCPR stated the need to 'ensure that our young people of school age have adequate opportunity to develop excellence in the context of a competitive and sporting environment' (DOE/DES 1986: 5). Other issues related to facilities, curriculum, manpower and objectives. The outcome was a decision to commission a 'desk study' and to establish a body which would consider the issues. The body, which became known as the School Sport Forum, had a number of members in common with the Council's existing Physical Education Advisory Panel. The terms of reference limited the Forum to an investigation of the 'place of sport in the school curriculum', and it was envisaged that the Forum would complete its work by 1991 (DOE 1986).

The CCPR provided strong support for the work of the Forum by conducting a questionnaire survey of governing bodies. To date two documents have been produced, associated with the work of the Forum, the first a desk study, *Sport in Schools*, which reviewed the major issues and was intended to set an agenda for the deliberations of the Forum (Murdoch 1987). The second document was the report of the School Sport Forum (1988).

The purpose of the 'desk study' was to identify strategic issues for the Forum. Although the remit was to focus on sport in schools the desk study covered a much broader range of issues on the grounds that:

> the study could not be confined solely to either the curriculum or schools since provision for sport for young people can only be understood and freely explored in the total context of school, out of school and post school. The need for a coherent, corporate and strategic approach is essential, incorporating all the agencies in any way involved.
>
> (Murdoch 1987: i)

The decision to move away from a narrow focus on the school, and to adopt a broader focus on the range of organisations involved, with the intention of developing a strategy for this age group, is a response to the issue echoed by a number of other organisations. However, adopting a strategic focus is much easier than achieving the co-operation of interested organisations on matters of policy development and implementation.

What the desk study showed was that the issue of sport in schools was an amalgam of a diffuse cluster of issues. There were those issues which concerned intellectual questions about the relationship between sport and physical education, and the contribution that PE makes to the education of a child. By contrast there were those questions that focused on the practical problems of persuading non-PE staff to take responsibility for an inter-school match out of normal school hours, and the problems of a shortage of secretarial support for PE departments. There was another cluster relating to the perceived decline in excellence in performance and in the quality of facilities available for training. Other issues related to the training needs of non-PE and primary school staff, the relationship between teaching and coaching, and the consequences of the continuing constraint on finance.

The broad sweep of the desk study is understandable, given the lack of any previous research which consolidated the variety of issues in the policy area. Unfortunately the broader the scope of a survey the more difficult it becomes to focus the analysis. This then creates the danger that recommendations arising from an analysis fail to target responsibility for action and implementation with sufficient precision. The danger is that organisations for whom the policy is of only marginal importance, yet who are crucial to its implementation, are able to sidestep responsibility more easily.

Using the desk study as the main basis of its discussions, the School Sport Forum met on ten occasions during the second half of 1987 and early 1988. It was given the following terms of reference:

To ensure that, within the resources available to local education authorities, voluntary sports and other organisations, the widest range of opportunities for, and thus benefits of, sport are available to all children of school age.

To consider the issues identified by the DES/DoE desk study, the seminar's report of proceedings and any other appropriate material; to identify means of overcoming any apparent problems; to recommend courses of action for all relevant bodies; and to report to government and the Sports Council by 31 May 1988.

Apart from giving the Forum a much broader remit than that for the desk study the most important element in the terms of reference was the explicit statement that no new resources would be made available.

The Forum was chaired by Audry Bambra, formerly principal of a PE college, a member of the Sports Council and, at the time, chair of the Council's PE Advisory Group. The membership was drawn from a wide range of representative organisations, including the CCPR, the National Council for Schools Sport, the local authority associations and the British Council for Physical Education. Selecting the membership of review bodies such as the Forum is always difficult. The ideal member is one who is knowledgeable in his/her own right, able to speak on behalf of a particular interest and able to commit resources. Of the nineteen members of the Forum only the two representatives from the Sports Council could claim to be in a position to commit resources, and even then not without negotiations within the Council.

The Forum made a total of sixty-nine recommendations. Recommendations were directed at each major participant in the policy area and at virtually all the issues identified in the desk study. Some were at the level of exhortations, for example the media were recommended to 'use their powerful influence to promote ethical attitudes in sport' and 'governing bodies of schools should encourage enthusiastic parents to give help in school under the general guidance of the PE teachers' (6, 15). Others were aspiring to a degree of influence way beyond any realistic expectation, such as the recommendation that the DOE should review its control over local authority capital spending. However, the majority of recommendations were fairly specific and pragmatic and suggested, for example, that 10 per cent of time in the national curriculum should be earmarked for PE. The main problems with the recommendations were, first, that there were too many of them, and second that there was no order of priority. A third criticism was that the Forum seemed to leave aside any serious consideration of the resource implications of its suggestions. Fourth, a large number of the recommendations inevitably relied heavily on co-operation between a number of organisations and interests for their success. Finally, from the point of view of policy development it is debatable whether the efforts of the Forum have facilitated the formation of a policy network for sport for school-age children by refining the exact nature of the problem to be addressed. As mentioned in chapter 6, a policy network will function effectively if the issue is clearly defined and responsibility for it is accepted and acknowledged. In summary, a comprehensive list of recommendations may be an important step in clarifying issues and setting a further agenda but its impact is reduced unless the problems of implementation are also addressed.

The response to the School Sport Forum report was generally positive, with, not surprisingly, the warmest response coming from the PE-related interest groups such as the British Council of Physical Education. But among other organisations doubts were expressed about the feasibility of many of its recommendations. The most serious reservations were voiced by the local authority associations. This is not surprising, as a substantial responsibility for implementation would fall on their members. A typical response was the following comments from one of the major associations:

> there is some doubt, because of the number of recommendations in the report, as to the success in achieving their implementation. There is a real danger that many of the extremely worthwhile points could be lost because there is no clear path for action. There is a concern that the report in its final tenor tries to be all things to all known pressure groups within sport and that it has not identified a clear path for action . . . It is considered to be full of generalities and short on specifics.

The government's response was a mixture of enthusiastic endorsement of some recommendations and rejection of others. Typically the government endorsed recommendations which encouraged other organisations to take action and rejected those that required action from central government (DES/DOE 1989).

While it is easy to be cynical about the government's response, the tone reflects not just a desire to avoid any additional commitment of resources but also the problems of gaining access to other policy communities. This can be illustrated by con- sidering the recommendations made concerning schools, teachers and the national curriculum. Suggestions about paying teachers for running extra-curricular sport, allotting a specific amount of time to PE within the curriculum and specifying the PE content of initial teacher training courses were all rejected, in the main, one might suggest, because they were seen as the property of other policy communities.

Finally, a central theme of the Forum's report is the need for greater co-ordination and partnership. The Forum is well aware of the fragmentation of responsibility for children's sport, and the key to progress in implementing its recommendations lies in an ability to forge a common purpose between a disparate range of interests. In order to assess the likelihood of success in forming an effective policy network it is necessary to appreciate the diversity of organisations involved and of their priorities and the problems that it poses for policy formation and implementation.

A RANGE OF POTENTIAL PROVIDERS AND POLICY MAKERS

The range of potential actors in the policy process for children's sport divides into two groups: first those that have a responsibility for children and young people, and second those that have a responsibility for sport's development. Into the first category come the youth service, the DES, local education authorities and teachers while the second category contains the Sports Council, the CCPR and the governing bodies of sport. This section explores the relationship between the core concerns of a number of these organisations and the issue of sport and school-age children. In addition it examines their capacity to contribute to policy development and implementation in this area.

The youth service

The youth service is a title that covers a wide range of organisations in the public and voluntary sectors and refers, very generally, to organisations concerned with young people between the ages of nine or ten up to the early twenties. The most common manifestation of the youth service is the 'youth club' run either by the local education authority or else by voluntary, frequently church, organisations with the help of a local authority grant. Sport has long been a prominent element in the activities of youth clubs and has prompted governing bodies to press for a more open acknowledgement of their importance in relation to sport and the young (Swain and Stead 1987). However, the role of sport in youth work is clearly ambiguous, with the most recent report on the youth service saying little about sport (DES 1982). For much of the post-war period youth work has occupied a no-man's-land between social work and education and has defined its central concern as being with 'social education'. Most youth service provision is offered as part of the range of services within the local authority education department. In a small number of authorities – Birmingham, for example – the youth service is located within leisure and recreation departments. Unfortunately such arrangements are rare and in general sport has not filled a prominent role in the philosophy of youth work.[4]

If sport does not figure prominently in discussions of the philosophy of the youth service there is evidence to suggest that in practice sport provides a significant focus for youth work. For example, there is evidence to suggest that sport is the basis of up to 80 per cent of youth work (Swain 1987). Unfortunately only a small proportion of those who participate in sport through the youth service see it as a point of entry to specialist sports clubs. Data from a Sports Council-sponsored project suggest that only 1 per cent of sports club members and 1 per cent of casual participants had been introduced to their sport through participation in youth organisations (Sports Council 1985a). Despite these low figures the fact that sport is such a prominent feature of youth work and that one child in eight is involved with a youth organisation is sufficient reason for the Sports Council and governing bodies to see such organisations as playing an important part in the sports development process, as they 'come into contact with young people at a crucial stage in their development' (Sports Council 1988: 43). Nevertheless the Sports Council acknowledges that 'they are neither a major route into sport nor yet a long-term sustainer of participation' (1988: 43).

Despite the strong social work and education policy context of youth work there has been some discussion of the relationship of youth work and sport. In 1987 a series of conferences was organised jointly by the Sports Council, the National Council for Voluntary Youth Services and the National Youth Bureau. What is clear from the contributions to the conferences is the uneasy relationship between sport and youth work. As Swain comments, 'the youth service has a love–hate relationship with sport. Some youth workers love it: others hate it' (1987). For most youth workers the emphasis was on using sport as a 'platform for personal and social development' (Howie 1987). The attitude of those in the youth service is ambiguous, for while there are those who complain of the intrusion of sport into youth work there are also those who object to not being consulted on sport policy for children. Indeed a strong complaint by the National Youth Bureau was that when the Sports Council launched its campaign 'Ever Thought of Sport?' it did so without prior consultation with the youth service. Despite this criticism the National Youth Bureau identified the Sports Council as the most appropriate body to act as the lead organisation in devising a strategy to improve the links between sport and the youth service.

There are some examples of the development of a closer relationship between sports bodies and youth organisations but in general the relationship is characterised by a significant degree of suspicion on the part of many youth workers. At one level there are those who are sceptical of the value of sport as a means of achieving youth work objectives. 'Sport is seen as a programme device which tended to overwhelm in the past and that tends to obscure and is insensitive to the multifaceted needs of young people' (National Council for Voluntary Youth Services 1987: 23). At another level there is the more sensitive concern among youth workers that the nature of their professionalism is at stake in the debate over the relationship with sport. Youth work as a relatively new occupation is keen to establish its professional credentials; a process which is particularly important in the local government context (Houlihan 1988). For many youth workers an association with the relatively powerful teaching profession is preferable to the development of closer links with the weaker leisure profession. 'Prejudice towards sport is further fuelled by moves to transfer the Youth Service into local authority recreation and leisure departments and away from its education base' (National Council for Voluntary Youth Services 1987: 23). If a partnership between sports bodies and the youth service is to be established it is likely to be against a background of limited enthusiasm from youth workers.

Sport and physical education in schools

The pattern of contact between the Sports Council and the world of education is better established than with the youth service but it is debatable whether its influence is any greater. Contact is largely through the Physical Education Advisory Group of the Sports Council, whose membership is broadly representative of the variety of interests in the world of PE. For the Sports Council this is its major point of contact with the educational policy community. The main role of the group is to provide advice for the Council but it also enables a valuable exchange of information and views on issues of mutual interest. However, it would not see its primary role as lobbying those involved in PE. In general it would be true to say that the Council has been wary of getting involved in educational matters such as curriculum design.

This self-imposed limit is partly owing to the low priority given to sport in schools in the past and also partly owing to an acknowledgement of the difficulty of attempting to join the education policy community, which claims ownership of physical education policy. The strength of the policy community for education and the specific policy networks within it have been well documented, most recently by McPherson and Raab (1988; Rhodes 1986; Kogan 1975; Lodge and Blackstone 1982). The problems of gaining access are compounded by the fact that the Council is linked, through the Minister for Sport, to the DOE and not to the DES. Consequently, contact between the Sports Council and the DES, for example over matters concerning the design of the national curriculum, are more difficult to develop. Within the Sports Council there is little day-to-day contact with the DES at senior management level and less at middle management level. Thus not only does the Sports Council have weak links with education but the education policy community is more firmly established and therefore finds it far easier to exclude sport-related priorities and rebuff attempts by the sports interests to gain access to the education agenda.

This problem is compounded by the difficulty the Sports Council has in persuading some governing bodies to become involved in children's sport, as many regard this as the teachers' responsibility.[5] Yet the significance of school sport for the future of many governing bodies is great. Traditionally the main point of access to specialist sports clubs was through school and through the PE teacher encouraging talented pupils to seek specialist coaching. What makes the situation worse for the Council is that within the world of education PE, and PE staff, are generally considered to hold low status. Therefore the capacity of PE teachers, local education authority advisers for PE and PE educationists to raise school sport as an issue within the broader education community is weak, as is their capacity to influence the outcome of policy discussions on school sport when they do take place.

Part of the explanation of the low status of PE in the curriculum is that, along with art and music, it is seen as representing a qualitatively different, and by implication intellectually inferior, category of subject. The problem for PE staff is illustrated by the well known way the subject is treated by R.S. Peters in his exploration of the philosophy of education. In the chapter where he examines the criteria to be used in assessing the suitability of a subject or activity for inclusion in the school curriculum he compares 'games' to 'serious pursuits'. Serious pursuits, such as science, history and literary appreciation:

> are 'serious' in that they illuminate other areas of life and contribute much to the quality of living. They have, secondly, a wide-ranging cognitive content which distinguishes them from games. Skills, for instance, do not have a wide-ranging cognitive content. There is very little to know about riding bicycles, swimming or golf.... Furthermore what there is to know throws very little light on much else.
>
> (1966: 159)

This is a view echoed by the historian and writer on cricket, C.L.R. James, who asked in the preface to his major social and political analysis of cricket (1963), 'What do they know of cricket that only cricket knows?'

For Peters the main justification for including 'games' in the curriculum is that they make an importance contribution to moral education (1966: 159–60). Claims of the character-building qualities of sport have long been an important element in the justification of PE in schools, others being its contribution to health, the cultural education of the nation (Gleeson 1985: 8; Murdoch 1990: 223), maintaining the nation's sporting heritage (PEA 1990), social skills and aesthetics. While all these justifications are open to challenge (Parry 1988a, 1988b) the mere fact that the debate about justification is still continuing is evidence of the fundamental insecurity of PE within the curriculum.[6] As Parry argues there are considerable dangers in justifying sport in terms of other objectives. If sport is only valuable in schools because it contributes to, for example, health or moral development then there is no justification for sport if these objectives can be achieved through other (cheaper, less time-consuming) vehicles.

Against this background PE in schools has had an uneasy relationship with the world of sport. Physical educationists have been keen to see PE accepted as having a status within the curriculum similar to that of other subjects and one consequence of this has been a reluctance to become too closely associated with sport and its administrative organisations.[7] A key objective has been to distinguish PE from sport and to identify the latter as simply one element in the PE curriculum. Therefore sport has to compete with other elements of the curriculum such as health and fitness. In other words, and only slightly cynically, the quest for acceptance within the school curriculum has been achieved by taking the sport out of PE. The debate about the nature and role of PE in the curriculum has developed slowly throughout the 1980s as the government has refined its plans for establishing a national curriculum.

A typical example of the wide range of definitions of PE is given by Bucher (1972), who sees PE as 'an integral part of the total education process which has as its aims the development of physically, mentally, emotionally, and socially fit citizens through the medium of physical activity'. Unfortunately there is a marked lack of consensus about the adequacy of this definition. As Ojeme, for example, makes clear there are a wide range of alternatives available most of which are keen to eschew a strong connection with sport (1984: 193). Thus 'movement studies', 'movement education' and 'movement science' have their supporters. As regards the suggestion that 'sports education' would be a suitable title Ojeme observes that:

> there is a very strong feeling against the use of the word 'sports' as a title for the field. Some feel that sport is one of the activities included in PE. Furthermore experience with sport has shown that it is characterised by unwholesome practices which may pollute or adulterate the meaning and significance of PE.

(1984: 193)

The question of the role of competitive sport in PE is symptomatic of the problems facing physical educationists. While it is acknowledged that the extent of the decline in competitive school sport and the lack of support of some local education authorities for competitive sport has been vastly overblown, the debate on the place of competition in the PE curriculum persists (Thomas 1987; Atkinson 1985; ILEA 1988; Secondary Heads' Association 1987).

Of greater significance is the trend to turn PE into an examinable subject and thereby secure one of the key ingredients of academic respectability. At higher education level, and slowly percolating down through the schools, is a redefinition of sport away from 'sport as skill' and towards 'sport as knowledge' (see Kirk *et al.* 1986). The curriculum is being augmented by, for example, sports psychology, sports history and bio-mechanics. Reviewing the growth of sports-related syllabuses at GCSE, 'A' level, and from other examining bodies such as BTEC and City and Guilds, Casbon regrets that 'the emphasis in the development of these courses seems to have been upon achieving 'academic' respectability on non-Physical Educationist terms' (1988: 217).

The confusion within the teaching profession about the nature of the PE curriculum and whether and how it might be assessed has been brought into sharp relief by the proposal in the 1988 Education Reform Act to establish a national curriculum for schools. The main concern of both PE teachers and of sport's governing bodies is that PE will become marginalised.[8] Although the National Curriculum Council has yet to publish a PE curriculum, and by mid 1990 the Secretary of State for Education had not appointed a curriculum working party, its potential impact on PE is not viewed with universal enthusiasm.

There are a number of factors which are causing concern among educationists about the status of the subject and, by implication, the status of PE teachers. Within the national curriculum subjects have been allocated to either core or foundation status. PE has been identified as a foundation subject, on a par with foreign languages, history and geography. However, there was some concern that despite its 'foundation' status PE might not figure in all the secondary school years. A DES discussion document commented that 'Provision for [PE] in secondary school years 1–3 is virtually universal and this position should continue. It is for consideration whether PE/games might be a free option in years 4 and 5' (DES 1984). This comment was made against a background where PE is frequently seen as an expendable subject within the curriculum. As Williams and Jenkins note, 'there are currently a number of schools in which physical education is seen as one subject from which those pupils who have other identified needs may be legitimately removed' (1988: 126).

A further cause for concern lies in the likely time allocated to PE in the curriculum. While the DES has, so far, not set the amount of time to be devoted to particular subjects, there is a clear perception among physical educationists that it will be PE that will be squeezed to enable other curriculum objectives, such as the priority for foreign languages, to be met. An allocation of time of 5 per cent has been suggested by the DES for fourth and fifth year pupils (1987), whereas the School Sport Forum argued for a minimum allocation of 10 per cent in secondary schools and a 'daily session of vigorous activity in each primary school' (1988: 27).

Finally, the DES discussion documents produced so far indicate that PE, along with art and music, will be provided with 'guidelines' for pupil attainment and will not have to work towards the specific attainment targets expected of other subjects. While this is an understandable point of view, given the importance of factors such as physical maturity for attainment, it has already been suggested that the DES position is indicative of the attitude that 'subjects like art, music and PE are not important subjects for the declaration of targets that subjects should be striving towards' (Thomason and Almond 1988). It is tempting for PE staff therefore to give priority within the PE curriculum to those aspects that are measurable, such as theory and fitness, possibly at the expense of the experience of participating in and practising specific sports.

Understandably the imminence of the national curriculum for PE has generated considerable debate within the PE profession and much activity by the various bodies representing PE interests. What is clear from the statements of these pressure groups is that an impending national curriculum is not going to make it easier for sports bodies to build partnerships with PE teachers and schools. This is best illustrated by examining the work of the British Council of PE, which, with the support of the DES, has established an Interim Working Group (IWG) on the PE curriculum. In its recent progress report the IWG enunciated a number of principles on which to base its work. Among these was a statement that PE should be treated in the same way as any other subject, i.e. establish attainment targets, levels of achievement, etc.; that PE is not synonymous with sport and that the educational elements of the subject must be stressed; and that the curriculum for PE should be more about how children learn than about what they learn. The message is clear that in this period of considerable uncertainty for teachers of PE they are unlikely to embark on any innovations which might jeopardise their status. Consequently, attempts by the CCPR and the governing bodies of sport to increase the amount of sport in the PE curriculum are unlikely to succeed. A degree of caution must also be expressed regarding the role of PE staff as the conduit through which able and gifted pupils reach specialist clubs, as there is some sensitivity to being labelled as the (unpaid) talent scouts of competitive sports clubs.

The National Children's Play and Recreation Unit

In the report of the Physical Education Association (1987) it is the primary school years which are identified as having the poorest PE provision in terms of facilities and trained PE teachers. The Sports Council has acknowledged the importance of an early introduction to sport as a foundation for lifelong involvement. One organisation which expressly addresses the needs of this five to fifteen age group is the National Children's Play and Recreation Unit (NCPRU). The NCPRU was created following the closure of Playboard, an organisation which was established in 1984 after lobbying by pressure groups and from MPs for the creation of a body to take responsibility for the promotion and co-ordination of children's play. Playboard was funded for three years by the DOE. But in 1987 the DOE proposed to abolish Playboard and broaden the responsibility of the Sports Council to cover children's play. However, after considerable protest the NCPRU was established, for a limited period of four years, as the replacement for Playboard. The Unit was to report to the DOE, but receive its finance via the Sports Council.

The Unit sees itself as an advocate of children's interests across a range of policy areas. Among the priorities of the Unit are to create an understanding of the importance of play, to encourage the development and dissemination of good practice, and to promote partnerships between agencies. Officers of the Unit rightly point to the almost total absence of a policy framework for children's development outside school and the generally poor level of funding for the scant services that exist.

For the Unit 'play' is defined very widely, covering the arts as well as informal physical play and sport. Given that the Unit's responsibilities include an interest in recreation and sport and that it has the potential to establish close management links with the Sports Council, it would seem a valuable basis for the creation of joint initiatives aimed at developing the interests of the child in sport and recreation. The Unit has contributed to a number of policy discussions relating to sport and young people and also made a submission to the School Sport Forum. However, the NCPRU has been keen to maintain its distance from the Council. Indeed the Unit was very reluctant to be linked with the Sports Council, as many of its initial problems concerned persuading other organisations that it was not simply a 'sports council' for the young. When the government decided to close Playboard and merge it with the Sports Council the trustees of Playboard opted for voluntary liquidation in protest. The main consequence of the brief history of the Unit is that it, like PE teachers, is extremely wary of being associated too closely with sport and therefore is possibly unduly unreceptive to partnership opportunities. In other words one way in which it can establish its distinctive character is by overemphasising the lines of demarcation between it and sports organisations.

Governing bodies

With some important exceptions, such as the Amateur Swimming Association and the Amateur Athletic Association, most governing bodies of sport have traditionally taken only a marginal role in nurturing sporting interest and talent among the young. This introductory or foundation level of the sports development hierarchy is generally considered as being best left to schools and PE staff. As a result the governing bodies have had high expectations of the contribution of schools to their aims. For many the primary role of the school was to provide the basis of sporting achievement. In a recent policy statement the CCPR identified as one of its aims 'To develop a strategy within the school PE programme whereby children of outstanding potential are referred to the county or regional governing body coach' (quoted in PEA 1987: 40).

Not surprisingly the governing bodies, the CCPR and related organisations such as the National Council for School Sport and the National Coaching Foundation have been in the forefront of the debate about school sport and the national curriculum, and the alleged decline in competitive and team sports in school. However, given the progress in the debate over the role of PE in the national curriculum, it is becoming clear that sport will be but one element of PE and that the inclusion of a wider range of sports will make specialisation at school more difficult. In addition the amount of extra-curricular sport will take a long time to return to its pre-1985 levels, if indeed it does so.

The CCPR and, by the mid 1980s, most governing bodies were well aware of the problems they faced and that the solution lay in developing closer links with schools and taking a greater share of the responsibility for nurturing sporting talent. However, scepticism concerning the capacity of clubs to fulfil the role expected of them was also evident. The DES/DOE seminar in 1986 noted that the fostering of talent in children through the club/school link:

> predicated the existence of specialist clubs not only structured and willing to accept young talented sportsmen and sportswomen but to provide . . . educational monitoring. . . . to make judgements concerning the likely effects of exercise, sports and games on the growth and development of young people across the physical, psychological and sociological areas.
>
> (DOE/DES 1986: 9)

Although there are a growing number of examples of close links between clubs, governing bodies and schools, a survey by the South West Sports Council (1985) painted a bleak picture of the co-operation between governing bodies and schools.

There are a number of governing bodies that have already taken steps to build better links with schools, including the Hockey Association, the Lawn Tennis Association, the All England Netball Association and the Amateur Athletic Association. The Hockey Association, in conjunction with the All England Women's Hockey Association, has established a strong youth development programme, part of which is aimed at encouraging clubs to appoint youth development officers who would then seek to develop links with schools through offers of coaching support, although taking responsibility for running school teams has proved more difficult to arrange.[9] The AAA has been very successful in gaining acceptance for its 10-Step and 5-Star award schemes, which are used by a large number of schools as performance targets. It has also been encouraging its clubs to build closer links with schools through its 'Adopt a School' scheme.

However, the governing bodies have not relied solely on trying to develop stronger links with schools. Many have taken steps to make their clubs more welcoming to children and, more importantly, to their parents, and to adapt their sports to the abilities of children. For example, the Midland Counties AAA has been encouraging clubs to prepare development plans which include policies for children and has also been funding clubs to make their publicity more professional and designed to reassure parents that their children will be well looked after.[10] Other governing bodies have developed children's versions of their sport, for example mini-hockey, kwik cricket and short tennis.

Although there has been considerable innovation within governing bodies with regard to sport for children there are major problems to be faced. First, the resources devoted to youth development work are still comparatively small. Much of the success of developing school/club links depends less on the number of development officers appointed than on the number of PE teachers who are club members. Second, there are still a number of sports and clubs that have no development policy for young people, and furthermore do not have the resources to initiate one. Finally, there is no guarantee that a sport development policy focused on schools will be sympathetically received by physical educationists. Even now when the youth development work of many governing bodies is hardly established their activities have brought some criticism from other quarters. The National Council for Schools Sports talks of the 'real danger that outside bodies [will] take over the organisation of sport for school children' (quoted in PEA 1987: 42). The PE Association commented that 'campaigns by governing bodies of sport to involve youngsters in particular sports place undue pressure on youngsters' (1987: 14). The PEA also reports some concern among Her Majesty's Inspectors of schools that governing body proficiency award schemes occasionally dominate the PE programme.

The Sports Council and problems of implementation

In the policy area of children's sport the picture that emerges is one where a number of relatively powerful interests have an involvement in policy but none see it as their rationale or primary role. For some policy actors children's sport is of only peripheral significance to their core functions and is consequently defined in terms of that core philosophy, for example the youth service and PE teachers. In addition there are actors, such as the NCPRU, who perceive an association with sport as compromising, or even undermining, their status in their primary policy community. This does not mean that the less sympathetic actors would support the Sports Council, the CCPR and the governing bodies in expanding their activities to take over, for example, the sporting aspects of PE or youth work. It would seem that the maintenance of territorial boundaries is important even if some of the territory is considered to be a liability.

The establishment of a policy network to address the issue of children's sport is not going to be easy or rapid. If success is to be achieved then one must turn to the policy actors whose primary responsibility is sport, and to the Sports Council in particular. The Council, through its lines of contact with local authority leisure departments on the one hand and governing bodies and the CCPR on the other, is in the best position to raise the profile of the issue and to co-ordinate policy discussion. However, the capacity of the Council to fulfil this leadership role must be open to question, given its lack of an established framework for policy implementation in this area. Apart from one or two important exceptions the Council has few policy programmes in operation designed to meet the needs of this age group.[11]

The Council acknowledges that it has been slow to recognise the needs of this group and is also aware of the barriers to successful policy development that must be faced. In seeking to explain its neglect of the school-age population the Council comments that 'This omission was partly because in the past the Council confined itself to adult and out-of-school sporting matters, by agreement leaving the national responsibility for school sport with the Department of Education and Science' (Sports Council 1988: 41). The clear implication of this statement is that any expansion of the role of the Council in the area of school-age children will entail a renegotiation of the line of demarcation between the Council (and the DOE) and the DES. In order to pursue its objectives the Council would be entering policy territory at present dominated by the DES and containing a number of other influential actors, including the teaching profession, the National Playing Fields Association and the Physical Education Association. The Council therefore is treading very carefully, for while on the one hand it refers to the crucial role which the 'physical education curriculum plays in developing post-school sporting attitudes and habits' (1988: 41), on the other it notes that 'In developing its own role, the Council will give particular attention to where it has a unique role to play . . .' (1988: 68). In essence the problem facing the Council is how to intervene in policy development without generating too much resentment from the other major organisations involved.

In the medium to long-term the picture is probably more optimistic. The School Sport Forum, although destined to disappear in 1991, has raised the profile of the issue and this should provide the PE Advisory Group of the Sports Council with sufficient momentum to keep the issue on the political agenda. The Sports Council is gradually adopting a more proactive role and accepting that it is the lead organisation in the policy area, even if only by default. While part of its reluctance is owing to the failure of the government to provide additional resources to enable the Council to meet these new responsibilities, it has nevertheless begun to develop partnerships with other interested organisations and has initiated one or two demonstration projects. For example, the Council grant-aids the National Council for Schools' Sport as well as providing financial support to help a number of governing bodies prepare youth teams for competition.

The Coventry 'Active Life Styles' project run in co-operation with Coventry City Council Education Committee and four of its comprehensive schools is a further example of the Council's support for innovation. The aim of the project is to increase the number of children who leave school committed to sport and active recreation as part of their adult life (Sports Council 1985b; Coventry City Council 1989). Similar joint projects with education authorities are taking place in Dudley (examining PE in primary schools) and in a group of North West authorities (exploring the impact of local management of schools). There are more examples of successful partnerships with local authority leisure services departments, including the organising of 'taster days' for children, where local authorities and clubs organise sports participation events for children to sample. Although the youth service does not see the development of sporting ability as its primary activity it is taking part in a series of initiatives to improve the capacity of youth workers to run sports. For example, the Eastern Region Sports Council organised a number of sport experience days for youth workers while the British Canoe Union has modified its training programme to meet the needs of people like youth workers, who require a level of skill lower than that of the water sport coach.

Governing bodies are also adopting a much more active role in encouraging clubs to take more responsibility for recruiting and developing school-age talent and are receiving Sports Council grant aid to appoint development officers. As well as funding development work by the governing bodies the Sports Council took a major policy decision in 1985 to fund youth organisations whose primary role was not sport. Thus YMCAs, Boys' Clubs and Youth Clubs UK have received grants. This decision should do much to reduce suspicion by youth organisations of the intentions of the Sports Council.

In conclusion, if an effective policy network for children's sport is to be formed then the Sports Council is best placed to fulfil the leadership role. At present the Council is a reluctant leader, partly owing to lack of DOE financial support for what the Council rightly sees as a major area of investment, partly because of the number of entrenched interests involved, and partly because of the lack of any consensus as to the direction that policy should take. There might be agreement on the means, most notably partnership, but there is far less agreement on the purpose of that partnership. Developing a policy for children's sport that can achieve the support of the PE establishment, the youth service and the governing bodies will take a long time, but without the Sports Council taking a vigorous lead it is doubtful whether it can be done at all.

10

CONCLUSION

It must never again be the case that the politicking inside sport makes the House of Commons look tame by comparison. The simple home truth is that if we are to put this chapter of the 1980s behind us we need one voice for sport, one lobby to Government and one body representing the Sports Council and the CCPR, the governing bodies, the SAF, the BOA – all organisations which seek to represent or serve sportsmen and women.

Colin Moynihan[1]

POLICY PROCESSES

In the opening chapter of this book attention was drawn to the steady growth of interest in the relationship between sport and politics. What puts that growth of interest into even sharper relief is that government intervention in sport has continued, if not increased, under a government that is avowedly anti-interventionist. Attempts to impose a boycott on participation in the 1980 Olympic Games and legislation concerning football hooliganism are the most obvious examples, but the government, through the Minister for Sport, has continued the interventionist tradition developed by Denis Howell in a number of other ways. Action at international level in the Council of Europe in particular has been strongly supported on hooliganism and drug abuse. Intervention by the government on education has been equally forceful, especially in the area of the national curriculum, with the implications that this has for physical education. The Minister for Sport has also supported the use of Sports Council grant aid

Table 8 Stages in the life cycle of a policy

	Hogwood and Gunn	Downs
1	Deciding to decide (issue search/agenda setting)	Issue exists but not recognised; alarmed discovery
2	Deciding how to decide (Issue filtration)	
3	Issue definition	
4	Forecasting	
5	Setting objectives	Realisation of costs;
6	Analysis of options	cooling of enthusiasm;
7	Policy implementation, monitoring and control	transfer to back-burner.
8	Evaluation and review	
9	Policy maintenance, succession or termination	

powers to influence the policy decisions of independent governing bodies of sport. Doubtless in a moment of exasperation brought on by the recalcitrance of the governing bodies to do everything he tells them, Colin Moynihan also threatened to introduce legislation 'to impose a single umbrella body on British sport, obliging it to speak with one voice, unless the administrators create one themselves' (*The Independent*, 30 November 1989).

The three case studies explored in the previous chapters provide an opportunity not only to illustrate the character of government intervention, but also to examine the role of other actors in the policy process. In chapter 6 reference was made to the policy cycle described by Hogwood and Gunn (1984) and in chapter 7 Downs's 'issue attention cycle' was outlined (summarised in Table 8). These descriptions of the policy process provide a useful way of organising an examination of sport policy. Let us turn first to how sports issues arrive on the policy agenda.

For football hooliganism there was certainly a period when the issue existed but was not recognised by those able to influence access to the policy agenda. Downs suggests that a number of issues arrive on the policy agenda as a result of a dramatic event which focuses the attention of the public and, more importantly, of political influentials. The Bradford City fire, the deaths at the

Heysel stadium and those at Hillsborough certainly were a series of dramatic events which focused public and political attention on a range of issues associated with football, including crowd management and safety, the physical fabric of and conditions within stadiums, and spectator violence. While these events were important in accelerating the pace of entry on to the agenda the issue was gradually surfacing through other routes, for example through the deliberations of the DOE working group, the attention of the media and, maybe more importantly, through the embarrassment caused to the Prime Minister and other senior politicians when hooliganism occurred overseas. The movement of the question of drug abuse by athletes on to the policy agenda was in some ways similar though more gradual than dramatic. The steady rise in prominence of the issue, prompted by the occasional scandal or death, dates from the late 1960s. The Ben Johnson episode certainly did raise the profile of the issue, but more so for the public than for governing bodies and organisations such as the IOC.

In order for an issue to enter the agenda swiftly a dramatic demonstration of urgency is not always sufficient. Rapid entry is best achieved when the issue has already begun to generate interest and therefore key actors, firmly established in existing policy communities, have begun to consider questions of issue filtration and the appropriate location/route for the issue.

By contrast, the issue of sport for school-age children is barely out of the pre-problem stage. In almost classical fashion the issue had been acknowledged within a tight professional circle of PE teachers, advisers and their various representative bodies for much of the 1960s and 1970s. It was not until the 1980s that organisations outside this group, such as the CCPR, major governing bodies and the Sports Council, began to recognise the issue as impinging on their interests. The main problem facing these groups in hastening the promotion of this issue on to the policy agenda is in determining the proper route for, and ownership of, the issue. Traditionally the issue of school sport has been one for the education policy community to resolve, and in chapter 9, the difficulty of redefining the issue as a sports issue was made clear. Not only is the education policy community more influential than that for sport, but also the members of the education community whose support is essential for any redefinition of the issue (PE teachers and advisers) are very conscious of the vulnerability of their status within education. They are consequently faced with the dilemma of preserving and defending their status in the education community while also trying to defend the role of sport within the PE curriculum and within the national curriculum. The evidence so far suggests that they are more concerned to preserve their status as teachers than as PE/sports teachers. Firmly establishing sport for school-age children as an issue to be resolved by a sports policy network is still a long way off but the recent activity by the Sports Council, through the School Sports Forum, is an important step in asserting an interest in the debate.

Crucial to deciding the route that an issue takes through the political system is the way in which the issue is defined. Whereas football hooliganism has been firmly defined as an issue to be resolved as a matter of law and order, drug abuse by athletes has been left largely as a matter for the sports policy community and the use of existing drug abuse and medicines legislation has been limited. Regarding children's sport, much of the activity of the sports policy actors has been aimed at broadening the existing narrow definition of the issue as one predominantly concerned with education.

It is at the stage of analysing and implementing policy options that the greatest difficulties arise for a policy community. Just as the ability to assert ownership of an issue is an important sign of a mature policy community, so too is the ability to determine the policy response. As regards football hooliganism much of the debate on the policy response, and many of the eventual policy choices, were made by actors from other policy communities. The football membership scheme is probably the best example where debate on the proposal treated representations from sports organisations with a mixture of condescension and contempt. However, the strong intervention from government is in large part the result of an absence of policy leadership from sports organisations, most notably the Football Association and the Football League.

For a policy network or community to act effectively within the policy process three ingredients are essential, namely leadership, resource control and legitimacy. Leadership refers not just to the actions of initiating policy discussion or suggesting solutions to problems, but also to the acknowledgement of the actor's focal role by other network members. Thus, while a community of interests may exist, it must be organised before it can have an impact on policy. Leadership is an important aspect of the organisation of that community of interests.

The second ingredient, resource control, has been explored in chapter 6. From the case studies it is clear that three resources are of particular importance in affecting the ability of actors to participate in the sport policy process. Control over financial and physical resources is of major importance. Although local authorities (and local education authorities) have considerable control over these resources, local management of schools, compulsory competitive tendering and the national curriculum may reduce their degree of discretion. Consequently the physical and financial resources controlled by other actors, including the Sports Council, governing bodies (and their clubs) and the BOA, although much smaller than those of the local authorities, may become more significant in shaping sport policy. Expert knowledge is the second important resource, and one which is unevenly distributed among the organisations with an interest in sport policy. In some, such as many of the governing bodies, knowledge is very narrowly based and is consequently a handicap to their participation in broader policy debates. Other participants, such as SARD, and by implication the Minister, have little expertise or capacity to gather it directly. The BOA, the CCPR and the Sports Council are among the policy actors that can claim both a broad knowledge of a range of sport-related issues and also a degree of expertise on specific issues.

The final major resource is legitimacy, which refers to the capacity to speak authoritatively on behalf of a group of interests, owing either to election or the operation of some other representative mechanism. Legitimacy also refers to the acknowledgement of an organisation's right to be consulted on, or to participate in, policy discussions. Legitimacy is the least tangible of the three resources but can give actors considerable influence over policy and can compensate for deficiencies in other resources. For example, the CCPR, which possesses few physical and financial resources and has spent much of the 1980s locked into a destructive squabble with the Sports Council, has none the less a high level of legitimacy due to its justifiable claim to represent a wide range of sports interests. Having Prince Philip as an active president and having had a Sports Minister as a chairman also helps an organisation to maintain its influence. The Sports Council on the other hand has to work hard to establish and maintain its legitimacy in the eyes of other policy actors. For many organisations the Council is compromised by its close relationship with government, while ironically for others the Council is weakened by its distance from government and its perceived inability to speak authoritatively on behalf of government. As a result the Council must develop its standing in the policy community by virtue of its expertise and its even-handed distribution of grant aid.

Returning to the examination of the case studies, for football hooliganism the policy network contained a number of potential leaders, especially the FA and the League, but both seemed reluctant to take on the role. Part of the explanation lies in a general reticence about expanding their activities beyond their traditional boundaries, but part also lies in the fragmentation of resources and interests within the policy area. The local authorities, the police, the football authorities, the Sports Council and the Minister for Sport all controlled different resources and had different policy priorities. In these circumstances policy leadership is difficult to develop and it was only the government that had the combination of determination, resources and legitimacy to attempt to impose a policy solution.

The development of greater cohesion within the football policy network is not going to be easy to achieve, despite many positive features. For example, there is an important degree of overlap of membership in some of the organisations involved in football, most clearly between the Football League and the FA. Unfortunately the representatives of the League who sit on the FA Council seem more concerned with ensuring that the Association does nothing that encroaches on the interests of the League. In a similar fashion many League clubs see the League Management Committee as a threat to their traditional autonomy rather than as a vehicle for the pursuit of collective interests. Indeed it is the difficulty of articulating collective interests that undermines the potential for effective lobbying to be derived from this overlap in membership. In such circumstances leadership within a policy network becomes extremely difficult to develop, as network members see links with other members as opportunities to monitor and restrain their activity rather than as opportunities for developing collective interests and objectives.

The peripheral role of football supporters is illustrative of the malaise within the network. In many other policy communities, such as education and health, the 'clients/customers' have been a vociferous, if not always influential, element in policy debate. Policy actors, especially service producers, have been keen to build alliances with their customers as a way of strengthening their bargaining power in relation to government. Although 'customers' can prove to be an inconveniently wilful ally they can play an important role in affecting government attitudes. Within football, spectators, and the Football Supporters' Association, have been treated by the football authorities as having little or nothing to contribute to the sport or the debate on hooliganism.

By contrast strong leadership and, more importantly, a clear overlap of interests among the influential actors was evident in the policy network for drug abuse. At the domestic level strong and consistent leadership came from the Sports Council, the Minister for Sport and the key governing body, the AAA. In addition, with only one or two minor exceptions the leadership was accepted as legitimate. The Sports Council's clear moral stand on the issue was undoubtedly helped by its ability to deploy resources to support its policy objectives. Underwriting the cost of testing was crucial to the success of the policy, as is the continuing funding of research into testing methods. This domestic action was complemented at international level by the strong leads from the IOC, a variety of ISFs and the Council of Europe. Although there was some disagreement within the policy network the broad consensus that existed was more than enough to ensure that the less enthusiastic governing bodies and athletes were unable to undermine the policy.

The main impediments to the successful establishment of a policy network for sport for school-age children are the absence of a policy leader capable of providing a focus for the interests of sports bodies and the lack of leverage derived from control over needed resources. As was shown, part of the explanation of the weakness of sports interests in the debate over children's sport lies in the strength of the education policy community. However, part of the explanation also lies in the fragmentation of sports interests and the narrowness of their concerns. It is only the Sports Council that has the capacity to take a leading role, but it seems reluctant to be too closely associated with the issue, owing to the perceived financial costs and other resource implications of leading policy development and implementation. In contrast to the issue of drug abuse few of the resources available to the Council constitute 'hard currency' with many of the other policy actors. In addition the clear leadership provided by the Minister on drug abuse is not present on school sport.

The sports interests in the nascent policy network are faced with an awkward dilemma. The ability of governing bodies, the CCPR and the Sports Council to intervene effectively in the discussion on school sport is limited. The key resources of staff, facilities and time (curriculum) are controlled by interests within the education policy community. The prospect is that major competitive sport in schools will continue to decline. Ironically, opportunities for greater influence over the sporting activities of school-age children are most likely to come only if school sport continues to decline and pressure grows on local authority recreation departments to increase provision and on governing bodies and their local clubs to establish or expand youth development programmes. Needless to say, such an eventuality would result in extremely uneven provision over the country and in different parts of cities and towns, as it would depend on parental support and the resources and location of clubs.

Finally, one aspect of the policy process that needs emphasis is the growing importance of the international dimension. For both hooliganism and drug abuse it was not possible to insulate the domestic response from the international debate on the problems. With regard to hooliganism the government used its participation at the international level to influence domestic policy. In the development of policy towards drug abuse the overlap and interpenetration of the domestic with the international policy discussions was also clear. One important consequence of internationalisation is that domestic policy actors need to develop a strategy to enable effective access to the international arena. At present, especially on the issues of drugs and hooliganism, it is the government which has demonstrated the greatest ability to pursue its interests effectively in both the international and domestic arenas.

POLICY COMMUNITIES

At the beginning of the book it was suggested that to conceptualise the policy process as taking place within a policy community was a potentially fruitful approach to explaining the development of policy for sport. There was, however, the difficulty in determining whether a policy community existed for sport or whether some other description was more appropriate. The evidence derived from the examination of the case studies would seem to confirm that in the policy area of sport a mature community does not yet exist. Nevertheless some of the characteristics of a policy community mentioned earlier, in chapter 6 are evident. There are signs of both vertical integration and horizontal compartmentalisation; there is also a membership which is stable and which involves Ministers, civil servants and representatives of voluntary and private interests, but there are also significant characteristics missing. Despite the existence of a central group of policy actors (Sports Council, CCPR, governing bodies and Ministry) there would appear to be little recognition of their respective roles or an implicit authority structure; more importantly there is only a weak value consensus among members. In addition there is a marked absence of a core of professionals to help give policy development a clear direction.

To conclude that a mature policy community for sport does not exist is not surprising, yet the case studies raise a number of interesting questions for the study both of communities and of the policy process of sport. In the earlier discussion of the transition of issues from the pre-problem stage to the policy agenda the emphasis was on the ways in which issues were sponsored by interest groups or else arose as a result of a crisis. In a mature policy community one would expect members to be involved in a scanning activity which would alert the community to issues of potential concern the community. A policy community may therefore be subject to lobbying by interest groups who are keen for it to accept responsibility for an issue; it may claim an issue as a result of scanning its environment; or it may have an issue thrust upon it by government or some other, more powerful actor. The three case studies provide interesting evidence relating to all three processes.

The cluster of organisations and interests concerned with football showed a great reluctance to accept the issues as their

258

own. Many thought either that there was no problem or, more commonly, that it was somebody else's responsibility. There was, in fact, a reversal of the traditional relationship between government and interest groups, as it was the government that was attempting to encourage a range of interest groups to accept the issue as their legitimate property. Throughout the case study it was clear that the government was keen to overcome the evident fragmentation within the policy area and would have supported the sport policy community if it had led to the establishment of a policy network. Indeed it may be argued that in a number of ways the government attempted to sponsor the emergence of a policy network for football hooliganism, though doubtless on terms and of a character to its own liking.

For the government the existence of a policy community (and its constituent networks) has a number of potential advantages. In particular it is a way of co-opting expertise, and of generating co-operation over policy selection, thereby easing the implementation of policy. It is also a way of routinising issues and providing a degree of consistency in treatment. Because these benefits do not always materialise the government must possess a sufficient presence, or capacity to intervene, in the community so as to be able to steer it towards, or away from, a particular course of action. The cluster of issues associated with football that arose in the 1980s (hooliganism, crumbling stadiums, quality of management and leadership) could well have been dealt with in this way. In the event the government failed in its attempt to encourage the development of a policy network able to deal with hooliganism and consequently selected policy options largely independent of football interests.

The situation regarding drug abuse was different. The acknowledgement, by a number of influential actors, of the issue as a problem requiring action, the existence of a broad value consensus regarding the problem and its solution, and the effective control of resources by key organisations, all contributed to the development of a much more effective policy network for the issue. In addition, the intervention by the government in the issue area was broadly consistent and supportive of the prevailing consensus. Indeed, the pattern of relationships developed over the issue was, and still is, both mutually supportive and complementary. If the effectiveness of policy networks was dependent upon the existence of a policy community then the evidence for a sport policy community would be strong. However, it seems that it is possible to have effective networks in the absence of a mature policy community.

The example of children's sport differs in that control over the issue has already been claimed by the education policy community. What the case study showed was the problem of gaining access to the policy network. As mentioned in chapter 6 a policy network does not necessarily draw all its members from the 'parent' community. For example, a number of representatives of the medical policy community are members of the policy network for drug abuse. As regards children's sport the sports organisations were attempting to gain access to the education debate and also trying to separate the debate on sport, competitive games and the sale of playing fields from the issues of more central concern to the educational community such as the nature of PE, the national curriculum and the status of PE teachers. At best the case study showed the development of a loose network of interested organisations capable of lobbying the education community but, owing in part to the weakness of the policy community for sport, not yet able to have their claims for participation in the policy process acknowledged as legitimate.

The situation therefore has arisen where sport policy networks, of varying degrees of organisation, exist but a complementary community is only weakly delineated, despite clear signals of support from government. Part of the problem for the government is that the culture within the policy area is one that stresses non-interference by government (financial support notwithstanding) and supports the fierce policy autonomy of the governing bodies of sport. This culture has been fostered by the governing bodies themselves with the support of the CCPR, the Sports Council and successive governments. It is therefore easy to appreciate the problems that the government faces in attempting to develop a culture which sees policy for sport as the outcome of a process of negotiation between itself and the governing bodies.

Despite the evidence which suggests the absence of an effective policy community there are some signs that one may emerge. Three key conditions for the successful development of a community are, first, an institutional focus within government, second, opportunities for routine contact and, third, a degree of value consensus. Regarding the first condition, while there has been a Minister with responsibility for sport for over twenty years none of them, with the exception of Denis Howell, who seemed to like the job, has been an impressive figure or politically influential. Nevertheless the greater salience of sports issues to government has raised the status of the Minister's position, if only temporarily, and has thereby provided a strong focus for policy development. In addition to a focus on the Minister, the Sports Council must be seen as fulfilling a similar role. The damaging rift with the CCPR and the suspicion of some governing bodies notwithstanding, the Council has gradually, during the 1980s, enhanced its role and reputation in sport. It is slowly expanding its span of interests, most notably into the area of children's sport, and if it can reach a working relationship with the CCPR its capacity to speed the development of the policy community will increase substantially.

Opportunities for routine contact is the second condition, and again these have existed for some time, mainly directed through the Sports Council and the CCPR, and would seem to be well established and extensive. It is the final condition, a value consensus, which seems to be missing. In two of the case studies, football and children's sport, there seemed to be only superficial agreement about objectives and a marked level of disagreement about the means of achieving them. In particular, even in the study of drug abuse, there was a problem in reconciling the individualist quality of sporting activity, the autonomy of the governing bodies of sport and the pressure for co-ordination and control coming from the government and the Sports Council. Indeed the best prospect for the strengthening of the policy community is as a reaction to persistent government intervention in what are considered to be areas of traditional autonomy for athletes and their governing bodies.

A fourth possible condition for the successful development of the policy community is the existence of a number of policy networks in the area. It is plausible to suggest that, as a specific issue arises, some of the interests affected by it will emerge (possibly at the prompting of government) to form a policy network. This might be to act as a sounding board concerning government proposals or to lobby to protect their interests. The contacts built up by the process of consultation/lobbying will lay the foundations for similar patterns of interaction as related issues arise in the future. In this way interested policy actors are identified and common membership emerges, thus laying the foundation for the development of a policy community and a transition from a reactive to a more proactive role in the policy process. The three case studies provide some support for this hypothesis, but given the immaturity of the policy community for sport it is too soon to draw conclusions regarding the significance of networks for the emergence of communities.

POLICY ISSUES IN SPORT

For Jordan and Richardson the growth of government interest in sport is but one further example of the tendency of modern governments to 'hyperactivity' and of the 'electoral pressure for any potential government to show an interest in all problems and to be confident that it can ameliorate the issue at hand' (1987: 25). The development of interest is hardly surprising, given the rapid growth of sport as an industry, the significance of sport as a leisure pastime, and the number of sport-related issues that arose during the 1980s. Whether a governmental concern with the arts would have drawn a similar response from Jordan and Richardson is open to question. Part of their response was possibly due, not so much to a disdainful attitude towards sport as a proper focus of government concern, but more to the deeply entrenched view that government involvement in sport is in some measure an intrusion into the private sphere.

Whatever attitude academics and politicians have towards the proper relationship between sport and government activity, it is undeniable that the 1980s have seen sport become firmly established as an area of policy activity for government. In the medium to long-term this poses serious problems for those who administer or participate in sport. The post-war consensus among political parties that sport should be supported by government but not become the subject of party political debate is weakening. Too many contemporary issues in sport touch on problems that are the property of other, more influential, policy communities, such as that for law and order, and foreign affairs. There is the risk that, if major organisations in sport fail to assert their interests in the sport-related issues being discussed by government, they will become increasingly peripheral to the policy process and lose what little capacity they have to influence policy development. The most likely consequence of any failure to assert sporting interests effectively is that it will give the government a free hand to exploit sport for its own purposes. Williams *et al.* (1984a), for example, feel that this has already taken place with regard to hooliganism and that the government may be using 'the problem of soccer hooliganism' to galvanise public opinion against all social deviants and to justify its law and order policies. While this is probably a premature assessment it is none the less a distinct possibility and an ominous sign for the future development of sports policy.

If sports organisations are to participate effectively in the policy process then a number of issues need to be considered and problems resolved. The foremost problem is the degree of rivalry and fragmentation among the major national sports organisations. Much has been said in this book about the detrimental effects of fragmentation, and particularly about the poor relationship between the Sports Council and the CCPR. At present the three major bodies, the Council, the CCPR and the British Olympic Association, duplicate a great deal of effort and resources and certainly do not provide the degree of mutual support over policy issues that one would expect, or at least hope for. To expect a merger between these organisations is to oversimplify their respective roles within sport and their overriding concern to protect their sovereignty, and also to ignore the failed attempts at merger between the Council and the CCPR and more recently between the CCPR and the BOA. Discussions are indeed still continuing between the CCPR, the BOA and organisations representing governing bodies in Scotland, Wales and Northern Ireland with a view to developing a closer relationship, short of merger. The aim is to produce a unified 'voice of British sport'. The creation of the British International Sports Committee to speak for British interests at international level is one result of these discussions, though the committee has yet to prove its value. At the domestic level slow progress is being made towards a 'British Sports Forum' which would speak on behalf of British sport and be capable of lobbying the government and the Sports Council. However, it remains to be seen how effective the organisation will turn out to be.

If these discussions fail to produce a strong lobby for British sport it may well be that it is the CCPR that is in the weakest position, as it is vulnerable to the steady improvement in the relationship between the Sports Council and governing bodies, particularly as sport development work becomes more prominent. The CCPR is also vulnerable to any expansion in the role of the BOA. Don Anthony, writing in 1980, also considered the question of how to overcome the 'petty squabbling and power struggles' within the national administration of sport (1980: 134). His solution was to enhance the role of the BOA, with the opportunity to do so arising from a successful bid to host a future Olympic Games. For Anthony the BOA was suitable as a focus for national sport administration because it:

> is the oldest of the British multi-sport bodies; it is the only truly *British* organisation; its membership is open to institutions *and* individuals; it is open to Olympic sports and non-Olympic sports; it is concerned with elite sport and mass sport; it has health and education as concurrent objectives; it has a special role in cultivating the fine arts.
>
> (1980: 135; emphasis in the original)

While the BOA has the potential to develop the range of interests and contacts indicated by Anthony, it has generally been reluctant, and, it must be said, has also lacked the resources to broaden its range of concerns. Britain's national Olympic association has consciously adopted a narrowly defined role in sport. Unlike many other national Olympic organisations (such as those in the United States and in Italy), which are the focus for national sports policy and administration, the BOA restricts itself to a concern with elite sport and Olympic competition. It has also been especially determined to maintain its distance from government since Mrs Thatcher's attempt to force a boycott of the Moscow Olympic Games on British athletes. However, the BOA is taking some tentative steps to widen the range of services it offers to elite athletes and, depending on how broad the range of services becomes, it may well be the case that some of the major governing bodies will find the Association a more valuable voice for their interests than the CCPR. There is also evidence that the BOA is beginning to develop a complementary and mutually rewarding relationship with the Sports Council. The combination of the Sports Council and the BOA would make a formidable lobbying partnership, but possibly at the expense of the CCPR.

Whatever the extent to which the major national sports bodies take Colin Moynihan's advice quoted at the start of this chapter to form a single representative body to speak on behalf of sport, a key requirement is that a capacity to consider policy strategically is developed. In the football hooliganism and children's sport case studies the importance of a sense of strategy is all too apparent. With regard to hooliganism the readmission of British clubs to European competition is as much the result of government fatigue and UEFA's indecision than a reflection of a successful policy to combat football spectator violence. It represents not a resolution of the problem but rather a lull in government interest. As such it provides an aspiring policy network with an opportunity to achieve greater influence and grasp the initiative.

Seeking organisational solutions to the problem of the weakness of sports organisations in many policy networks is of only limited utility. A further element in the explanation concerns the absence of any clearly articulated statement of the intrinsic values of sport. While there will always be those who will justify good health in terms of productivity gains at work, and justify high standards of education in terms of meeting the needs of the economy or the need to instil certain values in children, there will also be a highly vociferous group who will justify good health and education as being valuable in their own right; that to be healthy and to be well educated are both intrinsically desirable conditions. Where are the voices making the claims for the intrinsic worth of sport?

One of the missing ingredients in the development of an effective policy community for sport is a clearly articulated set of values for sport. Too many national bodies are willing, if not quite content, to accept statements of the value of sport similar to those used by the Minister in his open letter to John Smith, when he was chairman of the Sports Council, which justified sport in terms of its value for the nation's health, its contribution to the alleviation of social deprivation, and its contribution to national morale and international standing through sporting success. It would be naive to expect sports bodies to bid for government resources on the basis of the intrinsic value of sport alone. Even doctors and teachers will be sensitive to the priorities of the government of the day when they are framing their bids for resources. However, they will still articulate the intrinsic values of the service as part of their case. A clear expression of the values inherent in a service is an important ingredient in developing the cohesion of a policy community.

The range of issues facing sport in the 1990s includes not just those dealt with in this book but a number of others, such as the relationship to the media, the role of commercial sponsorship, racism, sexism and the amateur/professional distinction. If sportsmen and women are to be in a position to influence the policy decisions associated with these issues they need an organisationally and ideologically coherent presence within a range of policy networks. While some progress has been made during the 1980s it has been painfully slow and there still remain too many issues where the interests of sport are likely to be defined by organisations with no particular commitment to sport itself.

POSTSCRIPT

The administrative map of government is rarely fixed for any length of time. New priorities, the preferences of senior ministers, the need to reward loyal supporters and the appointment of a new Prime Minister may each prompt a review of the allocation of responsibilities between government departments. Responsibility for sport and recreation was initially located in the Ministry of Housing and Local Government, was later moved to the Department of Education and Science before finding a home for over twenty years in the Department of the Environment. In December 1990, following John Major's appointment as Prime Minister, sport and recreation responsibilities were moved again, back to the Department of Education and Science. On his transfer the Minister took with him the sport and recreation division (SARD) and responsibility for funding the Sports Council.

Given that the DOE has the main responsibility for financing local authority expenditure and that local authorities are the main providers of sport and recreation facilities for the general public, the transfer is indeed a curious decision. The transfer has left many of the general features of the organisation and responsibilities of SARD unaltered. Robert Atkins, the Minister appointed in July 1990 to replace Colin Moynihan, is still able to spend only a small proportion of his time on sports issues as these are only one part of the range of responsibilities within his new department. His rank has not changed and therefore his seniority within the DES is no greater than it was within the DOE. Finally, SARD is still a small division within a large and busy department.

The most likely strategic explanation for the move may be

267

found in the increasing prominence of school sport as a political issue. The CCPR has been lobbying intensively on the issue as has the Secondary Heads Association. Both organisations must feel a degree of satisfaction at the transfer, as it may be argued that the location of SARD within the DES provides it, and the Minister, with clearer access to key policy networks concerned with curriculum development, staff development, the use of playing fields and education finance. However, it may also be argued that while it was difficult for the Minister to criticise DES policy from his position in the DOE, it is all but impossible for him to do so from within the DES. The discipline of ministerial loyalty may therefore result in Robert Atkins being a less effective voice on behalf of school sport. Thus although school sport will undoubtedly have a higher profile in the DES due to the Minister's presence there is still no assurance that this alone will strengthen his hand sufficiently for it to affect the outcome of the policy deliberations.

Whatever the eventual impact that the Minister and SARD are able to make on education policy there will inevitably be a period of mutual adjustment as the new responsibilities are accommodated within the culture of the DES. Thus while the Minister will hope to affect education policy as it impinges on sport, and may well be successful, it will also be the case that sport policy will be affected by being viewed from an education perspective rather than from the perspective prevailing in the DOE.

The impact of the transfer of departmental responsibility on the Sports Council is one of the most important broader implications that needs to be considered. There can be little doubt that the Council would have preferred to have stayed in the DOE. In its new departmental home it is more remote from a cluster of sport-related functions including countryside recreation, land-use planning and local government finance. The disruption of the Council's established pattern of relationships is intensified by the current review of its future instigated by Robert Atkins. The review is expected to be completed by the middle of 1991, and it is clear that a number of radical options are being considered ranging from absorption into the ministry, to the devolution of substantial functions to the regional level along the lines recently announced for the Arts Council. What is probably more likely is that the Council will retain its independent status, but that the role of the regions will be enhanced and that the Council's role will be defined more narrowly. The uncertainty caused by the combination of a major review and the transfer to a new department is bound to limit the ability of the Council to act effectively on sports issues. It can only be hoped that clear decisions are taken soon and that the momentum on policies concerning drug abuse and widening participation is not lost.

NOTES

1 SPORT, POLITICS AND POLICIES

1 Quoted in Grayson (1988).
2 Quoted in Jones (1988: 75).
3 The major exception is Asian women, whose level of participation is significantly lower than for women in general.
4 For a sample of research material with a British focus see Ouseley (1983), DES (1983),Wolverhampton Borough Council (1985), Lewisham (1985).
5 Quoted in *The Independent*, 3 April 1990.
6 The comment was made during a BBC documentary, *Inside Story: The Race Game*, 2 May 1990.
7 Although generally referred to as the Minister for Sport or even the Sports Minister, the proper title of the incumbent is Under-Secretary of State with the Department of the Environment, which is a third-level ministerial position in the department. Those who have held the post under Mrs Thatcher have all had this title, although Denis Howell held a second-level position as Minister of State at the DOE in the late 1960s. Rather than use the lengthy title of the present holder I will use the conventional title of Minister for Sport throughout this text.

2 CENTRAL GOVERNMENT AND SPORT

1 The figure for the DOE is from *Civil Service Statistics, 1987, HMSO*, and is for full time equivalent staff. It excludes staff employed by the Property Services Agency and the Crown Suppliers.
2 Management Information System for Ministers (MINIS) is prepared on an annual basis by each division of the DOE and outlines objectives for the forthcoming twelve months and evaluates progress over the preceding twelve months in achieving objectives. See Metcalfe and Richards (1987: ch. 3) for more details.

3 THE ROLE OF LOCAL GOVERNMENT IN SPORT

1 Owing to the difficulty of defining leisure services any figures relating to expenditure need to be treated cautiously. This figure is taken from the analysis of local authority expenditure produced by CIPFA (1989).

4 THE SPORTS COUNCIL AND THE ROLE OF GOVERNMENT AGENCIES

1 The Sports Council employed in 1988–89 635 staff divided between headquarters (156), regional offices (207) and the national sports centres (272).
2 In 1988–89 the Sports Council distributed grants to over seventy national governing bodies, including £430,724 to basketball, £387,803 to swimming, and £6,000 to baseball. Among the other national organisations to receive grant aid were the British Association of National Coaches (£24,374), the British Sports Association for the Disabled (£143,000) and the British Polytechnics' Sports Association (£1,785). Grants for specific projects included £129,792 to help governing bodies play a full part in international affairs, £294,088 for doping control and £840,633 for the Action Sport scheme.
3 The CCPR covers the major sports organisations for England. Similar bodies exist in Scotland, Wales and Northern Ireland.
4 In 1988–89 the CCPR and the BOA discussed the possibility of a merger between the two organisations. The talks eventually broke down, with the BOA withdrawing from the CCPR. From the BOA's point of view there was little to be gained from a merger and there was the concern that the merger might compromise its independence. However, from the CCPR's point of view the merger was extremely attractive, arising not simply from the status of the BOA but also from its substantial income.
5 See chapter 5 for a fuller discussion of the role of the British International Sports Committee.

5 THE GOVERNING BODIES OF SPORT

1 Sports Council, *Annual report, 1980–81*, p.3.
2 Graham Kelly, interviewed on *Panorama*, 'Football: Safe in their Hands?', BBC Television, 10 April 1989.
3 *Panorama*, 'Football: Safe in their Hands?', BBC Television, 10 April 1989.
4 Ibid.

6 THE POLICY PROCESS FOR SPORT

1 Quoted in Fry (1985).
2 See, for example, Jordan and Richardson (1987), Hogwood and Gunn

(1984), Dunleavy and O'Leary (1987), McGrew and Wilson (1982), Burch and Wood (1983), Ham and Hill (1984).
3 See Offe (1981) and O'Conner (1973) for attempts to ground the state's relative autonomy in its control of resources rather than in its relationship to the ruling class.
4 The following references provide a fuller outline of the rational model and the incrementalist critique: McGrew and Wilson (1982: Section 2), Leach and Stewart (1982: ch. 1), Ham and Hill (1984: ch. 5), Richardson and Jordan (1979: ch. 1).

7   THE DEVELOPMENT OF POLICY FOR FOOTBALL HOOLIGANISM

1 Comments made by the Prime Minister in her statement to the House of Commons following the Heysel stadium disaster.
2 In May 1985 fire broke out at Bradford City football ground in one of its main stands during a football match. Over fifty people died as a result of the fire. In April 1989 ninety-five people were killed as a result of crushing on the terraces of Sheffield Wednesday's Hillsborough ground during the FA Cup semi-final between Nottingham Forest and Liverpool.
3 See Williams *et al.* (1984a) and Pearson (1983) for a summary of the extent and history of spectator violence.
4 See Canter *et al.* (1989) for a review of these and other research findings.
5 During this crucial period in the mid 1980s there were three Ministers for Sport. The rapid turnover can have done little to develop a consistent approach to policy and relations with the football authorities and may well have weakened the Minister's position *vis-à-vis* the Prime Minister and possibly the football authorities.
6 The value of all-seat stadiums as a solution to the problem of football hooliganism is debatable. What evidence there is suggests that its contribution will be limited (Williams *et al.* 1984b).

8   THE DEVELOPMENT OF POLICY TO COMBAT DRUG ABUSE BY ATHLETES

1 Dr Mario Astaphan was Ben Johnson's doctor and made this remark in his evidence to the Canadian government inquiry into drug taking in sport. Quoted in *The Independent*, 27 May 1989.
2 Quoted in *The Independent*, 7 February 1989.
3 The BCF carried out tests at the 1965 Milk Race and by 1967 had developed a set of regulations for cycling.
4 Testimony to a US Senate Committee in 1973.
5 Quoted in the *Observer*, 11 December 1988, p.20.
6 The reason that Delgado was not penalised for drug taking was a delay by the Union Cycliste Internationale (the ISF for cycling) in adding

Probenecid to its list of proscribed drugs. Although the IOC and the IAAF had added Probenecid to their list in January and April 1988 respectively the UCI did not include it on its list until August 1988, when the Tour de France had already taken place.

7 The phrase 'core list' is used because the aim of policy-making is not necessarily to encourage all governing bodies to adopt a uniform list of proscribed drugs. Increasingly the attitude of the Sports Council and of the IOC is to encourage governing bodies and ISFs to adapt the IOC list to the needs of particular sports.

8 Although the geographical distribution of accredited laboratories is worrying, as it inhibits the diffusion of expertise, it must be acknowledged that, in general, laboratories are most needed in those countries that hold the most international competitions, namely Europe and North America.

9 Quantitative analysis is a normal part of the analytical procedures for many drugs. The problem of attempting to set a quantity level which would be allowable for therapeutic purposes is best illustrated in events that take place over a period of time, for example long distance cycle races such as the Tour de France and the Milk Race. For example, what interpretation can be put on finding a small quantity of a banned substance in a cyclist's urine sample if it is found on the fifth day of the race? One possible conclusion is that it is the traces of a drug he/she took the previous night. Another interpretation is that it is a trace of a much larger quantity of the drug taken five or six days ago.

10 This decision follows the failure, in 1987, owing to lack of parliamentary time, of Menzies Campbell's Private Member's Bill which sought to have anabolic steroids declared a controlled drug under the Misuse of Drugs Act 1971.

11 For example, in Norway (Norman 1987), the USA (*Athletics Weekly*, 3 December 1987), Britain (*Athletics Weekly*, 26 November 1987),

9 SPORT POLICY FOR SCHOOL-AGE CHILDREN

1 Quoted in *Olympic Review*, No. 237, 1987, p.11.

2 See Murdoch (1987: section 2) for a summary of the range of organisations debating issues related to school sport. She also indicates the variety of ways in which pressure was brought to bear on the DOE and the DES to raise the political profile of the issue.

3 See, for example, CCPR (1983, 1984).

4 In a recent review of local authority youth work there is no discussion of the role of sport (National Youth Bureau 1987).

5 McStravick, in a report for the BAAB, noted that 'Damaging criticisms have been made of the PE profession by governing bodies of sport, its collective body the CCPR and corresponding comments have been returned, with equal amounts of force, by the PE profession . . .' (1989).

6 Sparkes (1990: 237) refers to 'the battle that physical educators are engaged in with other subjects for limited resources in schools', while

Evans (1986: 2) notes the concern of the physical education teachers 'not only for their own status within the school community but also for their very survival in the curriculum'. See also Carr (1983), Meakin (1983), ILEA (1988) and Parry (1986) for a fuller flavour of the debate.

7 This attitude no doubt accounts for the limited impact of the DES Circular 16/78, 'The Development of Sporting Talent in Children of School Age' (6 December 1978). The circular encouraged schools and local education authorities to give every opportunity for a pupil to develop his/her talent.

8 Not all educationists are pessimistic. Williams and Jenkins (1988) express the hope that the national curriculum may strengthen the bargaining position of PE staff in schools.

9 One interesting innovation concerns Timperley Lacrosse and Hockey Club, which has developed a close relationship with a local school. The school uses the club's facilities during the day and the club uses the school's gymnasium for training in the evenings. Some coaching support is also provided by the club.

10 The AAA/BAAB has probably gone further than most governing bodies in attempting to devise a strategy for school-age children. See in particular McStravick (1989).

11 The major exception is the Active Life Styles project in Coventry, which is discussed later in this chapter. But the PACE (Participation Athletics Community Enterprise) scheme is another successful example of the Sports Council supporting an initiative by a local athletic club (Wolverhampton and Bilston AC) to build links with schools.

10   CONCLUSION

1 Colin Moynihan made this remark during a speech to the CCPR's 1989 annual conference (29 November), having just quoted from the thirty-seventh report of the House of Commons Public Accounts Committee, which was severely critical of the relationship between the Sports Council and the CCPR.

BIBLIOGRAPHY

Acres, D. (1982) *Football Hooliganism*, London: Football Trust.

Alderman, G. (1978) *British Elections*, London: B.T. Batsford.

Allison, L. (ed.) (1986) *The Politics of Sport*, Manchester: Manchester University Press.

Arthur Anderson (1989) *The Football League Management*, London: Arthur Anderson.

Anderson, I.G. (1977) *Councils, Committees and Boards*, 3rd edition, Beckenham, Kent: CBD Research Ltd.

Anthony, D. (1980) *A Strategy for British Sport*, London: C. Hurst & Co.

Arthur, P. (1983) *The Government and Politics of Northern Ireland*, London: Longman.

Ashe, A. (1988) *A Hard Road to Glory: A History of the African–American athlete*, Vol. 1 *1619–1918*, Vol. 2 *1919–1945*, Vol. 3 . . . *since 1946*, New York: Warner Books.

Association of District Councils (1978) *Written Evidence to the Yates Committee on Recreation Management Training*, London: ADC.

Atkinson, J. (1985) 'Competition and the Child', in *Coaching Focus*, No. 2, autumn.

Audit Commission (1989) *Sport for Whom?*, London: HMSO.

Bachrach, P. and Baratz, M.S. (1970) *Power and Poverty*, New York: Oxford University Press.

Baddeley, S. (1988) 'Why Ban Drugs?', *Badminton Now*, 4.56.

Bailey, P. (1979) *Leisure and Class in Victorian England*, London: Routledge & Kegan Paul.

Bains Report (1972) *The New Local Authorities: Management and Structure, Working Party on Local Authority Management*, chairman M.A. Bains, London: HMSO.

Barker, A. (1981) *Quangos in Britain*, Basingstoke: Macmillan.

Barret, S. and Fudge, C. (eds) (1981) *Policy and Action*, London: Methuen.

Bauer, F. (1988) 'Leisure in France', *Leisure Management*, March.

Benington, J. and White, J. (1986) *The Future Role and Organisation of Local Government; Functional Study No. 4; Leisure*, Birmingham: Institute of Local Government Studies, University of Birmingham.

Benson, J.K. (1979) 'Interorganisational Networks and Policy Sectors: Notes towards Comparative Analysis', Mimeo, University of Missouri.

Benson, J.K. (1982) 'Networks and Policy Sectors: A Framework for extending Interorganisational Analysis', in Rogers, D. and Whitten, D., *Interorganisational Co-ordination*, Iowa: Iowa State University.

Bogdanor, V. (1981) *The People and the Party System*, Cambridge: Cambridge University Press.

Bottomley, M. (1987) *BAAB (Great Britain) report, Official Proceedings*, International Athletic Foundation World Symposium on Doping in Sport, Florence: IAF.

Bottomley, R. (1989) 'The Birth of a New Company', *Recreation Management 1989: Proceedings of the Sports Council's National Seminar*, London: Sports Council.

Bowen, G. (1978) *Survey of Fringe Bodies*, London: CSD.

Bowles, S. and Chappell, R. (1986) 'Women and Athletics', *Athletics Coach*, 20.2, June.

Bramham, P., Henry, I., Mommaas, H., and Van der Poel, H. (1989) *Leisure and Urban Processes: Critical Studies of Leisure Policy in Western European Cities*, London: Routledge.

Brohm, J-M. (1979) *Sport: A Prison of Measured Time*, London: Pluto Press.

Brown, W.M. (1984) 'Comments on Simon and Fraleigh', *Journal of the Philosophy of Sport*, XI.

Bucher, C. (1972) *Foundations of Physical Education*, New York: C.V. Moseby & Co.

Burch, M. and Wood, B. (1983) *Public Policy in Britain*, Oxford: Martin Robertson.

Byers, Lord (1968) *A Structure for British Sport*, London: AAA/BAAB.

Canter, D., Comber, M. and Uzzell, D.L. (1989) *Football in it Place: an Environmental Psychology of Football Grounds*, London: Routledge.

Carr, D. (1983) 'The Place of Physical Education in the School Curriculum', *Momentum*, 8.1.

Casbon, C. (1988) 'Examinations in PE – A Path to Curriculum Development', *British Journal of Physical Education*, 19.6.

Central Council of Physical Recreation (undated) *The CCPR. A Guide: What it is and What it Does*, London: CCPR.

Central Council of Physical Recreation (1983) *Multiple Use – Working for Everybody's Benefit*, London: CCPR.

Central Council of Physical Recreation (1984) *Sports Fields at Risk: An Assessment by the CCPR*, London: CCPR.

Central Council of Physical Recreation (1987) *Conference Report*, London: CCPR.

Chandler, J.A. (1988) *Public Policy-making for Local Government*, London: Croom Helm.

Chartered Institute of Public Finance and Accountancy (1980) *Leisure and Recreation Statistics, 1979–1980 Estimates*, London: CIPFA.

Chartered Institute of Public Finance and Accountancy (1989) *Leisure and Recreation Statistics*, London: CIPFA.

Clarke, J. (1978) 'Football and Working Class Fans: Tradition and Change', in Ingham (1978).

Clements, D.B. (1983) 'Drug Use Survey: Results and Conclusions', *Physician and Sports Medicine*, 11.

Coakley, J.J. (1986) *Sport in Society: Issues and Controversies*, 3rd edition, St Louis: Times Mirror/ Mosby College Publishing.

Coalter, F. (1984) 'Public Policy and Leisure', in *Leisure: Politics, Planning and People*, Vol. 1, *Plenary Papers*, ed. A. Tomlinson, Brighton: Leisure Studies Association.

Coalter, F. with Long, J. and Duffield, B (1986) *Rationale for Public Sector Investment in Leisure*, London: Sports Council and Economic and Social Research Council.

Cobham Report (1973) *Second Report of the Select Committee of the House of Lords on Sport and Leisure*, London: HMSO.

Conservative Party (1987) *The Next Moves Forward*, London: Conservative Party Central Office.

Cooter, G.R. (1980) 'Amphetamine Use, Physical Activity and Sport', *Journal of Drug Issues*, 10.

Council of Europe (1985) *European Convention on Spectator Violence and Misbehaviour at Sports Events and in Particular at Football Matches*, Strasbourg: Council of Europe.

Coventry City Council (1989) *Active Life Styles: Information Folder*, Coventry: Coventry City Council.

Crick, B. (1964) *In Defence of Politics*, Harmondsworth: Penguin.

Critcher, C. (1986) 'Radical Theorists of Sport: The State of Play', *Sociology of Sport Journal*, 3.

Cunningham, J. and Fahey, J. (1976) 'Administrators and Professionals in Local Government', *Local Government Studies*, 2.4.

Dahl, R. (1961) 'The Behavioural Approach to Political Science', *American Political Science Review*, 55.4, December.

Davies, A. (1979) *What's Wrong with Quangos?*, London: Outer Circle Policy Unit.

Delaney, T. (1984) *The Roots of Rugby League*, Keighley, published by the author.

Department of Education and Science (1968) *Report of Committee on Football*, chairman, Sir Norman Chester, London: HMSO.

Department of Education and Science (1981) Education (School Premises) Regulations (SI 1981/909), London: DES.

Department of Education and Science (1982) *Experience and Participation: Report of a Review Group on the Youth Service in England*, Cmd. 8686, London: HMSO.

Department of Education and Science (1983) *Young People in the 80s; A Survey*, London: HMSO.

Department of Education and Science (1984) *The Organisation and Content of the 5–16 Curriculum*, London: HMSO.

Department of Education and Science (1987) *The National Curriculum 5–16: a Consultation Document*, London: DES.

Department of Education and Science/ Department of the Environment

(1989) *The Government's Response to the School Sport Forum Report*, London, DES/DOE, 19 November.

Department of the Environment (1975) *Sport and Recreation*, Cmnd. 6200, London: HMSO.

Department of the Environment (1984) *Football Spectator Violence: Report of an Official Working Party*, London: HMSO.

Department of the Environment (1986) Press Release: Sport in Schools, 26 November, London: DOE.

Department of the Environment/Department of Education and Science (1986) *Sport in Schools Seminar; Report of Proceedings*, London: DOE/DES.

Doig, A. (1979) 'The Machinery of Government and the Growth of Governmental Bodies', *Public Administration*, 57.3.

Donike, M. (1987) Dope Analysis, *Official Proceedings*, International Athletic Foundation World Symposium on Doping in Sport, Florence: IAF.

Donnelly, P. (1986) 'The Paradox of Parks: the Politics of Recreational Land use before and after the Mass Trespass', *Leisure Studies*, 5.2.

Donohoe, T. and Johnson, N. (1986) *Foul Play: Drug Abuse in Sports*, Oxford: Blackwell.

Downs, A. (1967) *Inside Bureaucracy*, Boston: Little Brown.

Downs, A. (1972) 'Up and down with ecology – the "issue attention cycle"', *Public Interest*, 28.

Dror, Y. (1968) *Public Policy Making Re-examined*, San Francisco: Chandler.

Dunleavy, P.J. (1981) 'Professions and Policy Change: Notes towards a Model of Ideological Corporatism', *Public Administration Bulletin*, No.36, August.

Dunleavy, P.J. and O'Leary, B. (1987) *Theories of the State*, Basingstoke: Macmillan.

Dunning, E.G., Murphy, P. and Williams, J. (1982) *Working Class Social Bonding and the Sociogenesis of Football Hooliganism*, London: SSRC.

Dunning, E.G., Murphy, P. and Williams, J. (1986) 'Spectator Violence at Football Matches: Towards a Sociological Explanation', *British Journal of Sociology*, 37.2.

Dunning, E.G., Murphy, P. and Williams, J. (1988) *Roots of Football Hooliganism*, London: Routledge & Kegan Paul.

Dye, T. (1975) *Understanding Public Policy*, 2nd edition, Englewood Cliffs, N.J.: Prentice-Hall.

Easton, D. (1965) *A Systems Analysis of Political Life*, Chicago: Chicago University Press.

Eichberg, H. (1981) 'The unexplored areas in Olympic sports', *Eleventh Olympic Congress, Bulletin No. 8*, Baden-Baden: IOC.

Eichberg, H. (1984) 'Olympic Sport – Neocolonialism and Alternatives', *International Review for the Sociology of Sport*, 19.1.

Elcock, H. (1986) *Local Government: Politicians, Professionals and the Public in Local Authorities*, 2nd edition, London: Methuen.

Espy, R. (1979) *The Politics of the Olympic Games*, Berkeley: University of California Press.

Evans, H.J. (1974) *Services to Sport: The Story of the CCPR, 1935 to 1972*, London: Pelham Books.

Evans, J. (ed.) (1986) *Physical Education, Sport and Schooling*, Lewes: The Falmer Press.

Evans Report (1986) *A Structure for a British Athletics Federation*, London: British Amateur Athletic Board.

Evans, W.A.L. (1989) *British Athletics Federation, Introduction*, Birmingham: AAA.

Football League (1983) *Report of the Committee of Enquiry into Structure and Finance*, chairman Sir Norman Chester, Lytham St Anne's: Football League.

Football League (1986) *Hooliganism at Football Matches*, Lytham St Annes: The Football League.

Friend, J., Power, J.M. and Yewlett, C.J.L. (1974) *Public Planning: The Inter-corporate Dimension*, London: Tavistock.

Fry, G. (1985) 'The Career Civil Service under Challenge', paper presented at the Public Administration Conference, York, September.

Gaughan, J. (1989) 'The Contract and Specification', *Recreation Management 1989, Proceedings of the Sports Council's National Seminar*, London: Sports Council.

Gilbert, D. (1980) *The Miracle Machine*, New York: Coward McCann & Geoghegan.

Gleeson, G. (1985) 'Sport for Children – Necessary? Educational? Both?', *Coaching Focus*, No. 2, autumn.

Gold, Sir A. (1985) 'A Challenge to Coaches', *Coaching Focus*, 1. 12.

Grayson, E. (1988) *Sport and the Law*, London: Butterworth.

Greenwood, R. and Stewart, J. (1974) *Corporate Planning in Local Government*, London: Charles Knight.

Greenwood, R., Hinings, C.R., Ranson, S. and Walsh, K. (1976) *In Pursuit of Corporate Rationality: Organisational Developments in the Post-reorganisation Period*, Birmingham: Institute of Local Government Studies, University of Birmingham

Gunn Report (1986) *Management Training for Leisure and Recreation in Scotland*, Working Party Report, chairman L.A. Gunn, Edinburgh: Scottish Education Department.

Guttman, A. (1984) *The Games Must Go On: Avery Brundage and the Olympic Movement*, New York: Columbia University Press.

Ham, C. and Hill, M. (1984) *The Policy Process in the Modern Capitalist State*, Brighton: Wheatsheaf.

Hanley, D.F. (1979) *Sports Medicine and Physiology*, Philadelphia: Saunders.

Hantrais, L. (1984) 'Leisure policy in France', *Leisure Studies*, 3.

Hantrais, L. (1987) 'The Implications of Comparitive Research into Leisure for Social Policy: a Franco-British Example', *Society and Leisure*, 10.2, autumn.

Hantrais, L. (1989) 'Central Government Policy in France under the Socialist Administration, 1981–86', in Bramham *et al.* (1989).

Hardman, K. (1980) 'The Development of Physical Education in the German Democratic Republic', *Physical Education Review*, 3.2.

279

Hardman, K. (1987) 'Politics, Ideology and Physical Education in the German Democratic Republic', *British Journal of Physical Education*, 18.1.

Hargreaves, J. (1985a) 'From Social Democracy to Authoritarian Populism: State Intervention in Sport and Physical Recreation in Contemporary Britain', *Leisure Studies*, 4.

Hargreaves, J. (1985b) *Theatre of the Great: Sport and Hegemony in Britain*, Oxford: Blackwell/Polity Press.

Harrington, J.A. (1968) *Soccer Hooliganism: A Preliminary Report*, Bristol: John Wright & Son.

Harvey, J. and Proulx, R. (1988) 'Sport and the State in Canada', in *Not Just a Game*, J. Harvey and H. Cantelon (eds) Ottawa: University of Ottawa Press.

Henry, I. (1985) *The Politics of the New Right*, Part 3, in *Leisure Management*, 5, February.

Her Majesty's Inspectorate of Education (1978) *Physical Education Curriculum (11–16)*, London: HMSO.

Hill, J. (1987) '"First Class" Cricket and the Leagues', *International Journal of the History of Sport*, 4, May.

Hill, D. (1989) *Out of his Skin: the John Barnes Phenomenon*, London: Faber & Faber.

Hill, M. and Bramley, G. (1986) *Analysing Social Policy*, Oxford: Blackwell.

The Hockey Association (1989) *Official Handbook*, London: Hockey Association.

Hogwood, B. (1979) 'Analysing Industrial Policy: a Multi-perspective Approach', *Public Administration Bulletin*, No. 29, April.

Hogwood, B. (1987) *From Crisis to Complacency*, Oxford: Oxford University Press.

Hogwood, B. and Gunn, L. (1984) *Policy Analysis for the Real World*, Oxford: Oxford University Press.

Holt, R. (1989) *Sport and the British; A Modern History*, Oxford: Oxford University Press.

Home Office (1983) *Young People in the 80s: A Survey*, London: HMSO.

Hood, C. (1978a) 'The Crown Agents Affair', *Public Administration*, 56.

Hood, C. (1978b) 'Keeping the Centre Small: Explanations of Agency Type', *Political Studies*, 26.1, March.

Hood, C. (1979) 'The World of Quasi-government: Central Department Bodies and Government Growth', paper presented at the Public Administration Committee Annual Conference, York, 3–5 September.

Hood, C. (1980) 'The Politics of Quangoscide', *Policy and Politics*, 8.3.

Hoose, P.M. (1989) *Necessities: Racial Barriers in American Sport*, New York: Random House.

Hoppner, M. (1987) 'Recommendations for the Organisation and Conduct of Doping Controls at Official IAAF and Area Group Competitions', *Official Proceedings*, International Athletic Foundation World Symposium on Doping in Sport, Florence: IAF.

Houlihan, B. (1988) 'The Professionalisation of Public Sector Sport and Leisure Management', *Local Government Studies*, 14.3, May/June.

House of Commons (1957) *Report of the House of Commons Select Committee on Estimates, Session 1956/57*, London: HMSO.

House of Commons (1986) *Second Report from the Environment Committee, Session 1985/86, The Sports Council*, London: HMSO.

House of Commons (1987) *Fifteenth Report of the Public Accounts Committee, Session 1986/87*, London: HMSO.

House of Commons (1989) Public Accounts Committee, *The Sports Council*, London: HMSO.

House of Commons (1989) *Debates*, 20 March, vol. 149, col. 423w, Hansard, London: HMSO.

House of Commons Library Research Division (1985) Research Note No. 252, Football, House of Commons Library.

House of Commons Library Research Division (1989) Football Spectators Bill, Reference Sheet No. 89/10, London, House of Commons Library.

Howell, D. (1987) *Labour's Action Plan for Sport*, London: The Labour Party.

Howell, D. (1990) *Made in Birmingham: The Memoirs of Denis Howell*, London: Macdonald, Queen Anne Press.

Howie, D. (1987) 'Personal Perspectives', in G. Swain and D. Stead *Youth Work and Sport*, Leicester: National Youth Bureau.

Husbands, C.T. (1986) 'Race and Gender', in H. Drucker, P. Dunleavy, A. Gamble and G. Peele (eds), *Developments in British Politics*, Basingstoke: Macmillan.

Ingham, R. (ed.) (1978) *Football Hooliganism: the Wider Context*, London: Inter-action Imprint.

Inner London Education Authority (1988) *My Favourite Subject*, London: ILEA.

International Amateur Athletic Federation (1988) *IAAF Handbook, 1988–1989*, London: IAAF.

International Amateur Athletic Federation (1989) 'Review of the year', *IAAF Magazine*, 5.1.

International Olympic Committee (1976) *IOC Medical Controls: Games of the XXI Olympiad*, Montreal: IOC.

James, C.L.R. (1963) *Beyond a Boundary*, London: Stanley Paul.

Jenkins W.I. (1978) *Policy Analysis: Political and Organisational Perspectives*, London: Martin Robertson.

Jenkins, B. and Gray, A. (1983) 'Bureaucratic Politics and Power', *Political Studies*, 31.2.

Johnson, W. (ed.) (1980) *Sport and Physical Education around the World*, Champaign, Ill. : University of Illinois Press.

Jones, S.G. (1988) *Sport, Politics and the Working Class*, Manchester: Manchester University Press.

Jordan, A.G. (1981) 'Iron Triangle, Woolly Corporatism and Elastic Nets: Images of the Policy Process', *Journal of Public Policy*, 1.1.

Jordan, A.G. and Richardson, J.J. (1982) 'The British Policy Style or the Logic of Negotiation?', in J.J. Richardson (ed.), *Policy Styles in Western Europe*, London: Allen & Unwin.

Jordan, A.G. and Richardson, J.J. (1987) *British Politics and the Policy Process*, London: Allen & Unwin.

Kilmuir, Viscount (1961) House of Lords, *Debates*, 15 February, col. 867, Hansard, London: HMSO.

Kirk, D., McKay, J. and George, L.F. (1986) 'All Work and No Play? Hegemony in the Physical Education Curriculum', *Trends and Developments in PE, Proceedings of the VIII Commonwealth and International Conference on Sport, PE, Dance, Recreation and Health*, London: Spon.

Knox, C. (1986) 'Political Symbolism and Leisure Provision in Northern Ireland Local Government', *Local Government Studies*, September–October, 12.5.

Knox, C. (1987) 'Territorialism, Leisure and Community Centres in Northern Ireland', *Leisure Studies*, 6.

Knox, C. (1989) 'Local Government Leisure Services: Planning and Politics in Northern Ireland', unpublished PhD thesis, University of Birmingham.

Kogan, M. (1975) *Educational Policy-making*, London: Allen & Unwin.

Kroll, M. (1969) 'Policy and Administration', in F.J. Lyden, G.A. Shipman and M. Kroll, *Policies, Decisions and Organisation*, New York: Appleton-Century-Crofts.

Laffin, M. (1986) 'Professional Communities and Policy Communities in Central–Local Relations', in M. Goldsmith (ed.), *New Research in Central–Local Relations*, Aldershot: Gower.

Laffin, M. and Young, K. (1985) 'The Changing Role and Responsibilities of Local Authority Chief Executives', *Public Administration*, 63.1, spring.

Lasswell, H. (1958) *Politics, Who gets What, When and How*, New York: Meridian.

Lawrence, R.Z. and Pellegrom, J.D. (1989) 'Fools' Gold: How America Pays to Lose in the Olympics', *Brookings Review*, 22, fall.

Leach, S. and Stewart, J. (eds) (1982) *Approaches in Public Policy*, London: Allen & Unwin.

Leftwich, A. (1984) *What is Politics?* Oxford: Blackwell.

Lewisham Borough Council (1985) *Leisure Needs of Black People*, London: Borough of Lewisham.

Lightbown, C. and Schwartz, C. (1988) *Millwall in the Community*, London: Millwall FC.

Lindblom, C. (1977) *Politics and Markets*, New York: Basic Books.

Ljungqvist, A. (1975) 'The Use of Anabolic Steroids in top Swedish Athletes', *British Journal of Sports Medicine*, 9.

Ljungqvist, A. (1987) 'The Responsibility of the Medical Delegate at Athletic Competitions', *Official Proceedings*, International Athletic Foundation World Symposium on Doping in Sport, Florence: IAF.

Lodge, P. and Blackstone, T. (1982) *Educational Policy and Educational Inequality*, Oxford: Martin Robertson.

London Regional Council for Sport and Recreation (1989) *Black and Ethnic Minority Participation*, London: LRCSR.

Lovesey, P. (1979) *The Official Centenary History of the AAA*, Enfield: Guinness Superlatives.

McElhone Report (1977) *Report of the Working Group on Football Crowd Behaviour*, Scottish Education Department, Edinburgh: HMSO.

Macfarlane , N. (1986) *Sport and Politics: a World Divided*, London: Collins Willow.

McGrew, A.G. and Wilson, M.J. (eds) (1982) *Decision Making: Approaches and Analysis*, Manchester: Manchester University Press.

Macintosh, D. (1988) 'Federal Government and Voluntary Sports Associations', in J. Harvey and H. Cantelon (eds) *Not Just a Game*, Ottawa: University of Ottawa Press.

McIntosh, P. (1979) *Fair Play: Ethics in Sport and Education*, London: Heinemann.

McIntosh, P. and Charlton, V. (1985) *The Impact of Sport for All Policy, 1966–1984, and a Way Forward*, London: Sports Council.

McPherson, A. and Raab, C.D. (1988) *Education: A Sociology of Policy since 1945*, Edinburgh: Edinburgh University Press.

Macrory Report (1970) *Review Body on Local Government in Northern Ireland*, chairman P. Macrory, Cmnd. 546, London: HMSO.

McStravick, B. (1989) *Post Office Counters Schools Athletics Report*, Birmingham: BAAB.

Marsh, P., Rosser, E. and Harre, R. (1978) *The Rules of Disorder*, London: Routledge & Kegan Paul.

Mason, T. (1980) *Association Football and English Society*, Brighton: Wheatsheaf.

Mason, T. (1988) *Sport in Britain*, London: Faber & Faber.

Maud Report (1967) *Committee on the Management of Local Government*, chairman Sir John Maud, London: HMSO.

Meakin, D.C. (1983) 'On the Justification of Physical Education', *Momentum*, 8.3.

Metcalfe, L. and Richards, S. (1987) *Improving Public Management*, London: Sage.

Miliband, R. (1969) *The State in Capitalist Society*, London: Weidenfeld & Nicolson.

Millar, J.D.B. (1962) *The Nature of Politics*, London: Duckworth.

Millward, H.B. (1982) 'Interorganisational Policy Systems and Research on Public Organisations', *Administration and Society*, 13.4.

Moelwyn-Hughes Report (1946) *An Enquiry into the Collapse of Barriers at Bolton Wanderers Football Ground*, Cmnd. 6846, London: HMSO.

Morgan, T. (1979) 'Dual Use and Joint Provision', in Rees, B. and Parker, S. *Community Leisure and Culture: Arts and Sports Provision*, Bournmouth: The Leisure Studies Association.

Moynihan, C. (1988) letter to Jacques Georges, President of UEFA, 14 June.

Moynihan, C. and Coe, S. (1987) *The Misuse of Drugs in Sport*, London: Department of the Environment.

Munn, J. (1985) 'Working Together: The Roles of Education and Recreation Departments', *Sports Council Recreation Management Conference: Youth . . . Stepping into Leisure*, London: Sports Council.

Munro, J. (1970) *A Proposed Sport Policy for Canadians*, Ottawa: Queen's Printer.

Murdoch, E. (1987) *Sport in Schools*, London: Sports Council.

Murdoch, E. (1990) 'PE in the National Curriculum: Interim Working Group Progress Report', *British Journal of PE*, 21.1, spring.

National Audit Office (1986) *Report on the Sponsorship of Non-departmental Public Bodies*, London: HMSO.

National Audit Office (1989) *Financial Management and Control of the Sports Council*, London: HMSO.

National Council for Voluntary Youth Services (1987) 'Sport, Young People and the Youth Service', in *National Youth Bureau* (1987).

National Playing Fields Association (1989) *The State of Play*, London: NPFA.

National Youth Bureau (1987) *Reshaping the Youth Service*, Leicester: National Youth Bureau.

Nicholson, R.H. (1986) 'Drugs and Sport', *Institute of Medical Ethics Bulletin*, No.16.

Nicholson, R.H. (1987) 'Drugs in Sport', *National Rifle Association Journal*, LXVI.3.

Nixon, R. (1985) 'Working Together: The Role of Education and Recreation Departments', *Sports Council Recreation Management Conference: Youth . . . Stepping into Leisure*, London: Sports Council.

Norman, N. (1987) Norway report, *Official Proceedings*, International Athletic Foundation World Symposium on Doping in Sport, Florence: IAF.

Norton, A. (1987) *'The Future Role of Local Government: France'*, Birmingham: Institute of Local Government Studies, University of Birmingham.

O'Conner, J. (1973) *The Fiscal Crisis of the State*, New York: St Martin's Press.

Offe, C. (1981) 'The Attribution of Public Status to Interest Groups: Observations on the West German Case', in Berger, S. (ed.), *Organising Interests in Western Europe*, Cambridge: Cambridge University Press.

Ojeme, E.O. (1984) 'Has the Name Physical Education Outlived its Usefulness?', *The Physical Educator*, 41.4, December.

Ouseley H. (1983) 'London Against Racism in Sport and Recreation', paper presented to seminar *Sport and Recreation in London's Inner City; Special Needs – Special Measures*, Greater London and South East Council for Sport and Recreation, London, 23 November.

Parry, J (1986) 'Values in Physical Education', in Tomlinson, P. and Quinton, M. (eds) *Values Across the Curriculum*, Brighton: Falmer Press.

Parry, J. (1988a) 'Physical Education, Justification and the National Curriculum', *Physical Education Review*, 11.2.

Parry, J. (1988b), 'Value Judgements: Are there Good Reasons for Including Sport on the Curriculum?', *Sport and Leisure*, 29.1, March/April.

Pearson, G. (1983) *Hooligan: A History of Respectable Fears*, London: Macmillan.

Perrow, C. (1979) *Complex Organisations*, Chicago: Scott Foresman.

Peters, R.S. (1966) *Ethics in Education*, London: Allen & Unwin.

Physical Education Association (1987) *Report of a Commission of Enquiry*, London: PEA.

Physical Education Association (1990) 'PE within the School Curriculum: PEA Statement', *British Journal of Physical Education*, 20, spring.

Political and Economic Planning (1966) *English Professional Football*, London: PEP.

Polsby, N. (1963) *Community Power and Political Theory*, New Haven, Conn.: Yale University Press.

Poole, R.K. (1978) *The Local Government Service*, London: Allen & Unwin.

Popplewell Report (1986) *Committee of Enquiry into Crowd Safety and Control at Sports Grounds: Final Report*, chairman Oliver Popplewell, Cmnd. 9710, London: HMSO.

Poulantzas, N. (1978) *State, Power, Socialism*, London: New Left Books.

Pressman, J. and Wildavsky, A. (1973) *Implementation*, Berkeley: University of California Press.

Ranson, S. (1980) 'Changing Relations between Centre and Locality in Education', *Local Government Studies*, 6, November/December.

Redmond, G. (1985) 'Developments in Sport from 1939–1976', in M.L. and R.A. Howell (eds) *History of Sport in Canada*, Champaign, Ill.: Stipes.

Rhodes, R.A.W. (1985) 'Power – Dependence, Policy Communities and Intergovernmental Networks', *Public Administration Bulletin*, No. 49, 4–31.

Rhodes, R.A.W. (1986) *The National World of Local Government*, London: Macmillan.

Rhodes, R.A.W. (1988) *Beyond Westminster and Whitehall*, London: Unwin Hyman.

Rhodes, R.A.W. and Wistow, G. (1988) *The Core Executive and Policy Networks: Caring for Mentally Handicapped People*, Essex Papers in Policy and Government, No. 49, Colchester: University of Essex.

Richardson, J.J. and Jordan, A.G. (1979) *Governing under Pressure*, Oxford: Martin Robertson.

Rose, R. (1980) *Politics in England*, London: Faber.

Saunders, P. (1980) *Urban Politics*, Harmondsworth: Penguin.

School Sport Forum (1988) *Sport and Young People: Partnership and Action*, London: Sports Council.

Scruton, R. (1980) *The Meaning of Conservatism*, Harmondsworth: Penguin.

Secondary Heads' Association (1987) *No Ball*, London: SHA.

Sharpe, L.J. (1985) 'Central Co-ordination and the Policy Network', *Political Studies*, 33.2.

Shorrt Report (1924) *An Enquiry into the Control of Spectators at the Cup Final, 1923*, Cmnd. 2088, London: HMSO.

Simon, R.L. (1984) 'Response to Brown and Fraleigh', *Journal of the Philosophy of Sport*, XI.

Skinsley, M. (1987) 'The elite: whose responsibility?', *British Journal of Physical Education*, 18.2.

Smith, B. (1979) *Policy Making in British Government*, London: Martin Robertson.

Social Science Research Council/Sports Council (1978) *Public Disorder and Sporting Events*, London: SSRC/SC.

South West Sports Council (1985) *From School to Community*, Crewkerne: South West Sports Council.

Sparkes, A. (1990) 'School Governors and PE in the 1990s: On the Need for Effective Advocacy', *British Journal of Physical Education*, 20, spring.

Sport and Leisure (1985) 'Opening Time', 26.2, March/April.

Sports Council (1973) *Annual Report*, London: Sports Council.

Sports Council (1982) *Sport in the Community: The Next Ten Years*, London: Sports Council.

Sports Council (1985a) *Active Life Styles, Coventry City Council: Interim Report on the Results of the Pupils' Leisure Survey*, Manchester: North West Regional Council for Sport and Recreation.

Sports Council (1985b) *Active Life Styles, Coventry City Council: Phase 1 Monitoring Report – Establishing the Project*, Manchester: North West Regional Council for Sport and Recreation.

Sports Council (1986) *Drug Abuse in Sport*, London: Sports Council.

Sports Council (1987) Press Release, SC3O8, London: Sports Council.

Sports Council (1988) *Sport in the Community: Into the 90s*, London: Sports Council.

Sports Council for Wales (1988) *The Control of Drug Abuse in Sport: Advice on Action to be Taken on Detection of a Banned Substance*, Cardiff: Sports Council for Wales.

Strauss, A. (1978) *Negotiations: Varieties, Process and Social Order*, San Francisco: Jossey Bass.

Strauss, A., Schatzman, L., Bucher, R., Ehrlich, D. and Satshin, M. (1963) 'The Hospital and its Negotiated Order', in Friedson, E. (ed.) *The Hospital in Modern Society*, New York: Free Press.

Strietzel, D. and Heigel, E. (1987) 'The Social Consumption Fund as Main Financing Resource for Physical Culture and Sport in the GDR', *International Review for the Sociology of Sport*, 22.3.

Sugden, J. and Bairner, A. (1986) 'Northern Ireland: the Politics of Leisure in a Divided Society', *Leisure Studies*, 5.

Sutcliffe, P. (1988) 'The German Democratic Republic: an Overview', in K. Hardman (ed.), *Physical Education and Sport under Communism*, Manchester: Manchester University Press.

Sutherland, J. and Stewart, G. (1989) 'Community Football', *Leisure Management*, 9.7.

Swain, G. (1987) 'Sport, Youth Service and Young People', in Swain and Stead (1987).

Swain, G. and Stead, D. (1987) *Youth Work and Sport*, Leicester: National Youth Bureau.

Taylor, I. (1982) 'On the Sports Violence Question: Soccer Hooliganism Revisited', in J. Hargreaves (ed.), *Sport, Culture and Ideology*, London: Routledge & Kegan Paul.

Lord Justice Taylor (1990) *The Hillsborough Stadium Disaster; 15th April 1989*, Final Report, Home Office, Cm. 962, London: HMSO.

Taylor, T. (1986) 'Politics and the Olympic Spirit', in Allison (1986).

Theonig, J.C. (1978) 'State Bureaucrats and Local Government in France', in K. Hanf and F.W. Sharpf, *Interorganisational Policy Making*, London: Sage.

Thomas, A. (1987) 'Readiness for Competition', in *Children in Sport: A Report of a One Day Seminar*, London: Greater London and South East Region Sports Council.

Thomason, H. and Almond, L. (1988) 'Health and Physical Education in the National Curriculum', *Physical Education Review*, 11.2.

Tiger, L. (1969) *Men in Groups*, London: Nelson.

Tomlinson, A. (1986) 'Going Global: The FIFA Story', in A. Tomlinson and G. Whannel, *Off The Ball; The Football World Cup*, London: Pluto Press.

Torkildsen, G. (1986) *Leisure and Recreation Management*, 2nd edition, London: Spon.

Travis, A.S. (1979) *The State and Leisure Provision*, London: Sports Council/Social Science Research Council.

Travis, A.S., Veal, A.J. *et al.* (1981) *The Role of Central Government in Relation to the Provision of Leisure Services in England and Wales*, Research Memorandum 86, Birmingham: Centre for Urban and Regional Studies, University of Birmingham.

Turner Report (1983) *Report of the Working Party on a British Governing Body for Athletics*, London: Amateur Athletic Association.

University of Birmingham, Physical Education Department (1956) *Britain in the World of Sport*, London: Physical Education Association.

Veal, A.J. and Travis, A.S. (1979) 'Local Authority Services – The State of Play', *Local Government Studies*, 5.4, July/August.

West Midlands Chief Officers' Group (1987) *Indoor Recreation Facilities: The Challenge of Privatisation*, Birmingham: West Midlands Chief Officers' Group.

Whannel, G. (1983) *Blowing the Whistle: The Politics of Sport*, London: Pluto Press.

Whannel, G. (1989) 'The Shape of Things . . .', *Sport and Leisure*, 30.1 January/February.

Whannel, G. and Tomlinson, A. (1984) *Five Ring Circus: Money, Power and Politics at the Olympic Games*, London: Pluto Press.

White, A. and Brackenridge, J. (1985) 'Who Rules Sport? Gender Divisions in the Power Structure of British Sports Organisations from 1960', *International Review of the Sociology of Sport*, 20.

White, J. (1986) *The View From the Field*, Leisure Working Paper 4.8, Birmingham: INLOGOV, University of Birmingham.

Wilks, S. and Wright, M. (1987) *Comparative Government – Industry Relations: Western Europe, the United States and Japan*, Oxford: Clarendon Press.

Williams, A. and Jenkins, C. (1988) 'Reaction to Reform – the National Curriculum Proposals and Physical Education', *Physical Education Review*, 11.2.

Williams, J., Dunning, E.G. and Murphy, P.J. (1984a) *Hooligans Abroad*, London: Routledge and Kegan Paul.

Williams, J., Dunning, E.G. and Murphy, P.J. (1984b), *All Seated Grounds and Hooliganism: The Coventry City Experience 1981–84*, London: The Football Trust.

Williams, M.H. (1974) *Drugs and Athletic Performance*, Springfield, Ill.: Thomas.

Wilson, J.Q. (1973) *Political Organisations*, New York: Basic Books.

Wistow, G. and Rhodes, R.A.W. (1987) 'Policy networks and policy process: the case of care in the community', Paper, PSA Annual Conference, Aberdeen.

Wolfenden Report (1960) *Sport and the Community*, chairman Sir John Wolfenden, London: Eyre & Spottiswood.

Wolverhampton Borough Council (1985) *The Social Condition of Young People in Wolverhampton in 1984*, Wolverhampton: Wolverhampton BC.

Woodland, L. (1980) *Dope: The Use of Drugs in Sport*, Newton Abbot: David & Charles.

Woolley, B.H. (1987) 'Drugs in Society and Sport in the United States', in P. Bellotti, G. Benzi and A. Ljungqvist (eds), *Official Proceedings*, International Athletic Foundation World Symposium on Doping in Sport, Florence: IAF.

Wright, M. (1988) 'Policy Community, Policy Network and Comparative Industrial Policies', *Political Studies*, 36.4.

Yates Report (1984) *Recreation Management Training Committee*, chairman Mrs A. Yates, Final Report, London: HMSO.

INDEX